THE WROUGHT RESPONSE

THE
WROUGHT
RESPONSE

Reading and Writing About Literature
SECOND EDITION

RAY KYTLE
Central Michigan University

JUANITA LYONS
formerly of
Humboldt State College

DICKENSON PUBLISHING COMPANY, INC.
ENCINO, CALIFORNIA, AND BELMONT, CALIFORNIA

ISBN-0-8221-0183-1

Library of Congress Catalog Card Number: 76-3850

Printed in the United States of America

Printing (last digit): 9 8 7 6 5 4 3

Cover design: Preston J. Mitchell

FOR TOM

ACKNOWLEDGMENTS

Chatto and Windus Ltd.: Excerpt from "Arms and the Boy" from *The Collected Poems of Wilfred Owen*. Reprinted by permission of Mr. Harold Owen and Chatto and Windus Ltd.

J. M. Dent & Sons Ltd.: Excerpt from "Do Not Go Gentle Into That Good Night" by Dylan Thomas reprinted by permission of J. M. Dent & Sons Ltd. and the Trustees for the Copyrights of the late Dylan Thomas. Excerpt from "The Secret Sharer" by Joseph Conrad reprinted by permission of the Trustees of the Joseph Conrad Estate and J. M. Dent & Sons Ltd. London.

Doubleday & Company, Inc.: Excerpt from "Rain" by W. Somerset Maugham, from the book, *The Trembling of a Leaf*, copyright 1921 by Smart Set Company, Inc. Reprinted by permission of Doubleday & Company, Inc.

E. P. Dutton & Co., Inc.: "The Cat, A Goldfinch and the Stars" from the book *Horse on the Moon* by Luigi Pirandello. Trans. and with an introduction by Samuel Putnam. Copyright 1932 by E. P. Dutton & Co., Inc. Renewal, ©, 1960 by E. P. Dutton & Co., Inc., publishers and reprinted with their permission.

Norma Millay Ellis: "First Fig" from *Collected Poems* by Edna St. Vincent Millay; Harper & Row. Copyright 1922, 1950 by Edna St. Vincent Millay.

Faber and Faber Limited: "Snow" by Louis MacNeice. Reprinted by permission of Faber and Faber Ltd. from *The Collected Poems of Louis MacNeice*.

Farrar, Straus & Giroux, Inc.: Excerpt from "Life, Friends, Is Boring" by John Berryman. Reprinted with the permission of Farrar, Straus & Giroux, Inc. from *77 Dream Songs* by John Berryman, copyright © 1959, 1962, 1963, 1964 by John Berryman.

Harcourt Brace Jovanovich Inc.: "The Life You Save May Be Your Own," copyright 1973 by Flannery O'Connor; reprinted from her volume, *A Good Man Is Hard to Find*. Excerpt from *A Good Man Is Hard to Find* by Flannery O'Connor. Excerpt from "Sweeney Erect" from *Collected Poems 1909–1962* by T. S. Eliot. Excerpt from "Flowering Judas" from *Flowering Judas and Other Stories* by Katherine Anne Porter. All reprinted with the permission of Harcourt Brace Jovanovich, Inc.

Harvard University Press: "There Came a Wind Like a Bugle" by Emily Dickinson. Reprinted by permission of the publishers and the Trustees of Amherst College from Thomas H. Johnson, Editor, *The Poems of Emily Dickinson*, Cambridge, Mass.: The Belknap Press of Harvard University Copyright 1951, 1955, by The President and Fellows of Harvard College.

Holt, Rinehart and Winston, Inc.: Excerpt from "Birches" and "Design" by Robert Frost. From *The Poetry of Robert Frost* edited by Edward Connery Lathem. Copyright 1916, © 1969 by Holt, Rinehart and Winston, Inc. Copyright 1936, 1944 by Robert Frost. Copyright © 1964 by Lesley Frost Ballantine. Reprinted by permission of Holt, Rinehart and Winston, Inc.

Houghton Mifflin Company. "The End of the World" from *Collected Poems 1917–1952* by Archibald MacLeish. Reprinted by permission of Houghton Mifflin Company.

International Famous Agency. "The Portable Phonograph" from *Watchful Gods and Other Stories* by Walter van Tilburg Clark, Random House, 1950. Reprinted by permission of International Famous Agency. Copyright © 1941, 1969 by Walter van Tilburg Clark.

Kayak Press. Excerpt from "Confession" by Morton Markus. Reprinted by permission of Kayak, 3965 Bonnie Doon Rd., Santa Cruz, Cal. 95060.

Alfred A. Knopf, Inc. "A Cup of Tea" by Katherine Mansfield. Copyright 1923 by Alfred A. Knopf, Inc. and renewed 1951 by John Middleton Murry. Reprinted from *The Short Stories of Katherine Mansfield*, by permission of Alfred A. Knopf, Inc.

Little, Brown and Company. "Gold Coast" from *Hue and Cry* by James Alan McPherson, by permission of Atlantic-Little, Brown and Co. Copyright © 1968, 1969 by James Alan McPherson.

McClelland & Stewart Limited. "Go By Brooks" by Leonard Cohen, reprinted by permission of The Canadian Publishers, McClelland and Stewart Limited, Toronto.

The Macmillan Company. Excerpt from "Sailing to Byzantium" from *Collected Poems* by William Butler Yeats. Copyright 1928 by The Macmillan Company, renewed 1956 by George Yeats. "For Anne Gregory" from *Collected Poems* by William Butler Yeats. Copyright 1933 by The Macmillan Company, renewed 1961 by Bertha Georgie Yeats. Excerpt from "Mr. Flood's Party" from *Collected Poems* by Edward Arlington Robinson. Copyright 1921 by Edwin Arlington Robinson, renewed 1949 by Ruth Nivison. Excerpt from "Karma" from *Collected Poems* by Edward Arlington Robinson. Copyright 1925 by Edwin Arlington Robinson, renewed 1953 by Ruth Nivison and Barbara R. Holt. All reprinted with permission of The Macmillan Company.

The Macmillan Company of Canada Limited. Excerpt from "Eve" from *Collected Poems* by Ralph Hodgson, by permission of Mrs. Hodgson; Macmillan & Co. Ltd., London; and The Macmillan Company of Canada Limited.

Harold Matson Co. "The Chaser" by John Collier. Copyright 1940, 1968 by John Collier, reprinted by permission of Harold Matson Co., Inc.

New Directions Publishing Corporation. Excerpt from "Arms and the Boy" from *Collected Poems* by Wilfred Owen. Copyright Chatto & Windus, Ltd., 1946, © 1963. "Salutation" from *Personae* by Ezra Pound. Copyright 1926 by Ezra Pound. "Do Not Go Gentle Into That Good Night" from *Collected Poems* by Dylan Thomas. Copyright 1952 by Dylan Thomas. All reprinted by permission of New Directions Publishing Corporation.

Oxford University Press. "Snow" from *The Collected Poems of Louis MacNeice*, edited by E. R. Dodds. Copyright © The Estate of Louis MacNeice 1966. Reprinted by permission of Oxford University Press, Inc.

Random House, Inc. Excerpt from "The Bear" of *Go Down Moses* by William Faulkner. Excerpt from "As I Walked Out One Evening" by W. H. Auden. Excerpt from *A Tree of Night and Other Stories* by Truman Capote. All reprinted by permission of Random House, Inc.

St. Martin's Press, Incorporated. Excerpt from "Eve" from *Collected Poems* by Ralph Hodgson, by permission of St. Martin's Press, Inc., Macmillan & Co. Ltd.

Charles Scribner's Sons. "Cliff Klingenhagen" from *The Children of the Night* by Edward Arlington Robinson (1897). "The Invoice" and "Please—for James Broughton" from *For Love* by Robert Creeley. Copyright © 1962 by Robert Creeley. "A Clean, Well-Lighted Place" (Copyright 1933 Charles Scribner's Sons; renewal copyright © 1961 Ernest Hemingway) from *Winner Take Nothing* by Ernest Hemingway. Excerpts from *The Great Gatsby* by F. Scott Fitzgerald. Copyright 1925 Charles Scribner's Sons; renewal copyright 1953 Frances Scott Fitzgerald Lanahan. Excerpt from "Richard Cory" by Edwin Arlington Robinson. All reprinted by permission of Charles Scribner's Sons.

Sewanee Review. "Old Men Dream Dreams, Young Men See Visions" by John William Corrington first appeared in the *Sewanee Review*, 80 (Winter 1972). Copyright 1972 by the University of the South. Reprinted by permission of the editor.

Anne Stevenson. Excerpt from "Television" by Anne Stevenson. Reprinted by permission of the author.

Toni Strassman. "The Stone Boy" by Gina Berriault. First printed in *Mademoiselle*. Copyright 1957 by Gina Berriault. By permission of Toni Strassman, Agent.

Mrs. James Thurber. "The Bear Who Let It Alone," copyright © 1940 James Thurber. Copyright © 1968 Helen Thurber. From *Fables for Our Time*, published by Harper & Row. Originally printed in *The New Yorker*. "The Catbird Seat" excerpt, copyright © 1945 James Thurber. From "The Catbird Seat" in *The Thurber Carnival*, published by Harper & Row. Originally printed in *The New Yorker*. Both reprinted by permission of Mrs. James Thurber.

The Viking Press, Inc. "Go By Brooks" from *Selected Poems: 1956–1968* by Leonard Cohen. Copyright in all countries of the International Copyright Union. All rights reserved. Excerpt from "The Horse-Dealer's Daughter" from *The Complete Short Stories of D. H. Lawrence*, Volume II. Copyright 1922 by Thomas B. Seltzer, Inc., renewed 1950 by Frieda Lawrence. "Resume" from the Portable Dorothy Parker. Copyright 1926, renewed 1954 by Dorothy Parker. "Flight" from *The Long Valley* by John Steinbeck. Copyright 1938, copyright © renewed 1966 by John Steinbeck. All reprinted by permission of The Viking Press, Inc.

A. P. Watt & Son. "For Anne Gregory" and excerpt from "Sailing to Byzantium" from *The Collected Poems of William Butler Yeats*, by permission of Mr. M. B. Yeats and The Macmillan Company of Canada.

CONTENTS

PREFACE

Students asked to write critical analyses of literature, often for the first time, have a right to request, "Show me." They have a right to assert, "Don't just *tell* me how the essay should look, *show* me the process by which it is created." To show rather than to tell is what we have attempted in this text.

To this end, the first third of each chapter is devoted to "theory." Here we explain the nature of a particular element of literature and its significance. The second portion of each chapter consists of an illustrative work of literature. This is the touchstone to which the student can apply the general principles discussed, for it is our conviction that "rules" for interpreting literature have little merit and less validity when divorced from the specific context. In the third portion of each chapter we focus on "showing." We explain and exemplify the process by which a critical essay is created; we detail and illustrate the prewriting and writing activities that produce an effective analytical paper.

Throughout, our primary concern has been the student users of the text: their difficulties, their needs, their questions. For an effective critical essay about a work of literature is indeed a "wrought response," necessitating both critical insight and the ability to communicate that insight convincingly in essay form. To help students toward such insight and to illustrate the process by which their understanding can be convincingly communicated in writing are the complementary objectives of this text.

In the course of preparing this second edition we have become indebted to scores of professors around the country who shared with us their reactions to the book and, especially, to reviewers Charles Dawe, Orange Coast College; Ellyn Sue Lieberman, University of Cincinnati; John Wm. Martin, Moraine Valley Community College; and James Walter, Sinclair Community College. Although specific revisions are far too numerous to list, we would like to indicate the major changes. These are:

1. *New illustrative short stories for the chapters "Character" and "Point of View"*
2. *A completely new discussion of "Point of View"*
3. *Addition of a section on integrating and punctuating quotations*
4. *Addition of a mini-anthology of short stories for reading, discussion and writing.*
5. *Addition of a comprehensive index*

Ray Kytle
Juanita Lyons

ONE

SETTING

UNDERSTANDING SETTING

Look around. Look at the room you're in, the building the room's a part of. Look at your clothes, at your possessions. Go for a walk and take in the sights. What you see is *setting*. Your setting.

And you can be pretty sure that some stranger, nosing around and watching you in this setting, can tell a lot about you. He can examine your possessions, your clothes, the way your room is decorated, the books (or lack of them) on your shelves, the magazines lying about. And after doing so, he can make some fairly accurate guesses about what you're like. This is one function of setting in literature—to reveal character.

Setting Characterizes

Drawing by Koren; © 1970 The New Yorker Magazine, Inc.

How does the setting in this cartoon characterize the woman just inside the door? What does the setting suggest about her values? Her role in the family? Her personality? Her relation with her husband?

A person's surroundings and possessions inevitably reveal something, sometimes quite a lot, about that person. If an author takes the trouble to describe a character's home or office, possessions, or manner of dressing, you can be confident that the author is trying to tell you about that person's values and personality.

Take this passage from Poe's "The Fall of the House of Usher" in which the narrator describes Roderick Usher's chamber:

> The room in which I found myself was very large and lofty. The windows were long, narrow, and pointed, and at so vast a distance from the black oaken floor as to be altogether inaccessible from within. Feeble gleams of encrimsoned light made their way through the trellised panes, and served to render sufficiently distinct the more prominent objects around; the eye, however, struggled in vain to reach the remoter angles of the chamber, or the recesses of the vaulted and fretted ceiling. Dark draperies hung upon the walls. The general furniture was profuse, comfortless, antique, and tattered. Many books and musical instruments lay scattered about, but failed to give any vitality to the scene. I felt that I breathed an atmosphere of sorrow. An air of stern, deep, and irredeemable gloom hung over and pervaded all.

The floor is "black"; the light is "feeble" and "encrimsoned"; the draperies are "dark"; the remoter parts of the room are shrouded in shadow. The overall effect of these details of setting is "an air of stern, deep, and irredeemable gloom." We don't need to wait until Roderick speaks to deduce that he is himself in the throes of a deep and pervasive depression. No cheerful man, no man in good health and good spirits, would voluntarily dwell in such melancholy surroundings.

Other details of the setting reveal other aspects of Roderick's character. The furniture in the room is "profuse, comfortless, and antique, and tattered." These details bespeak Roderick's neglect of his physical comfort and reinforce our impression of a man too deeply preoccupied and troubled to concern himself with his surroundings. Further, the presence of "many books and musical instruments" reveals that Roderick is both artistic and intellectual. But the fact that they are "scattered about" suggests that their owner is restless and distracted, and no longer capable of enjoying his former artistic or intellectual pursuits. Thus, this single brief description of setting reveals to the reader numerous aspects of Roderick's character and mental state.

3

Similarly, setting may function as a metaphor for character. In other words, an analogy is suggested between the physical characteristics of setting and the mental or emotional characteristics of a person in a work of literature.

The analogy may be explicit, as in this scene from *Moby-Dick*:

> As they [the watch] narrated to each other their unholy adventures, their tales of terror told in words of mirth; as their uncivilized laughter forked upwards out of them, like the flames from the furnace; as to and fro, in their front, the harpooners wildly gesticulated with their huge pronged forks and dippers; as the wind howled on, and the sea leaped, and the ship groaned and dived, and yet steadfastly shot her red hell further and further into the blackness of the sea and the night, and scornfully champed the white bone in her mouth, and viciously spat round her on all sides; then the rushing *Pequod*, freighted with savages, and laden with fire, and burning a corpse, and plunging into that blackness of darkness, seemed the material counterpart of her monomaniac commander's soul.

Here, Ishmael *tells* us that certain qualities of the *Pequod* are analogous to the tortured, fiery, unholy, yet indomitable spirit of Captain Ahab; we don't have to discover the connection ourselves.

Often, though, the analogy is *implicit*. The reader has to discover for himself the metaphorical relation between setting and character. As the narrator approaches Usher's mansion, he describes it in these words:

> Its principal feature seemed to be that of an excessive antiquity. The discoloration of ages had been great. Minute fungi overspread the whole exterior, hanging in a fine tangled web-work from the eaves. Yet all this was apart from any extraordinary dilapidation. No portion of the masonry had fallen; and there appeared to be a wild inconsistency between its still perfect adaptation of parts, and the crumbling condition of the individual stones. In this there was much that reminded me of the specious totality of old woodwork which has rotted for long years in some neglected vault, with no disturbance from the breath of the external air. Beyond this indication of extensive decay, however, the fabric gave little token of instability. Perhaps the eye of a scrutinizing observer might have discovered a barely perceptible fissure, which, extending from the roof of the building in front, made its way down the wall in a zig-zag direction, until it became lost in the sullen waters of the tarn.

It is only after we have read further into the story, and have met Roderick, that we begin to see how the unstable, disintegrating mansion is analogous to Roderick Usher's unstable and disintegrating psyche.

Setting Heightens Probability

"Now here's my plan!"

Courtesy of *Penthouse*

What is the inevitable fate of the two white-hunter types pictured in the cartoon?

What are some of the details of setting that make this fate the only probable one?

What is the primary source of the humor in this cartoon?

5

In a particular setting, some actions are more probable than others. Witty sophisticated banter seems more believable in the drawing rooms of the rich than in the hovels of the poor. Violent, aggressive human behavior seems more believable in a raging storm or noisy, crowded, brawling tavern than at a formal state dinner for a visiting ambassador. These are extremes, but the point is clear—setting functions to heighten *probability*. It makes the action (and often the characters) believable. An appropriate setting for a certain pattern of action and a certain cast of characters contributes to the "willing suspension of disbelief" that effective imaginative literature evokes from the reader.

Setting Creates Atmosphere

It is not just that mysterious creakings and stealthy footsteps strike us as more credible in ancient, derelict mansions than in luxurious high-rise apartments. Setting also heightens probability by helping to create an appropriate *atmosphere*.

Again, all you need to do is look out your window. Is it sunny and clear? Is it overcast and gloomy? Is a storm impending and the air oppressive with natural fury soon to be released? Or is it violently stormy, with lightning flashing and crashing, wind raging, rain flying, clouds scudding? Or picture a desert with the sun beating down on a bleak, desolate, cruel, and lifeless barrenness.

The same terms that are used to describe the "real" or "outer" atmosphere are used to describe atmosphere in literature: *sunny, calm, somber, gloomy, oppressive, stormy, barren, bleak, desolate.* The atmosphere of a work of literature is its "emotional aura." It is created by the confluence of character, action, and setting. Hence, in Stephen Crane's "The Blue Hotel" the *character* of the Swede, who is alternately terrified and boisterously aggressive, the *action* of the story, in which the characters are thrown into greater and greater conflict, and the *setting*, a blizzard raging and howling over the Nebraska town, combine to create an atmosphere of violence and stress and furious unleashed elemental energy that, in turn, heightens our expectation of, and our willingness to accept as credible, violent and eventually murderous human behavior.

Similarly, the narrator's description of the Usher mansion, the setting of Poe's story, helps create an atmosphere of gloom, decay, disease, and eerieness that, in turn, predisposes us to accept the strange characters and events in that story.

The functions of setting that we've discussed so far have their counterparts in the nonfictional world, in "real life." In real life, setting establishes time and place, reveals character, makes certain events seem probable (witness the fear many have when walking on a dark deserted street), and creates atmosphere—just as it does in literature. There is another major function of setting in literature, however, that has no real life parallel, at least for most of us. In literature setting often functions to *communicate ideas*.

Setting Communicates Ideas

In the picture on page 8, setting and character interpenetrate. The boy is a real boy, the brick wall a real brick wall. But the two are merged in such a way that the setting also communicates an idea, makes a statement. The process in literature is the same.

As you read a work of literature, you should be alert for and receptive to possible symbolic values in the setting. But don't force conclusions, and keep your judgments tentative. If the symbolic value you've attached to an aspect of setting conflicts with the import of the plot, or with character, or with clearly emerging themes, abandon it.

When setting communicates ideas, it does so symbolically or metaphorically; the setting suggests meaning or ideas in addition to its literal descriptive function. Seasons, time of day, colors—all aspects of setting—often have thematic significance, as do dramatic changes in the setting in the course of a story. Thus, springtime, dawn, and soft pastel colors tend to suggest such ideas as hope, freedom of action, youthful-

Photo by Gene Ward

What is the setting in this picture?
How is the photographer using setting symbolically in this picture?
What does the setting symbolize?
What is the "idea" communicated through setting in this picture?

ness, and potential, whereas dark colors, winter, and nighttime often suggest emotional bleakness and despair.

The opening scene of Émile Zola's *Germinal* takes place on a "pitch-black starless night" in winter; the wind, "icy cold," is "blowing in great gusts like a storm at sea"; the protagonist is described as "trudging" through a "swirling sea of black shadows." At the end of the novel, the season is spring, the time of day dawn. The sun is bathing the earth in a "golden haze," birds are singing, "rosy wisps of clouds" are rising into a "limpid blue" sky, buds are "bursting into leaf," fields are "quickening with fresh green grass." Even a person unfamiliar with *Germinal* can readily infer that the novel ends on a positive and hopeful note.

Generally, when an author feels that it is important for the reader to recognize the symbolic significance of setting, the symbolic aspects of the setting are given extra emphasis. After you've read fictional literature extensively, you will develop a sort of sixth sense for recognizing settings with important symbolic functions because you will become familiar with the ways authors alert their readers:

1. An author may describe an aspect of setting with such *care* and in such *detail* that the need for special attention is obvious. Such minute description may also be combined with highly connotative terms that would be incongruous in a description intended to create a "realistic" or "photographic" picture in the mind's eye of the reader:

He slowly ventured into the pond. The bottom was deep, soft clay. He sank in, and the water clasped dead cold round his legs. As he stirred he could smell the cold, rotten clay that fouled up into the water. It was objectionable in his lungs. Still, repelled and yet not heeding, he moved deeper into the pond. The cold water rose over his thighs, over his loins, upon his abdomen. The lower part of his body was all sunk in the hideous cold element. And the bottom was so deeply soft and uncertain, he was afraid of pitching with his mouth underneath. He could not swim, and was afraid.

He crouched a little, spreading his hands under the water and moving them round, trying to feel for her. The dead cold pond swayed upon his chest. He moved again, a little deeper, and again, with his hands underneath, he felt all around under the water. And he touched her clothing. But it evaded his fingers. He made a desperate effort to grasp it.

And so doing he lost his balance and went under, horribly, suffocating in the foul earthy water, struggling madly for a few moments. At last, after what seemed an eternity, he got his footing, rose again into the air and looked around. He gasped, and knew he was in the world. Then he looked at the water. She had risen near him. He grasped her clothing, and drawing her nearer, turned to take his way to land again.

He went very slowly, carefully, absorbed in the slow progress. He rose higher, climbing out of the pond. The water was now only about his legs; he

was thankful, full of relief to be out of the clutches of the pond. He lifted her and staggered on to the bank, out of the horror of wet, grey clay.
—D, H. Lawrence, "The Horse Dealer's Daughter"

Note: The man described in this passage finds the pond evil, foul, clutching, hideous, horrifying. His exaggerated reaction to what is, after all, just a plain pond alerts us to study the passage for symbolic meaning.

2. An author may place *heavy emphasis* on a particular aspect of setting:

"It's the gun," Sam said. . . . *The gun,* the boy thought. *The gun.* . . .
—William Faulkner, "The Bear"

Note: In this passage the tri-fold repetition of the word "gun," its emphatic italicization, and the boy's own attempt to decipher the significance of Sam's statement alerts us that we, too, should seek to understand the symbolic significance of the gun.

3. An author may mention an aspect of setting *again and again* in the course of work. (In *Moby-Dick*, for example, sharks are alluded to so often that the reader is finally forced to examine their symbolic significance.)

Summary

We have seen that setting reveals character directly by its bearing on a character's social class, economic situation, tastes, personality, values, and state of mind. It reveals character indirectly by representing, metaphorically, some aspect or aspects of character. It also functions to heighten probability—directly, by matching time and place to character and action; indirectly, by contributing to an atmosphere appropriate to the action. Finally, we have seen that setting can function to communicate ideas, beliefs, and values by acquiring symbolic overtones.

In the short story "Flight" we can see various aspects of setting functioning in the ways we've mentioned. After you have read the story, we will discuss the three related matters of analyzing setting, determining its functions, and writing an essay about it.

FLIGHT

John Steinbeck

About fifteen miles below Monterey, on the wild coast, the Torres family had their farm, a few sloping acres above a cliff that dropped to the brown reefs and to the hissing white waters of the ocean. Behind the farm the stone mountains stood up against the sky. The farm buildings huddled like little clinging aphids on the mountain skirts, crouched low to the ground as though the wind might blow them into the sea. The little shack, the rattling, rotting barn were gray-bitten with sea salt, beaten by the damp wind until they had taken on the color of the granite hills. Two horses, a red cow and a red calf, half a dozen pigs and a flock of lean, multi-colored chickens stocked the place. A little corn was raised on the sterile slope, and it grew short and thick under the wind, and all the cobs formed on the landward sides of the stalks.

Mama Torres, a lean, dry woman with ancient eyes, had ruled the farm for ten years, ever since her husband tripped over a stone in the field one day and fell full length on a rattlesnake. When one is bitten on the chest there is not much that can be done.

Mama Torres had three children, two undersized black ones of twelve and fourteen, Emilio and Rosy, whom Mama kept fishing on the rocks below the farm when the sea was kind and when the truant officer was in some distant part of Monterey County. And there was Pepé, the tall smiling son of nineteen, a gentle, affectionate boy, but very lazy. Pepé had a tall head, pointed at the top, and from its peak, coarse black hair grew down like a thatch all around. Over his smiling little eyes Mama cut a straight bang so he could see. Pepé had sharp Indian cheekbones and an eagle nose, but his mouth was sweet and shapely as a girl's mouth, and his chin was fragile and chiseled. He was loose and gangling, all legs and feet and wrists, and he was very lazy. Mama thought him fine and brave, but she never told him so. She said, "Some lazy cow must have got into thy father's family, else how could I have a son like thee." And she said,

"When I carried thee, a sneaking lazy coyote came out of the brush and looked at me one day. That must have made thee so."

Pepé smiled sheepishly and stabbed at the ground with his knife to keep the blade sharp and free from rust. It was his inheritance, that knife, his father's knife. The long heavy blade folded back into the black handle. There was a button on the handle. When Pepé pressed the button, the blade leaped out ready for use. The knife was with Pepé always, for it had been his father's knife.

One sunny morning when the sea below the cliff was glinting and blue and the white surf creamed on the reef, when even the stone mountains looked kindly, Mama Torres called out the door of the shack, "Pepé, I have a labor for thee."

There was no answer. Mama listened. From behind the barn she heard a burst of laughter. She lifted her full long skirt and walked in the direction of the noise.

Pepé was sitting on the ground with his back against a box. His white teeth glistened. On either side of him stood the two black ones, tense and expectant. Fifteen feet away a redwood post was set in the ground. Pepé's right hand lay limply in his lap, and in the palm the big black knife rested. The blade was closed back into the handle. Pepé looked smiling at the sky.

Suddenly Emilio cried, "Ya!"

Pepé's wrist flicked like the head of a snake. The blade seemed to fly open in mid-air, and with a thump the point dug into the redwood post, and the black handle quivered. The three burst into excited laughter. Rosy ran to the post and pulled out the knife and brought it back to Pepé. He closed the blade and settled the knife carefully in his listless palm again. He grinned self-consciously at the sky.

"Ya!"

The heavy knife lanced out and sunk into the post again. Mama moved forward like a ship and scattered the play.

"All day you do foolish things with the knife, like a toy-baby," she stormed. "Get up on thy huge feet that eat up shoes. Get up!" She took him by one loose shoulder and hoisted at him. Pepé grinned sheepishly and came half-heartedly to his feet. "Look!" Mama cried. "Big lazy, you must catch the horse and put on him thy father's saddle. You must ride to Monterey. The medicine bottle is empty. There is no salt. Go thou now, Peanut! Catch the horse."

A revolution took place in the relaxed figure of Pepé. "To Monterey, me? Alone? *Si*, Mama."

She scowled at him. "Do not think, big sheep, that you will buy candy. No, I will give you only enough for the medicine and the salt."

Pepé smiled. "Mama, you will put the hatband on the hat?"

She relented then. "Yes Pepé. You may wear the hatband."

12

His voice grew insinuating, "And the green handkerchief, Mama?"

"Yes, if you go quickly and return with no trouble, the silk green handkerchief will go. If you make sure to take off the handkerchief when you eat so no spot may fall on it. . . ."

"*Si*, Mama. I will be careful. I am a man."

"Thou? A man? Thou art a peanut."

He went into the rickety barn and brought out a rope, and he walked agilely enough up the hill to catch the horse.

When he was ready and mounted before the door, mounted on his father's saddle that was so old that the oaken frame showed through torn leather in many places, then Mama brought out the round black hat with the tooled leather band, and she reached up and knotted the green silk handkerchief about his neck. Pepé's blue denim coat was much darker than his jeans, for it had been washed much less often.

Mama handed up the big medicine bottle and the silver coins. "That for the medicine," she said, "and that for the salt. That for a candle to burn for the papa. That for *dulces* for the little ones. Our friend Mrs. Rodriguez will give you dinner and maybe a bed for the night. When you go to the church say only ten Paternosters and only twenty-five Ave Marias. Oh! I know, big coyote. You would sit there flapping your mouth over Aves all day while you looked at the candles and the holy pictures. That is not good devotion to stare at the pretty things."

The black hat, covering the high pointed head and black thatched hair of Pepé, gave him dignity and age. He sat the rangy horse well. Mama thought how handsome he was, dark and lean and tall. "I would not send thee now alone, thou little one, except for the medicine," she said softly. "It is not good to have no medicine, for who knows when the toothache will come, or the sadness of the stomach. These things are."

"Adios, Mama," Pepé cried. "I will come back soon. You may send me often alone. I am a man."

"Thou art a foolish chicken."

He straightened his shoulders, flipped the reins against the horse's shoulder and rode away. He turned once and saw that they still watched him, Emilio and Rosy and Mama. Pepé grinned with pride and gladness and lifted the tough buckskin horse to a trot.

When he had dropped out of sight over a little dip in the road, Mama turned to the black ones, but she spoke to herself. "He is nearly a man now," she said. "It will be a nice thing to have a man in the house again." Her eyes sharpened on the children. "Go to the rocks now. The tide is going out. There will be abalones to be found." She put the iron hooks into their hands and saw them down the steep trail to the reefs. She brought the smooth stone *metate* to the doorway and sat grinding her corn to flour and looking occasionally at the road over which Pepé had gone.

13

The noonday came and then the afternoon, when the little ones beat the abalones on a rock to make them tender and Mama patted the tortillas to make them thin. They ate their dinner as the red sun was plunging down toward the ocean. They sat on the doorsteps and watched the big white moon come over the mountain tops.

Mama said, "He is now at the house of our friend Mrs. Rodriguez. She will give him nice things to eat and maybe a present."

Emilio said, "Some day I too will ride to Monterey for medicine. Did Pepé come to be a man today?"

Mama said wisely, "A boy gets to be a man when a man is needed. Remember this thing. I have known boys forty years old because there was no need for a man."

Soon afterwards they retired, Mama in her big oak bed on one side of the room, Emilio and Rosy in their boxes full of straw and sheepskins on the other side of the room.

The moon went over the sky and the surf roared on the rocks. The roosters crowed the first call. The surf subsided to a whispering surge against the reef. The moon dropped toward the sea. The roosters crowed again.

The moon was near down to the water when Pepé rode on a winded horse to his home flat. His dog bounced out and circled the horse yelping with pleasure. Pepé slid off the saddle to the ground. The weathered little shack was silver in the moonlight and the square shadow of it was black to the north and east. Against the east the piling mountains were misty with light; their tops melted into the sky.

Pepé walked wearily up the three steps and into the house. It was dark inside. There was a rustle in the corner.

Mama cried out from her bed. "Who comes? Pepé, is it thou?"

"*Si*, Mama."

"Did you get the medicine?"

"*Si*, Mama."

"Well, go to sleep, then. I thought you would be sleeping at the house of Mrs. Rodriguez." Pepé stood silently in the dark room. "Why do you stand there, Pepé? Did you drink wine?"

"*Si*, Mama."

"Well, go to bed then and sleep out the wine."

His voice was tired and patient, but very firm. "Light the candle, Mama. I must go away into the mountains."

"What is this, Pepé? You are crazy." Mama struck a sulphur match and held the little blue burr until the flame spread up the stick. She set light to the candle on the floor beside her bed. "Now, Pepé, what is this you say?" She looked anxiously into his face.

He was changed. The fragile quality seemed to have gone from his chin. His mouth was less full than it had been, the lines of the lips were straighter, but in his eyes the greatest change had taken place. There was no laughter in them any more nor any bashfulness. They were sharp and bright and purposeful.

He told her in a tired monotone, told her everything just as it had happened. A few people came into the kitchen of Mrs. Rodriguez. There was wine to drink. Pepé drank wine. The little quarrel—the man started toward Pepé and then the knife—it went almost by itself. It flew, it darted before Pepé knew it. As he talked, Mama's face grew stern, and it seemed to grow more lean. Pepé finished. "I am a man now, Mama. The man said names to me I could not allow."

Mama nodded. "Yes, thou art a man, my poor little Pepé. Thou art a man. I have seen it coming on thee. I have watched you throwing the knife into the post, and I have been afraid." For a moment her face had softened, but now it grew stern again. "Come! We must get you ready. Go. Awaken Emilio and Rosy. Go quickly."

Pepé stepped over to the corner where his brother and sister slept among the sheepskins. He leaned down and shook them gently. "Come, Rosy! Come, Emilio! The mama says you must arise."

The little black ones sat up and rubbed their eyes in the candlelight. Mama was out of bed now, her long black skirt over her nightgown. "Emilio," she cried. "Go up and catch the other horse for Pepé. Quickly, now! Quickly." Emilio put his legs in his overalls and stumbled sleepily out the door.

"You heard no one behind you on the road?" Mama demanded.

"No, Mama. I listened carefully. No one was on the road."

Mama darted like a bird about the room. From a nail on the wall she took a canvas water bag and threw it on the floor. She stripped a blanket from her bed and rolled it into a tight tube and tied the ends with string. From a box beside the stove she lifted a flour sack half full of black stringy jerky. "Your father's black coat, Pepé. Here, put it on."

Pepé stood in the middle of the floor watching her activity. She reached behind the door and brought out the rifle, a long 38–56, worn shiny the whole length of the barrel. Pepé took it from her and held it in the crook of his elbow. Mama brought a little leather bag and counted the cartridges into his hand. "Only ten left," she warned. "You must not waste them."

Emilio put his head in the door. "'Qui 'st 'l caballo, Mama."

"Put on the saddle from the other horse. Tie on the blanket. Here, tie the jerky to the saddle horn."

Still Pepé stood silently watching his mother's frantic activity. His chin looked hard, and his sweet mouth was drawn and thin. His little eyes followed Mama about the room almost suspiciously.

15

Rosy asked softly, "Where goes Pepé?"

Mama's eyes were fierce. "Pepé goes on a journey. Pepé is a man now. He has a man's things to do."

Pepé straightened his shoulders. His mouth changed until he looked very much like Mama.

At last the preparation was finished. The loaded horse stood outside the door. The water bag dripped a line of moisture down the bay shoulder.

The moonlight was being thinned by the dawn and the big white moon was near down to the sea. The family stood by the shack. Mama confronted Pepé. "Look, my son! Do not stop until it is dark again. Do not sleep even though you are tired. Take care of the horse in order that he may not stop of weariness. Remember to be careful with the bullets—there are only ten. Do not fill thy stomach with jerky or it will make thee sick. Eat a little jerky and fill thy stomach with grass. When thou comest to the high mountains, if thou seest any of the dark watching men, go not near to them nor try to speak to them. And forget not thy prayers." She put her lean hands on Pepé's shoulders, stood on her toes and kissed him formally on both cheeks, and Pepé kissed her on both cheeks. Then he went to Emilio and Rosy and kissed both of their cheeks.

Pepé turned back to Mama. He seemed to look for a little softness, a little weakness in her. His eyes were searching, but Mama's face remained fierce. "Go now," she said. "Do not wait to be caught like a chicken."

Pepé pulled himself into the saddle. "I am a man," he said.

It was the first dawn when he rode up the hill toward the little canyon which let a trail into the mountains. Moonlight and daylight fought with each other, and the two warring qualities made it difficult to see. Before Pepé had gone a hundred yards, the outlines of his figure were misty; and long before he entered the canyon, he had become a gray, indefinite shadow.

Mama stood stiffly in front of her doorstep, and on either side of her stood Emilio and Rosy. They cast furtive glances at Mama now and then.

When the gray shape of Pepé melted into the hillside and disappeared, Mama relaxed. She began the high, whining keen of the death wail. "Our beautiful—our brave," she cried. "Our protector, our son is gone." Emilio and Rosy moaned beside her. "Our beautiful—our brave, he is gone." It was the formal wail. It rose to a high piercing whine and subsided to a moan. Mama raised it three times and then she turned and went into the house and shut the door.

Emilio and Rosy stood wondering in the dawn. They heard Mama whimpering in the house. They went out to sit on the cliff above the ocean. They touched shoulders. "When did Pepé come to be a man?" Emilio asked.

"Last night," said Rosy. "Last night in Monterey." The ocean clouds turned red with the sun that was behind the mountains.

"We will have no breakfast," said Emilio. "Mama will not want to cook." Rosy did not answer him. "Where is Pepé gone?" he asked.

Rosy looked around at him. She drew her knowledge from the quiet air. "He has gone on a journey. He will never come back."

"Is he dead? Do you think he is dead?"

Rosy looked back at the ocean again. A little steamer, drawing a line of smoke, sat on the edge of the horizon. "He is not dead," Rosy explained. "Not yet."

Pepé rested the big rifle across the saddle in front of him. He let the horse walk up the hill and he didn't look back. The stony slope took on a coat of short brush so that Pepé found the entrance to a trail and entered it.

When he came to the canyon opening, he swung once in his saddle and looked back, but the houses were swallowed in the misty light. Pepé jerked forward again. The high shoulder of the canyon closed in on him. His horse stretched out its neck and sighed and settled to the trail.

It was a well-worn path, dark soft leaf-mold earth strewn with broken pieces of sandstone. The trail rounded the shoulder of the canyon and dropped steeply into the bed of the stream. In the shallows the water ran smoothly, glinting in the first morning sun. Small round stones on the bottom were as brown as rust with sun moss. In the sand along the edges of the stream the tall, rich wild mint grew, while in the water itself the cress, old and tough, had gone to heavy seed.

The path went into the stream and emerged on the other side. The horse sloshed into the water and stopped. Pepé dropped his bridle and let the beast drink of the running water.

Soon the canyon sides became steep and the first giant sentinel redwoods guarded the trail, great round red trunks bearing foliage as green and lacy as ferns. Once Pepé was among the trees, the sun was lost. A perfumed and purple light lay in the pale green of the underbrush. Gooseberry bushes and blackberries and tall ferns lined the stream, and overhead the branches of the redwoods met and cut off the sky.

Pepé drank from the water bag, and he reached into the flour sack and brought out a black string of jerky. His white teeth gnawed at the string until the tough meat parted. He chewed slowly and drank occasionally from the water bag. His little eyes were slumberous and tired, but the muscles of his face were hard set. The earth of the trail was black now. It gave up a hollow sound under the walking hoofbeats.

The stream fell more sharply. Little waterfalls splashed on the stones. Five-fingered ferns hung over the water and dripped spray from their fingertips. Pepe rode half over in his saddle, dangling one leg loosely. He picked a bay leaf from a tree beside the way and put it into his mouth for a moment to flavor the dry jerky. He held the gun loosely across the pommel.

Suddenly he squared in his saddle, swung the horse from the trail and kicked it hurriedly up behind a big redwood tree. He pulled up the reins tight against the bit to keep the horse from whinnying. His face was intent and his nostrils quivered a little.

A hollow pounding came down the trail, and a horseman rode by, a fat man with red cheeks and a white stubble beard. His horse put down its head and blubbered at the trail when it came to the place where Pepé had turned off. "Hold up!" said the man and he pulled up his horse's head.

When the last sound of the hoofs died away, Pepé came back into the trail again. He did not relax in the saddle any more. He lifted the big rifle and swung the lever to throw a shell into the chamber, and then he let down the hammer to half cock.

The trail grew very steep. Now the redwood trees were smaller and their tops were dead, bitten dead where the wind reached them. The horse plodded on; the sun went slowly overhead and started down toward the afternoon.

Where the stream came out of a side canyon, the trail left it. Pepé dismounted and watered his horse and filled up his water bag. As soon as the trail had parted from the stream, the trees were gone and only the thick brittle sage and manzanita and chaparral edged the trail. And the soft black earth was gone, too, leaving only the light tan broken rock for the trail bed. Lizards scampered away into the brush as the horse rattled over the little stones.

Pepé turned in his saddle and looked back. He was in the open now: he could be seen from a distance. As he ascended the trail the country grew more rough and terrible and dry. The way wound about the bases of great square rocks. Little gray rabbits skittered in the brush. A bird made a monotonous high creaking. Eastward the bare rock mountaintops were pale and powder-dry under the dropping sun. The horse plodded up and up the trail toward a little V in the ridge which was the pass.

Pepé looked suspiciously back every minute or so, and his eyes sought the tops of the ridges ahead. Once, on a white barren spur, he saw a black figure for a moment, but he looked quickly away, for it was one of the dark watchers. No one knew who the watchers were, nor where they lived, but it was better to ignore them and never to show interest in them. They did not bother one who stayed on the trail and minded his own business.

The air was parched and full of light dust blown by the breeze from the eroding mountains. Pepé drank sparingly from his bag and corked it tightly and hung it on the horn again. The trail moved up the dry shale hillside, avoiding rocks, dropping under clefts, climbing in and out of old water scars. When he arrived at the little pass he stopped and looked back for a long time. No dark watchers were to be seen now. The trail behind was empty. Only the high tops of the redwoods indicated where the stream flowed.

Pepé rode on through the pass. His little eyes were nearly closed with weariness, but his face was stern, relentless and manly. The high mountain wind coasted sighing through the pass and whistled on the edges of the big blocks of broken granite. In the air, a red-tailed hawk sailed over close to the ridge and screamed angrily. Pepé went slowly through the broken jagged pass and looked down on the other side.

The trail dropped quickly, staggering among broken rock. At the bottom of the slope there was a dark crease, thick with brush, and on the other side of the crease a little flat, in which a grove of oak trees grew. A scar of green grass cut across the flat. And behind the flat another mountain rose, desolate with dead rocks and starving little black bushes. Pepé drank from the bag again for the air was so dry that it encrusted his nostrils and burned his lips. He put the horse down the trail. The hooves slipped and struggled on the steep way, starting little stones that rolled off into the brush. The sun was gone behind the westward mountain now, but still it glowed brilliantly on the oaks and on the grassy flat. The rocks and the hillsides still sent up waves of the heat they had gathered from the day's sun.

Pepé looked up to the top of the next dry withered ridge. He saw a dark form against the sky, a man's figure standing on top of a rock, and he glanced away quickly not to appear curious. When a moment later he looked up again, the figure was gone.

Downward the trail was quickly covered. Sometimes the horse floundered for footing, sometimes set his feet and slid a little way. They came at last to the bottom where the dark chaparral was higher than Pepé's head. He held up his rifle on one side and his arm on the other to shield his face from the sharp brittle fingers of the brush.

Up and out of the crease he rode, and up a little cliff. The grassy flat was before him, and the round comfortable oaks. For a moment he studied the trail down which he had come, but there was no movement and no sound from it. Finally he rode out over the flat, to the green streak, and at the upper end of the damp he found a little spring welling out of the earth and dropping into a dug basin before it seeped out over the flat.

Pepé filled his bag first, and then he let the thirsty horse drink out of the pool. He led the horse to the clump of oaks, and in the middle of the

19

grove, fairly protected from sight on all sides, he took off the saddle and the bridle and laid them on the ground. The horse stretched his jaws sideways and yawned. Pepé knotted the lead rope about the horse's neck and tied him to a sapling among the oaks, where he could graze in a fairly large circle.

When the horse was gnawing hungrily at the dry grass, Pepé went to the saddle and took a black string of jerky from the sack and strolled to an oak tree on the edge of the grove, from under which he could watch the trail. He sat down in the crisp dry oak leaves and automatically felt for his big black knife to cut the jerky, but he had no knife. He leaned back on his elbow and gnawed at the tough strong meat. His face was blank, but it was a man's face.

The bright evening light washed the eastern ridge, but the valley was darkening. Doves flew down from the hills to the spring, and the quail came running out of the brush and joined them, calling clearly to one another.

Out of the corner of his eye Pepé saw a shadow grow out of the bushy crease. He turned his head slowly. A big spotted wildcat was creeping toward the spring, belly to the ground, moving like thought.

Pepé cocked his rifle and edged the muzzle slowly around. Then he looked apprehensively up the trail and dropped the hammer again. From the ground beside him he picked an oak twig and threw it toward the spring. The quail flew up with a roar and the doves whistled away. The big cat stood up: for a long moment he looked at Pepé with cold yellow eyes, and then fearlessly walked back into the gulch.

The dusk gathered quickly in the deep valley. Pepé muttered his prayers, put his head down on his arm and went instantly to sleep.

The moon came up and filled the valley with cold blue light, and the wind swept rustling down from the peaks. The owls worked up and down the slopes looking for rabbits. Down in the brush of the gulch a coyote gabbled. The oak trees whispered softly in the night breeze.

Pepé started up, listening. His horse had whinnied. The moon was just slipping behind the western ridge, leaving the valley in darkness behind it. Pepé sat tensely gripping his rifle. From far up the trail he heard an answering whinny and the crash of shod hooves on the broken rock. He jumped to his feet, ran to his horse and led it under the trees. He threw on the saddle and cinched it tight for the steep trail, caught the unwilling head and forced the bit into the mouth. He felt the saddle to make sure the water bag and the sack of jerky were there. Then he mounted and turned up the hill.

It was velvet dark. The horse found the entrance to the trail where it left the flat, and started up, stumbling and slipping on the rocks. Pepé's hand rose up to his head. His hat was gone. He had left it under the oak tree.

The horse had struggled far up the trail when the first change of dawn came into the air, a steel grayness as light mixed thoroughly with dark. Gradually the sharp snaggled edge of the ridge stood out above them, rotten granite tortured and eaten by the winds of time. Pepé had dropped his reins on the horn, leaving direction to the horse. The brush grabbed at his legs in the dark until one knee of his jeans was ripped.

Gradually the light flowed down over the ridge. The starved brush and rocks stood out in the half light, strange and lonely in high perspective. Then there came warmth into the light. Pepé drew up and looked back, but he could see nothing in the darker valley below. The sky turned blue over the coming sun. In the waste of the mountainside, the poor dry brush grew only three feet high. Here and there, big outcroppings of unrotted granite stood up like moldering houses. Pepé relaxed a little. He drank from his water bag and bit off a piece of jerky. A single eagle flew over, high in the light.

Without warning Pepé's horse screamed and fell on its side. He was almost down before the rifle crash echoed up from the valley. From a hole behind the struggling shoulder, a stream of bright crimson blood pumped and stopped and pumped and stopped. The hooves threshed on the ground. Pepé lay half stunned beside the horse. He looked slowly down the hill. A piece of sage clipped off beside his head and another crash echoed up from side to side of the canyon. Pepé flung himself frantically behind a bush.

He crawled up the hill on his knees and on one hand. His right hand held the rifle up off the ground and pushed it ahead of him. He moved with the instinctive care of an animal. Rapidly he wormed his way toward one of the big outcroppings of granite on the hill above him. Where the brush was high he doubled up and ran, but where the cover was slight he wriggled forward on his stomach, pushing the rifle ahead of him. In the last little distance there was no cover at all. Pepé poised and then he darted across the space and flashed around the corner of the rock.

He leaned panting against the stone. When his breath came easier he moved along behind the big rock until he came to a narrow split that offered a thin section of vision down the hill. Pepé lay on his stomach and pushed the rifle barrel through the slit and waited.

The sun reddened the western ridges now. Already the buzzards were settling down toward the place where the horse lay. A small brown bird scratched in the dead sage leaves directly in front of the rifle muzzle. The coasting eagle flew back toward the rising sun.

Pepé saw a little movement in the brush far below. His grip tightened

21

on the gun. A little brown doe stepped daintily out on the trail and crossed it and disappeared into the brush again. For a long time Pepé waited. Far below he could see the little flat and the oak trees and the slash of green. Suddenly his eyes flashed back at the trail again. A quarter of a mile down there had been a quick movement in the chaparral. The rifle swung over. The front sight nestled in the V of the rear sight. Pepé studied for a moment and then raised the rear sight a notch. The little movement in the brush came again. The sight settled on it. Pepé squeezed the trigger. The explosion crashed down the mountain and up the other side, and came rattling back. The whole side of the slope grew still. No more movement. And then a white streak cut into the granite of the slit and a bullet whined away and a crash sounded up from below. Pepé felt a sharp pain in his right hand. A sliver of granite was sticking out from between his first and second knuckles and the point protruded from his palm. Carefully he pulled out the sliver of stone. The wound bled evenly and gently. No vein nor artery was cut.

Pepé looked into a little dusty cave in the rock and gathered a handful of spider web, and he pressed the mass into the cut, plastering the soft web into the blood. The flow stopped almost at once.

The rifle was on the ground. Pepé picked it up, levered a new shell into the chamber. And then he slid into the brush on his stomach. Far to the right he crawled, and then up the hill, moving slowly and carefully, crawling to cover and resting and then crawling again.

In the mountains the sun is high in its arc before it penetrates the gorges. The hot face looked over the hill and brought instant heat with it. The white light beat on the rocks and reflected from them and rose up quivering from the earth again, and the rocks and bushes seemed to quiver behind the air.

Pepé crawled in the general direction of the ridge peak, zig-zagging for cover. The deep cut between his knuckles began to throb. He crawled close to a rattlesnake before he saw it, and when it raised its dry head and made a soft beginning whirr, he backed up and took another way. The quick gray lizards flashed in front of him, raising a tiny line of dust. He found another mass of spider web and pressed it against his throbbing hand.

Pepé was pushing the rifle with his left hand now. Little drops of sweat ran to the ends of his coarse black hair and rolled down his cheeks. His lips and tongue were growing thick and heavy. His lips writhed to draw saliva into his mouth. His little dark eyes were uneasy and suspicious. Once when a gray lizard pushed in front of him on the parched ground and turned its head sideways he crushed it flat with a stone.

When the sun slid past noon he had not gone a mile. He crawled exhaustedly a last hundred yards to a patch of high sharp manzanita, crawled desperately, and when the patch was reached he wriggled in among the tough gnarly trunks and dropped his head on his left arm. There was little shade in the meager brush, but there was cover and safety. Pepé went to sleep as he lay and the sun beat on his back. A few little birds hopped close to him and peered and hopped away. Pepé squirmed in his sleep and he raised and dropped his wounded hand again and again.

The sun went down behind the peaks and the cool evening came, and then the dark. A coyote yelled from the hillside. Pepé started awake and looked about with misty eyes. His hand was swollen and heavy; a little thread of pain ran up the inside of his arm and settled in a pocket in his armpit. He peered about and then stood up, for the mountains were black and the moon had not yet risen. Pepé stood up in the dark. The coat of his father pressed on his arm. His tongue was swollen until it nearly filled his mouth. He wriggled out of the coat and dropped it in the brush, and then he struggled up the hill, falling over rocks and tearing his way through the brush. The rifle knocked against stones as he went. Little dry avalanches of gravel and shattered stone went whispering down the hill behind him.

After a while the old moon came up and showed the jagged ridge top ahead of him. By moonlight Pepé traveled more easily. He bent forward so that his throbbing arm hung away from his body. The journey uphill was made in dashes and rests, a frantic rush up a few yards and then a rest. The wind coasted down the slope rattling the dry stems of the bushes.

The moon was at meridian when Pepé came at last to the sharp backbone of the ridge top. On the last hundred yards of the rise no soil had clung under the wearing winds. The way was on solid rock. He clambered to the top and looked down on the other side. There was a draw like the last below him, misty with moonlight, brushed with dry struggling sage and chaparral. On the other side the hill rose up sharply and at the top the jagged rotten teeth of the mountain showed against the sky. At the bottom of the cut the brush was thick and dark.

Pepé stumbled down the hill. His throat was almost closed with thirst. At first he tried to run, but immediately he fell and rolled. After that he went more carefully. The moon was just disappearing behind the mountains when he came to the bottom. He crawled into the heavy brush feeling with his fingers for water. There was no water in the bed of the stream, only damp earth. Pepé laid his gun down and scooped up a handful of mud and put it in his mouth, and then he spluttered and scraped the earth from his tongue with his finger, for the mud drew at his mouth like a poultice. He dug a hole in the stream bed with his fingers, dug a little basin to catch water; but before it was very deep his head fell forward on the damp ground and he slept.

The dawn came and the heat of the day fell on the earth, and still Pepé slept. Late in the afternoon his head jerked up. He looked slowly around. His eyes were slits of wariness. Twenty feet away in the heavy brush a big tawny mountain lion stood looking at him. Its long thick tail waved gracefully, its ears erect with interest, not laid back dangerously. The lion squatted down on its stomach and watched him.

Pepé looked at the hole he had dug in the earth. A half inch of muddy water had collected in the bottom. He tore the sleeve from his hurt arm, with his teeth ripped out a little square, soaked it in the water and put it in his mouth. Over and over he filled the cloth and sucked it.

Still the lion sat and watched him. The evening came down but there was no movement on the hills. No birds visited the dry bottom of the cut. Pepé looked occasionally at the lion. The eyes of the yellow beast drooped as though he were about to sleep. He yawned and his long thin red tongue curled out. Suddenly his head jerked around and his nostrils quivered. His big tail lashed. He stood up and slunk like a tawny shadow into the thick brush.

A moment later Pepé heard the sound, the faint far crash of horses' hooves on gravel. And he heard something else, a high whining yelp of a dog.

Pepé took his rifle in his left hand and he glided into the brush almost as quietly as the lion had. In the darkening evening he crouched up the hill toward the next ridge. Only when the dark came did he stand up. His energy was short. Once it was dark he fell over the rocks and slipped to his knees on the steep slope, but he moved on and on up the hill, climbing and scrabbling over the broken hillside.

When he was far up toward the top, he lay down and slept for a little while. The withered moon shining on his face awakened him. He stood up and moved up the hill. Fifty yards away he stopped and turned back, for he had forgotten his rifle. He walked heavily down and poked about in the brush, but he could not find the gun. At last he lay down to rest. The pocket of pain in his armpit had grown more sharp. His arm seemed to swell out and fall with every heartbeat. There was no position lying down where the heavy arm did not press against his armpit.

With the effort of a hurt beast, Pepé got up and moved again toward the top of the ridge. He held his swollen arm away from his body with his left hand. Up the steep hill he dragged himself, a few steps and a rest, and a few more steps. At last he was nearing the top. The moon showed the uneven sharp back of it against the sky.

Pepé's brain spun in a big spiral up and away from him. He slumped to the ground and lay still. The rock ridge top was only a hundred feet above him.

The moon moved over the sky. Pepé half turned on his back. His tongue tried to make words, but only a thick hissing came from between his lips.

When the dawn came, Pepé pulled himself up. His eyes were sane again. He drew his great puffed arm in front of him and looked at the angry wound. The black line ran up from his wrist to his armpit. Automatically he reached in his pocket for the big black knife, but it was not there. His eyes searched the ground. He picked up a sharp blade of stone and scraped at the wound, sawed at the proud flesh and then squeezed the green juice out in big drops. Instantly he threw back his head and whined like a dog. His whole right side shuddered at the pain, but the pain cleared his head.

In the gray light he struggled up the last slope to the ridge and crawled over and lay down behind a line of rocks. Below him lay a deep canyon exactly like the last, waterless and desolate. There was no flat, no oak trees, not even heavy brush in the bottom of it. And on the other side a sharp ridge stood up, thinly brushed with starving sage, littered with broken granite. Strewn over the hill there were giant outcroppings, and on the top the granite teeth stood out against the sky.

The new day was light now. The flame of sun came over the ridge and fell on Pepé where he lay on the ground. His coarse black hair was littered with twigs and bits of spider web. His eyes had retreated back into his head. Between his lips the tip of his black tongue showed.

He sat up and dragged his great arm into his lap and nursed it, rocking his body and moaning in his throat. He threw back his head and looked up into the pale sky. A big black bird circled nearly out of sight, and far to the left another was sailing near.

He lifted his head to listen, for a familiar sound had come to him from the valley he had climbed out of; it was the crying yelp of hounds, excited and feverish, on a trail.

Pepé bowed his head quickly. He tried to speak rapid words but only a thick hiss came from his lips. He drew a shaky cross on his breast with his left hand. It was a long struggle to get to his feet. He crawled slowly and mechanically to the top of a big rock on the ridge peak. Once there, he arose slowly, swaying to his feet, and stood erect. Far below he could see the dark brush where he had slept. He braced his feet and stood there, black against the morning sky.

There came a ripping sound at his feet. A piece of stone flew up and a bullet droned off into the next gorge. The hollow crash echoed up from below. Pepé looked down for a moment and then pulled himself straight again.

25

His body jarred back. His left hand fluttered helplessly toward his breast. The second crash sounded from below. Pepé swung forward and toppled from the rock. His body struck and rolled over and over, starting a little avalanche. And when at last he stopped against a bush, the avalanche slid slowly down and covered up his head.

Applications

Setting characterizes What does the lush, green, soft setting through which Pepé rides at the beginning of his flight suggest about his state of mind and mood at this point?

Setting heightens probability How does the setting described in the last portion of the story heighten the probability of Pepé's death?

Setting creates atmosphere How would you describe the atmosphere created by this description of setting:

Below him lay a deep canyon exactly like the last, waterless and desolate. There was no flat, no oak trees, not even heavy brush in the bottom of it. And on the other side a sharp ridge stood up, thinly brushed with starving sage, littered with broken granite. Strewn over the hill there were giant outcroppings, and on the top the granite teeth stood out against the sky.

Setting communicates ideas Why does Pepé want to wear his father's hatband and silk green handkerchief? What do the father's possessions—the knife, the hatband, the handkerchief, the saddle, the black coat, the gun—symbolize?

ANALYZING AND WRITING ABOUT SETTING

Analyzing Setting

It has been said that the greatest art seems the most artless. When an author writes an extremely good short story everything "clicks," all seems natural, we get involved in it. When we finish reading the story we have an impression, a feeling, but it is often difficult to explain exactly how the author managed to evoke that impression.

Now comes the critical analysis that many persons hate, for they regard it as "picking apart" the work. In a way, this reaction is akin to saying that studying how a noble building is constructed, or how a beautiful painting is composed, or how a moving symphony is orchestrated is to destroy one's appreciation of the beauty of the building or painting or symphony—which is not true.

Such analysis can heighten our appreciation of a work of art by letting us into the artist's mind, by letting us see him at work, by letting us admire both his techniques and the finished work created by these techniques. Such analysis enables us to enjoy a work on an intellectual, conscious level as well as on an emotional and intuitive level.

Limiting Our first step in analyzing the functions of setting in "Flight" is to determine *what* the major settings in the story are. Eventually, we will have to go back to the story and review, but not yet. We can start out using memory.

Two major elements of setting come readily to mind: the "things" that belonged to Pepé's father and the landscape, the mountains into which Pepé flees. Let's limit ourselves to one of these major elements, the landscape. When there are multiple settings in a piece of literature, or distinct elements of setting (in this case "nature" and man-made "things") it is best to limit your discussion to one of the major elements. Such limitation helps produce a tightly focused and unified paper.

After you have chosen a particular aspect of setting, you should note, in writing, its characteristics. Once you have got these characteristics written down, and documented with specific scenes, you can then turn to the matter of function and meaning.

Analyzing In "Flight," the further Pepé flees the more barren the landscape becomes.

I. In the first part of Pepé's flight, the setting is lush and green. The canyon that Pepé first passes through is rich with vegetation, perfumed, and well-watered by a flowing stream.

II. After the first sign of danger, the horseman with red cheeks, the landscape loses its earlier lushness. The trail grows steeper, the trees smaller.

III. As soon as the trail leaves the stream the country grows "more rough and terrible and dry."

IV. After Pepé passes through the V-shaped pass, the landscape becomes even more barren.
   A. There is only one sign of water in all the landscape and it is described as a "scar."
   B. At the watering place a wildcat looks at Pepé with "cold yellow eyes."

V. After Pepé leaves this second watering place, all is desolate, lifeless and "rotten."

VI. After Pepé's horse has been shot and his hand injured, he struggles into even more hostile country.
   A. At the third watering place there is no water, only damp earth.
   B. A mountain lion watches Pepé.

VII. As Pepé struggles up the "last slope" and over the ridge he discovers "a deep canyon exactly like the last." But this time, there is not even moisture at the bottom of the canyon. The landscape is essentially lifeless.

After you have analyzed the setting in the manner indicated, you are ready to turn to the matter of its function or functions in the story.

You should make a checklist of the various functions of setting and then examine each one in relation to the setting you are analyzing.

1. Does the setting directly reveal Pepé's character?
2. Does the setting characterize Pepé metaphorically?
3. Does the setting heighten the probability of the action?
4. Does the setting help create an appropriate atmosphere?
5. Does the setting communicate ideas, beliefs, or values by acquiring symbolic overtones?

Since the aspect of setting which we are concerned with is the natural setting, a setting independent of Pepé and not influenced by him, we can answer "no" to question 1, and go on to question 2.

When we look over our analysis of the setting, and then think of Pepé, it becomes clear that there *is* a connection between the changing nature of the setting and Pepé's situation and state of mind. Steinbeck doesn't tell us Pepé's thoughts or describe his emotions, but the setting does, metaphorically. We can infer that when Pepé first set out he had hope of escaping. Parallel to this state of mind is the lush green setting of the first part of his flight. Then, after his first scare, the setting becomes less attractive, less warm and soothing. This change can be seen as reflecting Pepé's changed attitude. The analogy between character and setting is sustained throughout the story: as Pepé's situation and (by inference) his outlook become bleaker and bleaker, so does the setting.

So, we can explain that setting in "Flight" reveals, by analogy or metaphorically, Pepé's progression from hope and confidence to despair. But, before we begin to write, we should see if the setting has other important functions.

Questions 3 and 4 can also be answered positively. As the countryside becomes increasingly barren and forbidding, the possibility of Pepé's surviving becomes less and less until, toward the end, Pepé's death seems inevitable. This sense of the inevitability of Pepé's death is reinforced by the bleak and sterile atmosphere which the setting helps create.

Question 5 is broader and more inclusive than the others. Insofar as the setting and the changes in the setting symbolize Pepé's progressive loss of hope and foreshadow his death, the answer would again be "yes." Certainly, to step outside our limitation for a moment, the various possessions of Pepé's father are invested with symbolic significance.

Writing About Setting

State your view about the function(s) of setting in the literary work   If, as in this case, you are going to deal with a limited part of the setting, make that limitation clear to the reader. Further, if you are going to assert that the setting has more than one function, state the less important functions first and the most important function last. This will give your paper an effective "climactic" order. Hence, you might begin by writing:

> In "Flight" the changing nature of the country into which Pepé flees increases the probability of his eventual death. As the landscape becomes increasingly barren, the possibility of life surviving in it becomes more and more remote. The increasingly forbidding landscape also creates an atmos-

29

phere of sterility and lifelessness, which, in turn, heightens our feeling that Pepé is doomed. But, even more importantly, the changing nature of the landscape functions to reveal to us Pepé's changing emotions and state of mind in the course of his flight.

Explain, amplify, and illustrate each of your assertions about setting   This explanation, amplification, and illustration will be the body of your essay. Your job is to convince the reader of the truth of *each* of the assertions about setting made in the introductory paragraph. In order to convince the reader you should develop your assertions, one at a time, in the order in which they appear in your first paragraph. Consider each assertion the central idea for a miniature essay. In other words, each must be developed in such a way that your treatment satisfies two demands which the reader makes whenever you make a general assertion: "How?" and "For instance?"

The answer to "how?" comes from your understanding of the function of setting. The answer to "for instance?" consists of references to or quotations from the text. Here's how you might proceed (the introductory paragraph is repeated so we can keep everything together):

Setting in "Flight"

In "Flight" the changing nature of the countryside into which Pepé flees increases the probability of his eventual death. As the landscape becomes increasingly barren, the possibility of life surviving in it becomes more and more remote. The increasingly forbidding landscape also creates an atmosphere of sterility and lifelessness which, in turn, heightens our feeling that Pepé is doomed. But even more importantly, the changing nature of the landscape functions to reveal to us Pepé's changing emotions and state of mind in the course of his flight.

In the first stage of Pepé's flight the landscape is lush and green. The light is "perfumed and purple," the path is "dark soft leaf-mold earth." It is a peaceful, kind setting with no hint of fear or threat. But as Pepé flees further, and especially after the trail leaves the stream, the landscape becomes increasingly barren and rugged. When Pepé turns into the mountains the country becomes "more rough and terrible and dry." After he rides through the V pass, he sees "another mountain . . . desolate with dead rocks and starving little black bushes." The landscape continues to deteriorate until, in the end, it is virtually lifeless:

> Below him lay a deep canyon exactly like the last, waterless and desolate. There was no flat, no oak trees, not even heavy brush in the bottom of it. And on the other side a sharp ridge stood up, thinly brushed with starving sage, littered with broken granite. Strewn over the hill there were giant outcroppings, and on the top the granite teeth stood out against the sky.

Even a strong and healthy man could not long survive without water and food and shelter in country like this. And Pepé, at this point, is already dying of gangrene poisoning and tormented by thirst. In such a setting, his death is inevitable.

> *Note: The preceding paragraph explains how the changing setting heightens the probability of Pepé's death, and includes numerous examples ("for instances") from the text in support of the explanation. We can now develop the second assertion in the first paragraph, which concerns the relation of setting to atmosphere.*

The increasingly forbidding landscape also creates an atmosphere of sterility and lifelessness which, in turn, heightens our feeling that Pepé is doomed. As we have already observed, the setting of the first stage of his flight is lush and moist and green. But the peaceful atmosphere created by this setting is soon dissipated as Pepé journeys into an increasingly barren and hostile countryside. The scenes we have already examined reveal a landscape gradually becoming a moonscape—arid, barren and sun-tortured. The "emotional aura" of starkness and bleakness that envelopes the latter portion of the story reinforces our conviction that Pepé is doomed.

> *Note: Here we explain and amplify, we tell how the setting creates an atmosphere that heightens probability. But, for our "for instance's" we refer the reader to passages previously mentioned. There is no point in repeating these allusions to the text; but if such scenes had not been previously cited, we would have to cite them here. For all assertions must be supported and documented by allusion to or quotation from specific scenes in the text. We are now ready to develop our view of the most important function of setting in "Flight."*

The setting in "Flight" has still another function, which is, in some respects, even more significant than the two uses already discussed. The changing landscape, the changing "outer" world, reveals to the reader Pepé's "inner" world, his changing emotions and state of mind. As the landscape changes from soft fertile lushness to hard, sterile barrenness we can infer Pepé's gradual loss of hope and his growing despair and desperation.

As we have already noted, Pepé's flight begins in a leisurely way, through a rich forest. This setting suggests Pepé's own emotions. He is not yet fatigued, he has not yet heard the sounds of pursuit, he is confident that he is a "man." Soon, however, this mood is shattered by a "hollow pounding" on the trail, and the horseman rides by. After this, Pepé's relaxed attitude vanishes, and he pumps a shell into the chamber of his rifle. Immediately, the landscape changes too: "The trail grew very steep. Now the redwood trees were smaller and their tops were dead, bitten dead where the wind reached them." The "wind of fear" generated by the galloping horseman may well have "bitten dead" the heights of Pepé's confidence and security.

When Pepé turns from the stream into the mountains, the country grows "more rough and terrible and dry." It is easy to imagine how Pepé's own spirits must have sunk as he turned away from water and vegetation into the barren and forbidding mountains. The full impact of his flight is brought home by this irrevocable act.

As Pepé grows more weary and as the "dark watchers" appear, the countryside becomes increasingly desolate. The only green is now described as a "scar of green grass." Where before there was a stream of water, now there is only a "little spring." And here, at the "grassy flat," a big spotted wildcat looks at Pepé with "cold yellow eyes." The setting can thus be seen as symbolizing Pepé's ebbing hope and, in the "cold yellow eyes" of the wildcat, his growing fearfulness.

After Pepé's horse is shot, buzzards appear, and later, after he is wounded, a rattlesnake threatens him. Both are associated with death and deadliness and suggest Pepé's own increasing awareness of impending death.

Finally, when Pepé's situation has become hopeless, when he must know that he is dying, when the only choice left for him to make is the manner of his dying, we come to the long descriptive passage quoted on the first page of this paper. The total desolation of the landscape reflects the total desolation of Pepé's hope of escape. Outer world and inner world are exactly parallel. Setting has become character.

Note: In a relatively short paper (500–700 words), a separate "conclusion" paragraph is often unnecessary and may, in fact, reduce the impact of your essay by being anticlimatic. But you don't want to just "drop" the reader, either. In this theme the last two sentences are, in effect, conclusion. The final sentence, with its note of finality, signals the end of the paper without dragging the matter out or inflicting upon the reader unnecessary or incongruous summary.

Sometimes, however, a paragraph of "conclusion" is desirable. In deciding, ask yourself whether the ending you have is logical, natural, and smooth. If it seems abrupt, or if the main points you've made need to be brought together, then you should write a brief conclusion paragraph. You can get a feeling for the distinction by examining other sample essays in this book.

TWO

CHARACTER

UNDERSTANDING CHARACTER

Appearance Characterizes

"Don't judge a book by its cover," runs one cliché. "Appearances are deceiving," says another. "Beware of first impressions," goes a third. The widespread currency of these admonitions reveals the strength of our impulse to characterize people on the basis of their appearance. For, in everyday life, a person's appearance is often deceiving.

In literature, as in life, we find characters whose appearance is at odds with their character: frail, bespectacled little men who turn out to be brave; muscular "he-men" who reveal themselves as cowardly. But, more typically, the description of a character's appearance is intended to evoke from us certain judgments about what he or she is like. The author uses aspects of a character's appearance to suggest aspects of personality.

Physiognomy, the art of inferring character from facial and body characteristics, has a long history, and even today there are reputable scientists who maintain its validity. W. H. Sheldon postulated three basic body types, the tall and bony (ectomorph), the muscular and proportional (mesomorph), the chubby and flaccid (endomorph):

Each body type is associated with certain personality traits. The ectomorph is seen as being introverted and intellectual; the mesomorph as being aggressive and physical; the endomorph as being complacent and self-indulgent.

Similarly, a jutting chin is popularly associated with forcefulness and decisiveness, a receding chin with indecision and lack of moral fibre. Shifty eyes suggest deceitfulness; beady eyes, calculation and coldness.

Authors often exploit our tendency to equate details of appearance with particular character traits. Steinbeck, for instance, refers repeatedly to Pepé's "little eyes," a physical characteristic that suggests a sly and untrustworthy character and which makes us doubt Pepé's emphatic claims to manhood and maturity. The Swede in Stephen Crane's "The Blue Hotel" is described as "shaky and quick-eyed," two details of appearance that suggest suspiciousness, nervousness, and fearfulness. In *The Great Gatsby* Tom Buchanan's appearance is explicitly equated with his character:

> Now he was a sturdy straw-haired man of thirty with a rather hard mouth and a supercilious manner. Two shining arrogant eyes had established dominance over his face and gave him the appearance of always leaning aggressively forward.

Here the terms used to evoke a picture of Buchanan in the mind's eye of the reader reveal aspects of his personality: *hardness, superciliousness, arrogance, dominance, aggressiveness.*

Names Characterize

Imagine yourself as Personnel Director for a large company. You have been instructed to hire a person whose primary duty will be to solicit new accounts by writing personal letters to businessmen. There are two equally qualified applicants: a Mr. Mortimer Snerd and a Mr. Victor Trueblood. Which man would you hire?

The name of the game is image. By sound and association, a name can suggest broad aspects of character—personality, disposition, competency, trustworthiness—as well as appearance and ethnic background. Recognizing this, authors often use names to characterize, especially when presenting one-dimensional or stereotyped characters. Wolf Larson is the hard, amoral, "wolfish" protagonist of Jack London's novel *The Sea Wolf*. In Joseph Heller's *Catch 22*, Major Major is a comical and ridiculous figure—as silly as his name. Framton Nuttel in Saki's "The Open Window" is, quite literally, "nutty." Often, too, authors employ names with biblical antecedents for their associative value. An "Eve" might suggest either innocence or seductiveness, a "Ruth" quite different qualities.

35

Speech Characterizes

Consider for a moment the vast difference between everyday conversation with friends and acquaintances, and the intimate talk of two people newly in love, or falling in love. The first is often a pretty casual sort of thing—we're getting along with people we already know. But the quiet, intimate talk of two people falling in love, that's something else altogether. Everything counts: what is said, and what isn't said, too. Tone, pitch, pauses—all are important. In this sort of talk the two people are deeply committed; they listen intently to each other's speech—for they are revealing their character, their being, to each other.

In serious literature *all* speech is like the talk of lovers: everything counts and everything is important because everything that is said reveals something significant about the character of the person speaking or about the character of the person he is speaking to, or both. We should listen to all speech in literature with the intensity and receptivity with which we would listen to the words of a lover.

Speech characterizes by implication   In conversation people seldom make explicit statements about their own "character." It's a rare man who tells others, "I think I'm great!" or who tries to win a woman's affection by saying, "I'm an unhappy and lonely person in need of love." Yet, after a conversation with another, we may say to ourselves, "He's conceited," or, "He's a lonely, unhappy person who is looking for a combination mother-mistress." We have inferred certain character traits, probably quite accurately, even though the person hasn't said a word about "what he's like."

In literature the process is exactly the same. But we have to pay close attention. We have to be alert for the implications. Notice how speech reveals character in this scene:

> "Oh look at the cute little pickaninny!" she said and pointed to a Negro child standing in the door of a shack. "Wouldn't that make a picture, now?" she asked and they all turned and looked at the little Negro out of the back window. He waved.
>
> "He didn't have any britches on," June said.
>
> "He probably didn't have any," the grandmother explained. "Little niggers in the country don't have things like we do. If I could paint, I'd paint that picture," she said.
>
> —Flannery O'Connor, "A Good Man Is Hard to Find"

The grandmother's use of the terms "pickaninny" and "nigger" reveals her racial prejudice. She regards a scene of wretchedness as picturesque and would like to "paint a picture" of it, not as a damning social indictment but as a bit of "local color." This expressed wish reveals how completely she has accepted racist values and reveals her inability to perceive either the social injustices that produced the scene or the wretchedness of the people in it.

Student reactions to close reading Let's digress for a moment in order to discuss two common student reactions to the close reading of literature. We *think* that both of these reactions can be traced to a single misconception, and we *know* that both of them seriously interfere with an instructor's ability to teach literature and with the ability of many students to fully understand and enjoy literature.

Reaction 1: BULL! Many students in basic literature courses respond to their instructor's "deep" and "involved" explication of a story or poem with the unvoiced sentiment, "Bull!" They think the instructor is reading into the work meanings and ideas that aren't really there. Such students may look disgustedly out a window while their instructor rants on and on. Or they may slouch resentfully in their chairs. Or they may just turn off and tune out. They know bull when they hear it.

Reaction 2: GEE! Sometimes this reaction is an honest one—the student really is impressed by the depth of the instructor's insight into a literary work. Such students exalt the instructor's intellectual capacities and marvel at the great gap between their own ignorance and the instructor's insight. Often, though, this reaction is simply a dishonest version of "BULL!" The student remains unconvinced. But he or she has learned that some teachers reward admiration with higher grades. So why not? "GEE!"

Even when this reaction is an honest one it is just as destructive of full enjoyment and understanding of literature as the "bull" reaction. For it involves looking at the instructor as a kind of god whose powers of perception are far beyond the reach of a mere student. Hence, it encourages a passive "Tell me, Teach" attitude. "Gee" students feel that they can't possibly rival their instructor's depth of insight, so they don't even try. They just wait for the instructor to tell them, and then write down the revealed truth.

We believe that both of these reactions can be traced to one all-important misconception. *This misconception is that dialogue in literature is like conversation in everyday life.*

In our everyday conversation with others we generally say what we mean and mean what we say. We may wish to inform: "English 320 meets on Tuesday and Thursday at 2:00 P.M." We may wish to express an emotion: "Ouch!" "Great!" "Damn!" We may wish to direct: "Please shut the door." But whatever our purpose, what we say can generally be taken at face value. There's no "hidden" meaning. What is actually said is what's important, not the implications of what is said. So, we develop the habit of listening to speech on one level only, the level of expressed content.

In literature, however, speech often functions on two levels. What is said, expressed content, is important. But often more important is the unexpressed content, the *implications* of what is said.

Close reading   In the passage quoted earlier, when June observes that the Negro boy wasn't wearing any pants, the grandmother responds:

> "He probably didn't have any . . . . Little niggers in the country don't have things like we do. If I could paint, I'd paint that picture . . . ."

Three sentences, that's all. But the implications—about the grandmother, about racial prejudice, about American society, about mankind—are devastating.

Notice first of all the literal meaning of the grandmother's first sentence: the Negro family is too poor to afford even one ragged pair of pants for the child. In the second sentence the grandmother casually "explains" the boy's lack of clothing with the observation, "'Little niggers in the country don't have things like we do.'" If someone said, "The Harold's have lots of *things*," what would come to mind? A car or maybe two cars, a nice house or apartment containing a television set and record player; appliances and gadgets such as a dishwasher, an electric can opener, a Waring blender, a Mixmaster, a clothes washer and dryer; other items, radios, a tape recorder, cameras, a movie projector, a power lawnmower, lawn chairs—the list can go on and on, a list of *luxury items*. Never would we think of "things" as enough food to sustain health, enough clothes to cover our nakedness, and shelter sufficient to protect us from the weather. These aren't *things*, these are the necessities for subsistence. Yet the Negro family lacks even these.

But none of this occurs to the grandmother. In the third sentence she returns to her desire to "paint a picture of that." The author is the one who has painted the picture, a three-sentence picture of misery and suffering casually ignored, a picture of an affluent racist society, a picture of people's incredible capacity for complacency and self-satisfaction, a picture of us and our America painted in the casual speech of a "nice old grandmother" who talks too much.

In short, serious literature of whatever genre—fiction, drama, poetry—has a "density" which both rewards and demands close reading. This density (sometimes called "economy" or "compactness"), is not just characteristic of dialogue in literature; it is also characteristic of all the other elements discussed in this book. Readers who realize this have taken a giant step toward enriched enjoyment and understanding of serious literature.

Behavior Characterizes

Actions speak louder than words in literature as well as in life. Behavior is character. What we do reveals what sort of person we are.

There is, however, a major difference between behavior in life and behavior in literature, a difference that parallels the distinction between conversation in everyday life and conversation in literature that we have discussed. In life much behavior is automatic, virtually meaningless robot behavior: get up, get dressed, go to school or job, run errands, and so forth. It doesn't really tell us very much about a person's nature or character. So, we tend to equate behavior and character only in gross ways. When a man beats his dog or his wife, when he lets people boss him around, when he singlehandedly kills twenty "enemy" soldiers—then we make some judgment about character.

In serious literature all behavior, like all speech, is meaningful and reveals significant aspects of character. The little things count as well as the big things. And the author expects us to know this.

Of course, behavior is action; it advances the plot. When the action of a narrative is exciting and suspenseful, it is easy to get so caught up in the plot that we may overlook the relation of behavior to character. Or the significance of a certain act may be overlooked because the act seems incidental and unimportant.

But the art of fiction is one of selection and compression. If the author intends more than simple entertainment, behavior must be studied for what it reveals about character.

At the end of Steinbeck's "Flight," Pepé, exhausted, dying of thirst and gangrene poisoning, obviously doomed, climbs one last ridge, painfully draws himself erect, and turns to face his pursuers. A bullet strikes the rock near his feet. He looks down for a moment and then pulls himself straight again. The next bullet strikes his chest and kills him. Had Pepé continued to crawl forward, or had he simply collapsed and waited passively for the pursuers to overtake him, he would have died miserably and abjectly. His action here, recognizing the inevitable, drawing himself erect, and facing death without panic, suggests that he has finally, and truly, achieved the courage that constitutes the manhood he had earlier falsely claimed.

Often, behavior is revealed in the course of a character's speech. In "Rain" Somerset Maugham lets a missionary couple damn themselves in the course of recounting their behavior upon being assigned to a group of Polynesian islands. The wife is speaking here:

> "Mr. Davidson and I talked it over and we made up our minds the first thing to do was to put down the dancing. The natives were crazy about dancing. . . . I'm thankful to God that we stamped it out, and I don't think I'm wrong in saying that no one has danced in our district for eight years."

39

Thoughts and Emotions Characterize

A recurrent figure in the literature of science fiction is the person who is able to read other people's minds, to hear their thoughts. Most of us would like to possess this ability, for then, we feel, we could really know other people: we could distinguish our false friends from our real friends, we could tell what a person really felt about us, we could get past the face and the sincere smile and the firm handshake to the person inside. When authors exercise their godlike prerogatives and lets us into a character's mind, they are opening to us an avenue for enriched understanding which is denied us in everyday life.

Appearance, speech, behavior—these are only the visible tip of the iceberg of character. They are supported and determined by the submerged workings of the mind. When we know a person's most private thoughts, shameful secrets, buried fantasies and fears, despair and joy, then we truly "know" that person. When a character's thoughts and emotions are revealed, either by the omniscient author or by the character himself, we should listen for implications with the attentive ear of a psychiatrist.

To illustrate:

> "Well, Mabel, and what are you going to do with yourself?" asked Joe, with foolish flippancy. He felt quite safe himself. Without listening for an answer, he turned aside, worked a grain of tobacco to the tip of his tongue, and spat it out. He did not care about anything, since he felt safe himself.
> —D. H. Lawrence, "The Horse-Dealer's Daughter"

In this passage Joe's question, taken by itself, suggests some concern for his sister. But the narrator's comment on Joe's tone and his description of Joe's emotions prevent such an interpretation. When we read "He did not care about anything, since he felt safe himself," we recognize the brother's hard and implacable selfishness.

Here is another illustrative passage:

> But what I felt most was my being a stranger to the ship; and if all the truth must be told, I was somewhat of a stranger to myself. The youngest man on board (barring the second mate), and untried as yet by a position of the fullest responsibility, I was willing to take the adequacy of the others for granted. They had simply to be equal to their tasks; but I wondered how far I should turn out to be faithful to that ideal conception of one's own personality every man sets up for himself secretly.
> —Joseph Conrad, "The Secret Sharer"

The young captain's statement of his thoughts and emotions on the first day of his first command reveals the most salient aspects of his character.

40

He does not know himself, he is unsure of his own adequacy. The entire story is a symbolic account of how he does come to know himself, of how he determines his adequacy.

Biography Characterizes

In literature biography characterizes with a good deal more reliability than it does in life. Again, the explanation of the discrepancy lies in authors' unwillingness to include irrelevant or nonfunctional material and in their desire to create characters who are representative.

In everyday life we are on dangerous ground if we infer character traits from a "life history" or "biographical sketch." People keep changing, developing. Their biography isn't complete until they're dead, and even then it only tells what they accomplished, not who they were. It reveals only the "public" person, not the inner or private person. But authors have full control over the biographies of their characters. They can use a few biographical details to suggest a lot about character.

In *The Great Gatsby*, for example, Nick Carraway's brief biography of Tom Buchanan suggests some of Buchanan's most significant character traits, his arrogance, his restlessness, his lack of fixed purpose or achievement, his carelessness:

> Her husband, among various physical accomplishments, had been one of the most powerful ends that ever played football at New Haven—a national figure in a way, one of those men who reach such an acute limited excellence at twenty-one that everything afterward savors of anti-climax. His family were enormously wealthy—even in college his freedom with money was a matter for reproach—but now he'd left Chicago and come East in a fashion that rather took your breath away: for instance, he'd brought down a string of polo ponies from Lake Forest. It was hard to realize that a man in my own generation was wealthy enough to do that.
>
> Why they came East I don't know. They had spent a year in France for no particular reason, and then drifted here and there unrestfully wherever people played polo and were rich together. This was a permanent move, said Daisy over the telephone, but I didn't believe it—I had no sight into Daisy's heart, but I felt that Tom would drift on forever seeking, a little wistfully, for the dramatic turbulence of some irrecoverable football game.
>
> —F. Scott Fitzgerald, *The Great Gatsby*

Images Characterize

A basic principle of effective writing is that *showing* is better than *telling*. Images "show"—they make us see, or hear, or feel, or taste, or smell. But they also "tell"—so an author gets two jobs done at the same time.

Images characterize by linking the associations they evoke to character and personality. "Screech," for example, is an unpleasant, grating

41

sound that gets on our nerves. Hence, if Mable is described as "screeching" at Henry, the author is not only describing the tone of Mable's voice but is *also*, in all likelihood, characterizing her as an unpleasant woman whose voice and personality grate on others.

Notice how images characterize in these passages (italics ours):

> Wilson looked at Macomber with his *flat, blue machine-gunner's eyes* . . . .
> —Ernest Hemingway, "The Short Happy Life of Francis Macomber"

Think of the qualities one might associate with a "machine gunner": extreme self-control and self-possession, intentness, courage, pitilessness. The image transfers all of these qualities to Wilson.

> I see him there
> Bringing a stone grasped firmly by the top
> In each hand, like an *old-stone savage armed.*
> —Robert Frost, "Mending Wall"

The simile conveys the spiritual and intellectual benightedness of the neighbor who "will not go behind his father's saying" and communicates the speaker's view of the potential savagery that lurks in those whose minds are closed.

> Pepé's wrist flicked like the *head of a snake.* The blade seemed to fly open in mid-air, and with a thump the point dug into the redwood post, and the black handle quivered.
> —John Steinbeck, "Flight"

The motion of Pepé's wrist is compared to the striking of a snake. The qualities that we associate with a deadly snake are thus transformed to Pepé.

> This withered root of knots of hair
> Slitted below and gashed with eyes,
> This oval O cropped out with teeth:
> The sickle motion from the thighs
>
> Jacknifes upward at the knees
> Then straightens out from heel to hip
> Pushing the framework of the bed
> And clawing at the pillow slip.
> —T. S. Eliot, "Sweeney Erect"

The various images and metaphors in this excerpt characterize Sweeney as a nauseating animal, as a "hairy ape."

Statements and Reflections of Other Characters Characterize

In literature, as in life, characters speak and think about others. And, as in life, a character's response to another may be as interesting for what it reveals about him as it is for what it reveals about the other person. Hence, the comments or thoughts of one character about another should be examined from both perspectives.

In *Moby-Dick* we find the following description of Starbuck's reaction to Ahab:

> My soul is more than matched; she's overmanned; and by a madman! Insufferable sting, that sanity should ground arms on such a field! But he drilled deep down, and blasted all my reason out of me! I think I see his impious end; but feel that I must help him to it. Will I, nill I, the ineffable thing has tied me to him; tows me with a cable I have no knife to cut. Horrible old man!

Starbuck's impassioned condemnation of Ahab is quite suspect; we must be wary of accepting his "horrible old man" label. For Starbuck's will has just shown itself weaker than Ahab's; his soul has been "overmanned." Thus, Starbuck's response actually reveals more about his own character—the limits of his will, his inability to resist the force of Ahab's monomania—than it does about Ahab's character.

Determining how much weight to give to a character's response to another is a matter of determining that character's *reliability*. The statements and reflections of characters who are presented sympathetically, who appear intelligent and perceptive, and who seem to reflect the norms and values of the author can generally be considered trustworthy. On the other hand, the observations of stupid, petty, shallow, or vicious characters may be totally unreliable.

Statements by the Author Characterize

Most of us would feel a good deal less comfortable in our daily lives if God had the habit of interrupting our everyday chatter and behavior with sudden judgments. Fortunately for our peace of mind He evidently lost His appetite for this sort of thing quite awhile back, and so did authors. Occasionally, however, especially in fiction from earlier periods, you may encounter authors who interrupt in their own voice, as author, to make a comment on character. Here, for example, is a passage from *Vanity Fair* in which the author, William Makepeace Thackeray, shares his feelings about one of his characters with the reader:

> I defy any one to say that our Becky, who has certainly some vices, has not been presented to the public in a perfectly genteel and inoffensive manner. In describing this syren singing and smiling, coaxing and cajoling, the

author, with modest pride, asks his readers all round, has he once forgotten the laws of politeness, and showed the monster's hideous tail above water? No! Those who like may peep down under waves that are pretty transparent, and see it writhing and twirling, diabolically hideous and slimy, flapping amongst bones, or curling round corpses; but above the water line, I ask, has not everything been proper, agreeable, and decorous, and right to cry fie? When, however, the syren disappears and dives below, down among the dead men, the water of course grows turbid over her, and it is labour lost to look into it ever so curiously. . . . And so, when Becky is out of the way, be sure that she is not particularly well employed, and that the less that is said about her doings is in fact the better.

When authors interrupt in this way, they reveal what *they* think about a particular character. They also reveal, implicitly, some of their own values, and standards and concepts of right and wrong. If your values are different, or if you interpret the character differently, you should feel free to disagree with the author's views.

Though modern authors seldom comment on or sketch character in their own voice, undramatized narrators* do indulge in direct and explicit characterization. If there is no character in the story to whom a statement can be ascribed, and the statement is not made by the author speaking as such, it can be regarded as a statement by the undramatized narrator. Such statements are generally reliable and, for this reason, well worth close attention.

Depth of Characterization

A fictional character may be characterized a little or a lot, superficially or in depth, simplistically or complexly. Author-scholar E. M. Forster has provided us with a classic distinction: "flat" characters vs. "round" characters. Flat characters are "constructed round a single idea or quality." Round characters, in contrast, possess the "incalculability of life"; they are "capable of surprising in a convincing way."

"Flat" and "round," as Forster uses the terms, are descriptive, not judgmental, labels. Some of the most memorable characters in literature are "flat," in the sense of being one-dimensional. Charles Dickens' Wilkins Micawber, the eternal optimist; James Thurber's Walter Mitty, the quintessential "little man"; Conan Doyle's Dr. Watson; Herman Melville's Billy Budd; Mark Twain's Tom Sawyer—all are technically "flat" characters.

Nevertheless, despite the memorableness of many one-dimensional characters (master-spy, super-stud James Bond and shuffling TV detective Lt. Columbo are further examples), those characters in literature who

---

*See "Point of View," pp. 64–65.

most enrich our understanding of ourselves and others are typically "round." Hamlet, Macbeth, Lear, Hedda Gabler—such characters confront and grapple with the eternal dilemmas of the human condition. Unlike flat characters, round characters such as these can never be captured in a single tag line or phrase.

Summary

We have examined nine ways in which character is communicated: appearance, names, speech, behavior, thoughts and emotions, biography, images, statements and reflections of other characters, and statements by the author or undramatized narrator. As you read the story that follows, try to identify at least one example of each of these techniques of characterization. After you have read Katherine Mansfield's story, we will use it to exemplify the process of analyzing and writing about character.

A CUP OF TEA

Katherine Mansfield

Rosemary Fell was not exactly beautiful. No, you couldn't have called her beautiful. Pretty? Well, if you took her to pieces. . . . But why be so cruel as to take any one to pieces? She was young, brilliant, extremely modern, exquisitely well dressed, amazingly well read in the newest of the new books, and her parties were the most delicious mixture of the really important people and . . . artists—quaint creatures, discoveries of hers, some of them too terrifying for words, but others quite presentable and amusing.

Rosemary had been married two years. She had a duck of a boy. No, not Peter—Michael. And her husband absolutely adored her. They were rich, really rich, not just comfortably well off, which is odious and stuffy and sounds like one's grandparents. But if Rosemary wanted to shop she would go to Paris as you and I would go to Bond Street. If she wanted to buy flowers, the car pulled up at that perfect shop in Regent Street, and Rosemary inside the shop just gazed in her dazzled, rather exotic way, and said: "I want those and those and those. Give me four bunches of those. And that jar of roses. Yes, I'll have all the roses in the jar. No, no lilac. I hate lilac. It's got no shape." The attendant bowed and put the lilac out of sight, as though this was only too true; lilac was dreadfully shapeless. "Give me those stumpy little tulips. Those red and white ones." And she was followed to the car by a thin shopgirl staggering under an immense white paper armful that looked like a baby in long clothes. . . .

One winter afternoon she had been buying something in a little antique shop in Curzon Street. It was a shop she liked. For one thing, one usually had it to oneself. And then the man who kept it was ridiculously fond of serving her. He beamed whenever she came in. He clasped his hands; he was so gratified that he could scarcely speak. Flattery, of course. All the same, there was something . . .

"You see, madam," he would explain in his low respectful tones, "I love my things. I would rather not part with them than sell them to some

46

one who does not appreciate them, who has not that fine feeling which is so rare. . . ." And, breathing deeply, he unrolled a tiny square of blue velvet and pressed it on the glass counter with his pale finger-tips.

Today it was a little box. He had been keeping it for her. He had shown it to nobody as yet. An exquisite little enamel box with a glaze so fine it looked as though it had been baked in cream. On the lid a minute creature stood under a flowery tree, and a more minute creature still had her arms around his neck. Her hat, really no bigger than a geranium petal, hung from a branch; it had green ribbons. And there was a pink cloud like a watchful cherub floating above their heads. Rosemary took her hands out of her long gloves. She always took off her gloves to examine such things. Yes, she liked it very much. She loved it; it was a great duck. She must have it. And, turning the creamy box, opening and shutting it, she couldn't help noticing how charming her hands were against the blue velvet. The shopman, in some dim cavern of his mind, may have dared to think so too. For he took a pencil, leant over the counter, and his pale bloodless fingers crept timidly towards those rosy, flashing ones, as he murmured gently: "If I may venture to point out to madam, the flowers on the little lady's bodice."

"Charming!" Rosemary admired the flowers. But what was the price? For a moment the shopman did not seem to hear. Then a murmur reached her. "Twenty-eight guineas, madam."

"Twenty-eight guineas." Rosemary gave no sign. She laid the little box down; she buttoned her gloves again. Twenty-eight guineas. Even if one is rich. . . . She looked vague. She stared at a plump tea-kettle like a plump hen above the shopman's head, and her voice was dreamy as she answered: "Well, keep it for me—will you? I'll . . ."

But the shopman had already bowed as though keeping it for her was all any human being could ask. He would be willing, of course, to keep it for her for ever.

The discreet door shut with a click. She was outside on the step, gazing at the winter afternoon. Rain was falling, and with the rain it seemed the dark came too, spinning down like ashes. There was a cold bitter taste in the air, and the new-lighted lamps looked sad. Sad were the lights in the houses opposite. Dimly they burned as if regretting something. And people hurried by, hidden under their hateful umbrellas. Rosemary felt a strange pang. She pressed her muff to her breast; she wished she had the little box, too, to cling to. Of course, the car was there. She'd only to cross the pavement. But still she waited. There are moments, horrible moments in life, when one emerges from shelter and looks out, and it's awful. One oughtn't to give way to them. One ought to go home and have an extra-special tea. But at the very instant of thinking that, a young girl, thin, dark, shadowy—where had she come from?—

was standing at Rosemary's elbow and a voice like a sigh, almost like a sob, breathed: "Madam, may I speak to you a moment?"

"Speak to me?" Rosemary turned. She saw a little battered creature with enormous eyes, some one quite young, no older than herself, who clutched at her coat-collar with reddened hands, and shivered as though she had just come out of the water.

"M-madam," stammered the voice. "Would you let me have the price of a cup of tea?"

"A cup of tea?" There was something simple, sincere in that voice; it wasn't in the least the voice of a beggar. "Then have you no money at all?" asked Rosemary.

"None, madam," came the answer.

"How extraordinary!" Rosemary peered through the dusk, and the girl gazed back at her. How more than extraordinary! And suddenly it seemed to Rosemary such an adventure. It was like something out of a novel by Dostoevsky, this meeting in the dusk. Supposing she took the girl home? Supposing she did do one of those things she was always reading about or seeing on the stage, what would happen? It would be thrilling. And she heard herself saying afterwards to the amazement of her friends: "I simply took her home with me," as she stepped forward and said to that dim person beside her: "Come home to tea with me."

The girl drew back startled. She even stopped shivering for a moment. Rosemary put out a hand and touched her arm. "I mean it," she said, smiling. And she felt how simple and kind her smile was. "Why won't you? Do. Come home with me now in my car and have tea."

"You—you don't mean it, madam," said the girl, and there was pain in her voice.

"But I do," cried Rosemary. "I want you to. To please me. Come along."

The girl put her fingers to her lips and her eyes devoured Rosemary. "You're—you're not taking me to the police station?" she stammered.

"The police station!" Rosemary laughed out. "Why should I be so cruel? No, I only want to make you warm and to hear—anything you care to tell me."

Hungry people are easily led. The footman held the door of the car open, and a moment later they were skimming through the dusk.

"There!" said Rosemary. She had a feeling of triumph as she slipped her hand through the velvet strap. She could have said, "Now I've got you," as she gazed at the little captive she had netted. But of course she meant it kindly. Oh, more than kindly. She was going to prove to this girl that—wonderful things did happen in life, that—fairy godmothers were real, that—rich people had hearts, and that women *were* sisters. She turned impulsively, saying: "Don't be frightened. After all, why shouldn't you come back with me? We're both women. If I'm the more fortunate, you ought to expect . . ."

But happily at that moment, for she didn't know how the sentence was going to end, the car stopped. The bell was rung, the door opened, and with a charming, protecting, almost embracing movement, Rosemary drew the other into the hall. Warmth, softness, light, a sweet scent, all those things so familiar to her she never even thought about them, she watched that other receive. It was fascinating. She was like the little rich girl in her nursery with all the cupboards to open, all the boxes to unpack.

"Come, come upstairs," said Rosemary, longing to begin to be generous. "Come up to my room." And, besides, she wanted to spare this poor little thing from being stared at by the servants; she decided as they mounted the stairs she would not even ring for Jeanne, but take off her things by herself. The great thing was to be natural!

And "There!" cried Rosemary again, as they reached her beautiful big bedroom with the curtains drawn, the fire leaping on her wonderful lacquer furniture, her gold cushions and the primrose and blue rugs.

The girl stood just inside the door; she seemed dazed. But Rosemary didn't mind that.

"Come and sit down," she cried, dragging her big chair up to the fire, "in this comfy chair. Come and get warm. You look so dreadfully cold."

"I daren't, madam," said the girl, and she edged backwards.

"Oh, please,"—Rosemary ran forward—"you mustn't be frightened, you mustn't, really. Sit down, and when I've taken off my things we shall go into the next room and have tea and be cozy. Why are you afraid?" And gently she half pushed the thin figure into its deep cradle.

But there was no answer. The girl stayed just as she had been put, with her hands by her sides and her mouth slightly open. To be quite sincere, she looked rather stupid. But Rosemary wouldn't acknowledge it. She leant over her, saying: "Won't you take off your hat? Your pretty hair is all wet. And one is so much more comfortable without a hat, isn't one?"

There was a whisper that sounded like, "Very good, madam," and the crushed hat was taken off.

"Let me help you off with your coat, too," said Rosemary.

The girl stood up. But she held on the chair with one hand and let Rosemary pull. It was quite an effort. The other scarcely helped her at all. She seemed to stagger like a child, and the thought came and went through Rosemary's mind, that if people wanted helping they must respond a little, just a little, otherwise it became very difficult indeed. And what was she to do with the coat now? She left it on the floor, and the hat too. She was just going to take a cigarette off the mantelpiece when the girl said quickly, but so lightly and strangely: "I'm very sorry, madam, but I'm going to faint. I shall go off, madam, if I don't have something."

"Good heavens, how thoughtless I am!" Rosemary rushed to the bell.

"Tea! Tea at once! And some brandy immediately!"

The maid was gone again, but the girl almost cried out: "No, I don't want no brandy. I never drink brandy. It's a cup of tea I want, madam." And she burst into tears.

It was a terrible and fascinating moment. Rosemary knelt beside her chair.

"Don't cry, poor little thing," she said. "Don't cry." And she gave the other her lace handkerchief. She really was touched beyond words. She put her arm round those thin, birdlike shoulders.

Now at last the other forgot to be shy, forgot everything except that they were both women, and gasped out: "I can't go on no longer like this. I can't bear it. I shall do away with myself. I can't bear no more."

"You shan't have to. I'll look after you. Don't cry any more. Don't you see what a good thing it was that you met me? We'll have tea and you'll tell me everything. And I shall arrange something. I promise. Do stop crying. It's so exhausting. Please!"

The other did stop just in time for Rosemary to get up before the tea came. She had the table placed between them. She plied the poor little creature with everything, all the sandwiches, all the bread and butter, and every time her cup was empty she filled it with tea, cream and sugar. People always said sugar was so nourishing. As for herself she didn't eat; she smoked and looked away tactfully so that the other should not be shy.

And really the effect of that slight meal was marvelous. When the tea-table was carried away a new being, a light, frail creature with tangled hair, dark lips, deep, lighted eyes, lay back in the big chair in a kind of sweet languor looking at the blaze. Rosemary lit a fresh cigarette; it was time to begin.

"And when did you have your last meal?" she asked softly.

But at that moment the door-handle turned.

"Rosemary, may I come in?" It was Philip.

"Of course."

He came in. "Oh, I'm so sorry," he said, and stopped and stared.

"It's quite all right," said Rosemary, smiling. "This is my friend, Miss—"

"Smith, madam," said the languid figure, who was strangely still and unafraid.

"Smith," said Rosemary. "We were going to have a little talk."

"Oh, yes," said Philip. "Quite," and his eye caught sight of the coat and hat on the floor. He came over to the fire and turned his back to it.

"It's a beastly afternoon," he said curiously, still looking at that listless figure, looking at its hands and boots, and then at Rosemary again.

"Yes, isn't it?" said Rosemary enthusiastically. "Vile."

Philip smiled his charming smile. "As a matter of fact," said he, "I wanted you to come into the library for a moment. Would you? Will Miss Smith excuse us?"

The big eyes were raised to him, but Rosemary answered for her. "Of course she will." And they went out of the room together.

"I say," said Philip, when they were alone. "Explain. Who is she? What does it all mean?"

Rosemary, laughing, leaned against the door and said: "I picked her up in Curzon Street. Really. She's a real pick-up. She asked me for the price of a cup of tea, and I brought her home with me."

"What on earth are you going to do with her?" cried Philip.

"Be nice to her," said Rosemary quickly. "Be frightfully nice to her. Look after her. I don't know how. We haven't talked yet. But show her—treat her—make her feel—"

"My darling girl," said Philip, "you're quite mad, you know. It simply can't be done."

"I knew you'd say that," retorted Rosemary. "Why not? I want to. Isn't that a reason? And besides, one's always reading about these things. I decided—"

"But," said Philip slowly, and he cut the end of a cigar, "she's so astonishingly pretty."

"Pretty?" Rosemary was so surprised that she blushed. "Do you think so? I—I hadn't thought about it."

"Good Lord!" Philip struck a match. "She's absolutely lovely. Look again, my child. I was bowled over when I came into your room just now. However . . . I think you're making a ghastly mistake. Sorry, darling, if I'm crude and all that. But let me know if Miss Smith is going to dine with us in time for me to look up *The Milliner's Gazette*."

"You absurd creature!" said Rosemary, and she went out of the library, but not back to her bedroom. She went to her writing-room and sat down at her desk. Pretty! Absolutely lovely! Bowled over! Her heart beat like a heavy bell. Pretty! Lovely! She drew her check book towards her. But no, checks would be of no use, of course. She opened a drawer and took out five pound notes, looked at them, put two back, and holding the three squeezed in her hand, she went back to her bedroom.

Half an hour later Philip was still in the library, when Rosemary came in.

"I only wanted to tell you," said she, and she leaned against the door again and looked at him with her dazzled exotic gaze, "Miss Smith won't dine with us tonight."

Philip put down the paper. "Oh, what's happened? Previous engagement?"

Rosemary came over and sat down on his knee. "She insisted on going," said she, "so I gave the poor little thing a present of money. I couldn't keep her against her will, could I?" she added softly.

Rosemary had just done her hair, darkened her eyes a little, and put on her pearls. She put up her hands and touched Philip's cheeks.

"Do you like me?" said she, and her tone, sweet, husky, troubled him.

"I like you awfully," he said, and he held her tighter. "Kiss me."

There was a pause.

Then Rosemary said dreamily, "I saw a fascinating little box today. It cost twenty-eight guineas. May I have it?"

Philip jumped her on his knee. "You may, little wasteful one," said he.

But that was not really what Rosemary wanted to say.

"Philip," she whispered, and she pressed his head against her bosom, "am I *pretty*?"

Applications

Appearance characterizes   What details of Rosemary's appearance suggest character traits?

Names characterize   Look up the various meanings of the word "fell" in the dictionary. Does one of the definitions suggest Rosemary's character? Consider, also, her full name, Rosemary Fell. Is there a contrast between first and last name that suggests a tension or contradiction in her character?

Speech characterizes   What does the way Rosemary speaks suggest about her?

Behavior characterizes   What does Rosemary's decision to send Miss Smith away reveal about her?

Thoughts and emotions characterize   Rosemary's act of inviting the destitute girl to come home with her might seem a sign of generosity and magnanimity. How do Rosemary's thoughts and emotions during this incident cause the reader to make quite a different interpretation?

Biography characterizes   What aspects of Rosemary's character are suggested by the biographical details in the first two paragraphs of the story?

Images characterize   What is suggested about Rosemary by the image of her "dazzled exotic gaze"? by her holding the three pound notes "squeezed" in her hand?

Statements and reflections of other characters characterize   Toward the end of the story, Philip playfully calls Rosemary "little wasteful one."

Do his words characterize her in a deeper and more profound way than he realizes?

Statements by the author characterize   What does the following "statement by the author" suggest about Rosemary?

> She was young, brilliant, extremely modern, exquisitely well-dressed, amazingly well read in the newest of the new books, and her parties were the most delicious mixture of the really important people and . . . artists—quaint creatures, discoveries of hers, some of them too terrifying for words, but others quite presentable and amusing.

Is the description above an authorial intrusion like Thackeray's comments about Becky (pp. 43–44), or is it a statement by the "undramatized narrator"? How can you tell?

ANALYZING AND WRITING ABOUT CHARACTER

Analyzing Character

After we've met someone for the first time, a friend of a friend, a co-worker, a roommate, we're often asked, "What's she like?" or, "How did you like him?" Usually, our response comes readily—"I liked her," "I didn't like him," and so forth. But explaining our reaction, to ourselves or to another—that's a bit harder. We have to review the person's appearance, speech, behavior to understand why he or she impressed us in a certain way and to convince another that our impression is correct.

Similarly, after reading a literary work, we will often have an "impression" of character. The purpose of *analyzing character* is to explain to ourselves the reasons for this impression, so we can then, when we write, convince our reader of its accuracy.

First, select the fictional person whose character you wish to analyze. If you are dealing with a short story or poem, it is usually best to select the main character; in such short works the author tends to develop only one character in breadth and depth. If you are dealing with a play or novel, you can choose either the main character or an important character other than the protagonist.

Next, make a chart like the one below, allowing plenty of room for each item.

Technique of Characterization	Significant Examples	Character Traits
Appearance		
Name		
Speech		
Behavior		

Thoughts and emotions	
Biography	
Images	
Statements and reflections of other characters	
Statements by the author	

The third step is to pair off each technique with significant examples from the fictional work. Then, indicate in the third column the character trait or traits suggested by each item in the second column.

In a short work, you may discover that the author has relied on two or three techniques of characterization to the virtual exclusion of others. Generally, too, far more is revealed about an important character through that character's speech, behavior, and thoughts and emotions than through the other techniques of characterization.

The chart below illustrates this analytical procedure.

THE CHARACTER OF ROSEMARY FELL IN "A CUP OF TEA"

Technique of Characterization	Significant Examples	Character Traits
Appearance	Not beautiful. Apparently not really pretty. Dresses "exquisitely" well.	Her lack of beauty is one source of her insecurity. She feels jealous and threatened when Philip calls Miss Smith "lovely."
Name	Rosemary Fell	"Fell" can mean "a rocky or barren hill," suggesting Rosemary's spiritual "barrenness." Another usage of the word connotes cruelty and deadliness.
Speech	Rosemary is given to exclamations and breathless enthusiasm ("'There!' 'Charming!,' 'Tea! Tea at once!'" etc.)	Affected, "fakey" quality of her speech suggests similar character traits.
	"'How extraordinary!'" Rosemary exclaims when the girl says she has no money at all.	Condemns her as shallow and superficial; poverty is scarcely "extraordinary."

Chart continued on following page.

Technique of Characterization	Significant Examples	Character Traits
	"'Don't cry, poor little thing,'" and later, "'Do stop crying. It's so exhausting.'"	She is condescending and self-centered. She finds another's misery "exhausting."
	Tells Philip that the girl insisted on going. Says "'I couldn't keep her against her her will, could I?'"	She is a liar and a hypocrite.
	Pleads with her husband, "'Philip . . . am I *pretty?*'"	Suggests her deep insecurity, self-doubt, sense of basic worthlessness.
Behavior	Invites girl home on impulse, without forethought.	Impulsive, given to indulging whims.
	Takes out five pound notes, puts two back.	Not really generous. Will spend large sums to indulge herself, but not to help others.
	Sends girl away.	Jealous, insecure, self-centered.
	Makes herself up, putting on makeup, doing her hair, donning pearls.	Attempt to be "pretty" and thereby get reassurance. Insecure.
Thoughts and Emotions	Likes little antique shop because "one usually had it to oneself."	Prefers to monopolize attention, afraid of competition, wants to be the single and sole center of interest.
	Believes that antique dealer thinks she is special, has extraordinary sensitivity.	Loves flattery, is taken in by it.
	Considers her act of inviting poor girl home "an adventure . . . like something out of a novel."	Incapable of deep feeling or empathy for others. Likes to dramatize herself.
	Has various noble thoughts about helping girl, all abandoned in an instant after Philip calls girl lovely.	Deceives herself about herself. Lacks real generosity of spirit. Actually petty, self-centered, selfish.
	Hurries girl upstairs, "longing to begin to be generous."	Not truly generous or warm-hearted; wants to "be generous" so she can have that flattering image of herself.

Technique of Characterization	Significant Examples	Character Traits
Biography	Gives parties for the "really important people"; invites artists only because they are "amusing."	Superficial and materialistic values.
	Reads "the newest of the new books."	Reads not for knowledge or insight but to be "in." Superficial and insecure.
Images	The term "duck" is applied with equal casualness to both her son and the enamel box.	Suggests superficiality of her emotions. Both people and possessions are valued solely for their "cuteness."
	Holds the three pound notes "squeezed" in her hand.	Suggests the degree of her anger at the girl for being "pretty" when she may not be. Suggestion, too, of Rosemary's potential for coldness and cruelty in this image.
Statements and reflections of other characters	"'little wasteful one,'" Philip says jokingly at end.	His words have a more serious meaning. Rosemary is "wasteful" both of money and of other people.
Statements by the author	The omniscient narrator characterizes Rosemary directly in the first two paragraphs, ironically and unsympathetically.	Rosemary is characterized as passably attractive at best, superficial, entirely devoted to being "with it" and "in."

Writing about Character

Once you have filled in the chart, you have three major options open to you. You can focus your paper on: (1) the major techniques used to characterize a particular fictional person; or (2) a sequence of important incidents or speeches that reveal character; or (3) particular character traits. The distinctions here are really matters of focus and emphasis. Whichever approach you take, your purpose remains the same—to explain character.

Our chart reveals that Rosemary Fell is primarily characterized by her behavior, her speech, and her thoughts and emotions. All reveal a woman who is superficial, insecure, and self-centered. So, let's choose option 3 and write a paper focusing on particular character traits.

Step one: determine the major character traits By consulting the third column of your chart, you can determine the fictional person's major character traits. In our example, the chart reveals that Rosemary is insecure, jealous, affected, superficial, condescending, self-centered, hypocritical, impulsive, self-deceiving, selfish, materialistic, wasteful, and cruel—clearly she is not an attractive woman. But an essay which laboriously demonstrated each of these character traits would be neither attractive nor effective. The key word is "major." Be selective rather than exhaustive. Confine yourself to delineating the most significant and telling character traits.

Step two: formulate a thesis statement After you have determined the major character traits, you should assert them in a thesis statement. The thesis should reflect the order in which you intend to discuss the traits mentioned. Hence, you might write: "Rosemary Fell is a superficial, self-centered woman, self-deceived and self-deceiving, and deeply insecure. There is also a suggestion of a darker strain in her character, a potential for callousness and cruelty."

Step three: construct an outline in support of your thesis Each character trait (or cluster of closely related traits) which you have asserted in the thesis should appear in the outline after a roman numeral. Examples can be drawn directly from the chart and should be designated by either capital letters or arabic numerals, depending on how your outline is structured. As you prepare your outline, check for order, proper classification, and unity. Be sure that the order in which the examples appear is the most effective order. And check each example to be sure it does indeed illustrate the characteristic that you intend it to illustrate.

Outline

I. Rosemary is superficial and self-centered.
  A. She is superficial.
    1. Rosemary's reading habits, the way she dresses, and the sort of people she invites to her parties are all determined by a desire to be "with it" or "in." No deeper or more meaningful motives are suggested.
    2. When Miss Smith confesses she has no money at all, Rosemary exclaims " 'How extraordinary!' "
  B. She is self-centered.
    1. She likes the little antique shop because "one usually had it to oneself." That way, the owner's attention is entirely centered on her.
    2. When Miss Smith cries in despair, Rosemary finds the girl's tears "exhausting," and exclaims impatiently, " 'Do stop crying.' "
II. Rosemary is self-deceived and self-deceiving.
  A. She fancies that she possesses a special sensitivity which the

shopkeeper recognizes, whereas we know his smooth flattery is just that and nothing more.

    B. She has various noble thoughts about helping the girl, all of which are abandoned instantly when Philip calls Miss Smith "lovely."

III. Rosemary is deeply insecure.

    A. Her extravagant buying sprees seem motivated largely by her need for reassurance. The almost grotesque deference of the clerks, their bowing and scraping and flattery, help her feel important and special.

    B. The way she immediately dismisses Miss Smith after Philip calls the girl lovely is further evidence of Rosemary's deep-seated insecurity.

    C. Her pleading demand at the end of the story, "'Philip . . . am I *pretty?*'" reemphasizes her insecurity as well as the superficiality of her values (To her, to be "pretty" is to be valued and valuable).

IV. Rosemary's superficiality, coupled with her insecurity, make her a sterile and cruel person.

    A. She displays no emotions that go beyond herself.

    B. Her act of building Miss Smith's hope of escape from misery, only to give her a token sum of money and send her away is destructive and callous.

    C. Her name also emphasizes this darker strain in her character. "Fell" has connotations of both sterility and deadliness.

Step four: write your paper directly from your outline As you write the paper, you should keep two principles in mind:

1. Acknowledge the complexity of your character. Many fictional characters are quite as complex as "real life" people. They often possess both virtues and vices, both strengths and weaknesses. When you write about character, you will typically concentrate on a few characteristics, or even on one particular aspect of character—Ahab's megalomania or Lord Jim's romanticism, for instance. But it is important to let the reader know that you recognize the complexity of the character you are writing about. If you fail to acknowledge aspects of character other than those you discuss, your reader may feel that you are oversimplifying, or that you are unaware of important facets of a fictional person's character.

2. When you write a critical paper on character, you should employ the three-stage process that typifies writing on any aspect of a literary work: **assertion→example(s)→explanation.** It is not enough simply to assert a character trait and then give an example illustrating it. These two

steps must be followed by a third, *explanation*. You must explain to the reader why and how the incident, speech, thought, image, or whatever, characterizes in the way you say it does.

The Character of Rosemary Fell in
Katherine Mansfield's "A Cup of Tea"

Although first published in 1923, Katherine Mansfield's "A Cup of Tea" seems scarcely dated. Rosemary Fell, the principal character, could easily be one of today's so-called "beautiful people." Ironically, she possesses no beauty of either person or spirit. She is a superficial, self-centered woman, self-deceived and self-deceiving, and deeply insecure. There is also a suggestion of a darker strain in her character, a potential for callousness and cruelty.

> *Note: The first paragraph begins with a general comment about the story, focused on character, which provides a lead-in or transition to the thesis statements about Rosemary's character. Succeeding paragraphs will explain and document each thesis assertion, beginning with the first (that Rosemary is superficial).*

Rosemary's superficiality is emphasized from the very beginning of the story, where we are told about her reading habits, the way she dresses, and her parties. All three are dictated by her desire to be "in" or "with it." One sign of "in-ness" is knowledge of the books currently in fashion, so those are the books Rosemary reads. Similarly, a fashionable person should give the appearance of being interested in the arts. Naturally, Rosemary does so, inviting "quaint" artists as well as "the really important people." More damning than this rather harmless diversion, however, is her exclamation when Miss Smith confesses she has no money at all. "'How extraordinary!'" Rosemary cries, as though abject poverty were a sort of diverting condition to be marvelled at, much like a curiously designed ring or strange-looking hat.

Rosemary's self-centeredness is a natural consequence of her superficiality; her only real interest is herself. Thus, she especially likes the little antique shop because "one usually had it to oneself." As a result, of course, the owner's attention is entirely centered on her. Another indication of her self-centeredness is the way she responds to Miss Smith's tears. Instead of feeling for the girl's misery, Rosemary responds entirely in terms of the effect the girl's crying has on her. "'Do stop crying,'" she insists. "'It's so exhausting.'"

> *Note: In the two paragraphs above (and those that follow), explanation is interwoven with assertion-example. The writer must explain how and why a certain passage or scene reveals the character traits alleged. It is not enough simply to cite passages without accompanying clarification.*

Another aspect of Rosemary's character is her lack of self-knowledge; she is both self-deceived and self-deceiving. We recognize the antique dealer's oily flattery for what it is, but Rosemary convinces herself that he sincerely admires her, that his protestation of her "rare" feeling for beauty is true. More damning still is the way Rosemary deceives herself about her true motives in "picking up" the girl. She fancies herself motivated by altruism, by a feeling of "sisterhood," and other similarly high-minded sentiments. We know her motives are purely selfish; she wants to see herself as a heroine rescuing a poor waif in distress, as in a romantic novel. When Philip calls the girl "lovely," she becomes a threat to Rosemary's self-esteem, and Rosemary quickly and brutally disposes of her.

Most of Rosemary's behavior—her craving for flattery, her need to be "chic" and "in," her desire to act out the role of a fictional heroine—can be largely ascribed to her deep-seated, almost pathetic insecurity. Certainly, she is materialistic, but her extravagant buying sprees have a deeper significance. The almost grotesque deference of the clerks, their bowing and scraping and flattery—all help Rosemary feel important and special; they provide desperately needed reassurance. It is completely in character that she should turn on Miss Smith the moment Philip admits to being "bowled over" by the girl's beauty, for Rosemary has an insatiable need to feel "special" and superior in everyone's regard. The plea with which the story ends, "'Philip . . . am I *pretty?*'" emphasizes this all-important aspect of her character. If she is not pretty, she must feel, she is nothing.

Such terrible, soul-destroying insecurity might be pathetic, might even evoke pity, if Rosemary were less self-centered, more vulnerable. But, as she is characterized, she evokes no sympathy from the reader. Her superficiality, self-centeredness, and insecurity make her both sterile and cruel. Incapable of empathy or emotional involvement with others, she is spiritually barren and sterile, just as her name, "Fell," implies. And, Mansfield definitely suggests, there may be a deadly quality about her as well, a dark destructiveness. For "fell" connotes "fierce, terrible, cruel," and also "deadly." In the story, the final confrontation between Rosemary and Miss Smith is played "off stage"; it is not dramatized. But it is, for that very reason, the more terrible. We can only imagine the words spoken, the payoff with the three pound notes "squeezed" in Rosemary's hand. But we do know that the enemy is vanquished. Miss Smith has been defeated; Rosemary returns to the study triumphant.

Note: In the paragraphs above, each thesis assertion about Rosemary's character is taken up, one by one, and then amplified, clarified, and explained.

THREE

POINT OF VIEW

UNDERSTANDING POINT OF VIEW

Point of view in literature does not mean "opinion" or "idea," as in, "What's your *point of view* on the public health care issue?" Instead, the term refers to the angle of vision or vantage point from which a story is narrated.

Broadly speaking, there are four major points of view:

1. Omniscient
2. Limited omniscient
3. First person
4. Objective

In the *omniscient* point of view, the author tells the story, giving us the thoughts and emotions of several characters.

In the *limited omniscient* point of view, the story is presented through the eyes of a *single* character, who is referred to in the third person (a proper name, such as "Alan," or "Mary" and the pronouns "he" or "she"). We see what this character sees, hear what he hears, learn his thoughts—but not the thoughts of other characters. Hence the descriptive phrase *"limited* omniscient." As with the omniscient point of view, the author is telling the story*, but it is presented through the eyes of, and as perceived by, a single character.

The *first person* point of view, although it may seem very different, is really quite similar to the limited omniscient. A single character tells the story, referring to himself or herself in the first person (as "I").

In the *objective* point of view, the author stays out of the characters' minds entirely, giving us only setting, actions, and speech—as in the theatre.

Practically speaking, if you wish to analyze point of view, it's best to choose a story which uses either the *limited omniscient* or *first person* point of view. In these two points of view, the author presents the story *as*

---

* To discuss the complex relation of author, implied author, and narrator would violate the focus of this text. An excellent discussion of this relation can be found in chapters 3, 5, and 6 of Wayne c. Booth's *The Rhetoric of Fiction* and in "Makers and Persons," by Patrick Cruttwell, *Hudson Review*, XII (Winter, 1959–60), 487–507.

perceived by a single character (often referred to as the "point of view character"), whose perception is often significantly different from the perception of the author.

In approaching such a story, ask yourself:

1. *What is the character of the point of view character?* Try to determine the point of view character's depth of perception, intelligence, values, maturity and sophistication, self-image, educational background, and so forth.

2. *What is the author's attitude toward the point of view character?* Is the point of view character presented sympathetically or unsympathetically? Does he or she have damning weaknesses? Is the point of view character perceptive and insightful, or lacking in these qualities?

3. *How reliable is the point of view character?* Try to determine how closely the point of view character resembles the implied author in intelligence, sophistication, values, outlook, perceptiveness. The closer the resemblance, the more reliable the perception and judgments of the point of view character will be.

After answering these questions, you can investigate the functions of point of view by asking:

1. *How does the method of narration (point of view) serve to communicate the author's central ideas?*

2. *How does the point of view influence or shape the effect of the story on the reader?*

3. *How does the point of view serve to heighten the effectiveness of the story?*

Summary

The four major narrative points of view are omniscient, limited omniscient, first person and objective. When the story is told through the eyes of a single character (limited omniscient and first person) who does not reflect the author's own norms and values, point of view has a major impact on the meaning and effect of the story. John Collier's "The Chaser" is a case in point.

THE CHASER

John Collier

Alan Austen, as nervous as a kitten, went up certain dark and creaky stairs in the neighborhood of Pell Street, and peered about for a long time on the dim landing before he found the name he wanted written obscurely on one of the doors.

He pushed open this door, as he had been told to do, and found himself in a tiny room, which contained no furniture but a plain kitchen table, a rocking-chair, and an ordinary chair. On one of the dirty buff-colored walls were a couple of shelves, containing in all perhaps a dozen bottles and jars.

An old man sat in the rocking-chair, reading a newspaper. Alan, without a word, handed him the card he had been given. "Sit down, Mr. Austen," said the old man very politely. "I am glad to make your acquaintance."

"Is it true," asked Alan, "that you have a certain mixture that has—er,—quite extraordinary effects?"

"My dear sir," replied the old man, "my stock in trade is not very large—I don't deal in laxatives and teething mixtures—but such as it is, it is varied. I think nothing I sell has effects which could be precisely described as ordinary."

"Well, the fact is—" began Alan.

"Here, for example," interrupted the old man, reaching for a bottle from the shelf. "Here is a liquid as colorless as water, almost tasteless, quite imperceptible in coffee, milk, wine, or any other beverage. It is also quite imperceptible to any known method of autopsy."

"Do you mean it is a poison?" cried Alan, very much horrified.

"Call it a glove-cleaner if you like," said the old man indifferently. "Maybe it will clean gloves. I have never tried. One might call it a life-cleaner. Lives need cleaning sometimes."

"I want nothing of that sort," said Alan.

"Probably it is just as well," said the old man. "Do you know the

66

price of this? For one teaspoonful, which is sufficient, I ask five thousand dollars. Never less. Not a penny less."

"I hope all your mixtures are not as expensive," said Alan apprehensively.

"Oh dear, no," said the old man. "It would be no good charging that sort of price for a love potion, for example. Young people who need a love potion very seldom have five thousand dollars. Otherwise they would not need a love potion."

"I am glad to hear that," said Alan.

"I look at it like this," said the old man. "Please a customer with one article, and he will come back when he needs another. Even if it *is* more costly. He will save up for it, if necessary."

"So," said Alan, "you really do sell love potions?"

"If I did not sell love potions," said the old man, reaching for another bottle, "I should not have mentioned the other matter to you. It is only when one is in a position to oblige that one can afford to be so confidential."

"And these potions," said Alan. "They are not just—just—er—"

"Oh, no," said the old man. "Their effects are permanent, and extend far beyond casual impulse. But they include it. Bountifully, insistently. Everlastingly."

"Dear me!" said Alan, attempting a look of scientific detachment. "How very interesting!"

"But consider the spiritual side," said the old man.

"I do, indeed," said Alan.

"For indifference," said the old man, "they substitute devotion. For scorn, adoration. Give one tiny measure of this to the young lady—its flavor is imperceptible in orange juice, soup, or cocktails—and however gay and giddy she is, she will change altogether. She will want nothing but solitude, and you."

"I can hardly believe it," said Alan. "She is so fond of parties."

"She will not like them any more," said the old man. "She will be afraid of the pretty girls you may meet."

"She will actually be jealous?" cried Alan in a rapture. "Of me?"

"Yes, she will want to be everything to you."

"She is, already. Only she doesn't care about it."

"She will, when she has taken this. She will care intensely. You will be her sole interest in life."

"Wonderful!" cried Alan.

"She will want to know all you do," said the old man. "All that has happened to you during the day. Every word of it. She will want to know what you are thinking about, why you smile suddenly, why you are looking sad."

67

"That is love!" cried Alan.

"Yes," said the old man. "How carefully she will look after you! She will never allow you to be tired, to sit in a draught, to neglect your food. If you are an hour late, she will be terrified. She will think you are killed, or that some siren has caught you."

"I can hardly imagine Diana like that!" cried Alan, overwhelmed with joy.

"You will not have to use your imagination," said the old man. "And, by the way, since there are always sirens, if by any chance you *should*, later on, slip a little, you need not worry. She will forgive you, in the end. She will be terribly hurt, of course, but she will forgive you—in the end."

"That will not happen," said Alan fervently.

"Of course not," said the old man. "But, if it did, you need not worry. She would never divorce you. Oh no! And, of course, she herself will never give you the least, the very least, grounds for—uneasiness."

"And how much," said Alan, "is this wonderful mixture?"

"It is not as dear," said the old man, "as the glove-cleaner, or life-cleaner, as I sometimes call it. No. That is five thousand dollars, never a penny less. One has to be older than you are, to indulge in that sort of thing. One has to save up for it."

"But the love potion?" said Alan.

"Oh, that," said the old man, opening the drawer in the kitchen table, and taking out a tiny, rather dirty-looking phial. "That is just a dollar."

"I can't tell you how grateful I am," said Alan, watching him fill it.

"I like to oblige," said the old man. "Then customers come back, later in life, when they are rather better off, and want more expensive things. Here you are. You will find it very effective."

"Thank you again," said Alan. "Good-by."

"*Au revoir*," said the old man.

Applications

1. What is the narrative point of view in "The Chaser"?
2. Through whose eyes and perception is the story narrated? Who is the point of view character?
3. What central irony or ironies emerge in the course of the story? How is the irony related to the point of view?

ANALYZING AND WRITING ABOUT POINT OF VIEW

Analyzing Point of View

As indicated earlier, the impact of point of view on meaning and effect is most demonstrable when the author filters the story through the eyes of a first person narrator or a third person center of consciousness (limited omniscient). In "The Chaser," Alan Austen is such a center of consciousness. In order to analyze the point of view, we should attempt to determine the *character*, the author's *attitude* toward, and the *reliability* of, the point of view character.

1. *What is the character of the point of view character?*

Alan Austen seems to be a typical romantic young man (note his unremarkable, "typical" name). Blindly in love with an indifferent young lady, he is entranced and enchanted by the idea of a potion which will render her insatiably passionate, jealously possessive, madly solicitous, and determinedly faithful. To Alan, such emotions spell everlasting happiness; they signify Love. He is a fool.

2. *What is the author's attitude toward the point of view character?*

Alan is shown to be totally benighted. The author seems to regard him as absurdly, and to some degree, pathetically, naive.

3. *How reliable is the point of view character?*

Since the apothecary, the author, and the reader all know that Alan is purchasing a "hate" potion, whereas he thinks he is purchasing a formula for bliss, we can only concede that he is totally unreliable. None of his values or perceptions can be trusted.

Determining the Functions of Point of View

Point of view may bear on the meaning, effect, and effectiveness of a story. We need to ask:

1. *How does the method of narration serve to communicate the author's central ideas?*

In "The Chaser," John Collier is exposing and satirizing the popular

69

myth of romantic love. To the young and foolish—to the Alan Austens of the world, whether male or female—such love seems glorious. Actually, Collier suggests, it is ultimately destructive. Possessive, jealous, all-consuming, such "love" becomes suffocating, stifling individuality, freedom, personal growth. It becomes a blight on life.

These central ideas are communicated by the ironic contrast between the apothecary's cynical knowledge and the naive self-delusion of the point of view character.

2. *How does the point of view influence or shape the effect of the story on the reader?*

In "The Chaser," the point of view is largely responsible for the ironic tone and effect of the story. Throughout the story there exists an ironic tension resulting from the contrast between the apothecary's insight and perception and the lack of insight and understanding on Alan's part. Appearance and reality, intention and achievement are at odds throughout the narrative. Alan thinks the potion will bring him happiness; we know it will bring him misery. Alan is full of gratitude at the potion's cheapness; we know it is the worst "bargain" he will ever make. Alan says "'Good-by'"; the apothecary says, "'*Au revoir.*'"

3. *How does the point of view serve to heighten the effectiveness of the story?*

In addition to the satiric and ironic effects mentioned above, the method of narration enhances the story's effectiveness by allowing Collier to get his message across without appearing either preachy or didactic. By filtering the narrative through Alan's eyes, Collier is able to mock false romanticism, expose the foolish naivety of those taken in by it, and achieve a sardonic humor—all without ever entering an explicit moral judgment or overt thematic statement.

Writing About Point of View

An essay on point of view should explain how the point of view used helps convey meaning or ideas, how it reinforces or even creates the particular effect of the work, and how it heightens (or, in rare cases, lessens), the work's effectiveness. If you're writing a short paper on a longer work, such as a novel, you might want to limit yourself to one function of point of view. If you're writing a longer essay or if you're analyzing point of view in a short story, you would probably want to analyze two or three functions. In either case, the process is the same:

First, describe the method of narration used.

Second, describe the character of the first person narrator or third person center of consciousness.

Third, explain how narration through the eyes of this character bears on one or more aspects of the work: meaning, effect, effectiveness.

Note: The focus of a paper on point of view should be on step three—the function or functions of point of view. Be careful to avoid blurring this focus when you discuss the point of view character. Keep that discussion relatively short, and keep such words as "narrator," "method of narration," and "point of view" before the reader.

Your answers to the six questions we have discussed are the basis for your essay about point of view in a particular literary work. But, before you begin to write, you should embody these answers in an outline. Putting them in outline form will allow you to see the overall structure of your paper, will allow you to perceive assertions that need further illustration and explanation, and will make it easier to formulate a thesis statement.

Outline

I. "The Chaser" uses the limited omniscient point of view.
  - A. The point of view character is a young man by the name of Alan Austen.
  - B. Everything presented to the reader is filtered through Alan's consciousness.

II. Alan is a naive and foolish young man obsessed with the supposed glories of romantic love.
  - A. To him, it is "wonderful" that the potion will make his beloved sexually insatiable, insanely jealous, and graspingly possessive.
  - B. He has no understanding of the destructiveness of these emotions.

III. The method of narration enables Collier to expose and satirize the popular myth of romantic love.
  - A. The theme of the story concerns the destructive effect of emotions and behavior often thought to be romantic and wonderful.
  - B. By presenting a "romantic" who is blind to the implications of his actions, foolish, self-deceived, and incapable of perceiving reality, the author is able to deride false romanticism without overt moralizing.

IV. The ironic effect of the story is also a function of point of view.
  - A. By definition, irony involves an incongruous tension between appearance and reality. In "The Chaser," the apothecary is able to distinguish illusion from truth, but not so Alan. Throughout the story, Alan's vision is distorted by the reality-blocking lens of his romanticism. Thus, an ironic tension pervades the entire narrative.
  - B. The sardonic humorousness of the story is also a direct result of its ironic tone. Alan cries "'Wonderful!'" when he should be

feeling horror. And, at the end of tale, a final ironic twist is added. Alan never expects to see the apothecary again. For him, it's "'Good-by'" But the apothecary knows better. His farewell means, "Till we meet again."

Thesis

We can now formulate a thesis statement and write the essay on point of view directly from the outline. As always, the thesis should indicate the main points you intend to make, and the order in which you intend to make them. On the basis of the outline above, the thesis might read:

> In "The Chaser," John Collier employs the limited omniscient point of view to expose and satirize the popular myth of romantic love. By filtering the narrative through the eyes of a naive and foolish young man, the author achieves a sustained ironic tension that both enhances the story's impact and gives it a biting humorousness.

Point of View in "The Chaser"

In "The Chaser," John Collier employs the limited omniscient point of view to expose and satirize the popular myth of romantic love. By filtering the narrative through the eyes of a naive and foolish young man, the author achieves a sustained ironic tension that both enhances the story's impact and gives it a biting humorousness.

Alan Austen, the point of view character, is a benighted young man obsessed with the supposed glories of romantic love. He is enraptured by the prospect of his beloved becoming insanely jealous, finds "wonderful" the apothecary's promise that she will make him her sole interest in life, is "overwhelmed with joy" at the prospect of her unflagging solicitude. In short, he is a fool.

> *Note: The focus of a critical paper on point of view must always be on the functions of point of view, the bearing of point of view on meaning, effect, effectiveness. Hence, the preceding paragraph sketches Alan's character, but does not go into great detail. It provides just enough supporting evidence from the story to validate the writer's contention that Alan is naive and foolish. Now the writer must show how narration through the eyes of the point of view character creates the particular effect alleged in the thesis.*

By filtering the narrative through Alan's eyes, Collier exposes and satirizes the popular myth of romantic love. He presents a "romantic" who is blind to implications of his actions, grossly self-deceived, and incapable of perceiving reality; by implication and association, all romantics are similarly ridiculed. Yet Collier's theme goes beyond mere ridicule. The emotions and attitudes which Alan so cherishes—jealousy, possessiveness, exclusive preoccupation with another—all are ultimately destructive of human growth, independence, and individuality. The apothecary knows this truth; after all, it is the source of his "repeat" business. But Alan has yet to learn it.

Note: In the paragraph above the writer turns to the relation between point of view and meaning, supporting and clarifying the thesis assertion that Collier is exposing and satirizing the popular myth of romantic love.

The ironic effect of the story is also a function of the point of view. By definition, irony involves an incongruous tension between appearance and reality. In "The Chaser," the apothecary is able to distinguish illusion from truth, but not so Alan, for his vision is distorted by the reality-blocking lens of his romanticism. As a consequence, dramatic irony is pervasive throughout the story. The reader knows Alan is buying misery; he believes he is buying bliss. The reader knows that the "love" potion is grotesquely mislabeled; Alan has no such insight. The reader understands that Alan will be back, years later, to purchase the poisonous "chaser"; but Alan is blind to the apothecary's veiled warnings. These ironies, and others, permeate the story, creating a constant tension.

Note: In the paragraph above, the writer amplifies the second assertion made in the thesis, that the point of view creates "a sustained ironic tension."

Finally, the grim humor of the story is a direct result of the ironic tone, a tone created, as we have seen, by the narrative perspective. Alan is enraptured when he should be horrified, cries "'Wonderful!'" when he should run, exclaims, "'That is love'" at a description of suffocating solicitude. And, at the very end of the tale, a final ironic twist is added. Alan, never expecting to see the apothecary again, says "'Good-by.'" But the apothecary, and the reader, knows better. "'Au revoir,'" the apothecary tells him—till we meet again.

Note: The final paragraph of the essay addresses itself to the final assertion in the writer's thesis, that the point of view gives the story a "biting humorousness."

FOUR

STRUCTURE

UNDERSTANDING STRUCTURE

The analysis of structure in a work of literature is the analysis of the arrangement of its parts. It consists of *identifying* the major parts, *describing* how they are arranged in relation to one another, and *explaining* the way in which the parts and their arrangement complement the meaning of the work.

Identifying the Major Parts

Everything is relative here. You might want to analyze the structure of a single scene involving a single character in a single chapter of a long novel. In this case, you would start out by identifying the major parts of this scene. Conversely, you might want to analyze the overall structure of the entire novel. In this case, you would start out by identifying the major divisions in the novel as a whole.

There is usually both internal and external evidence of structural divisions in literature. In poetry the various stanzas often correspond to structural divisions. In drama, the major divisions of the play often correspond to the acts, the minor divisions to scenes within a given act. In novels, chapter divisions offer a clue to structure. In short stories the arrangement of typography—the use of blank space and the setting of passages in italics—sometimes serves the same function.

Describing How the Parts Are Related

The second step in analyzing structure in literature is to determine how the parts are arranged in relation to each other. We can illustrate this step with Yeats' poem, "For Anne Gregory":

> 'Never shall a young man
> Thrown into despair
> By those great honey-coloured
> Ramparts at your ear,
> Love you for yourself alone
> And not your yellow hair.'

'But I can get a hair-dye
And set such colour there,
Brown, or black, or carrot,
That young men in despair
May love me for myself alone
And not my yellow hair.'

'I heard an old religious man
But yesternight declare
That he had found a text to prove
That only God, my dear,
Could love you for yourself alone
And not your yellow hair.'

There are two speakers in the poem, a young woman and an older man. The young woman apparently wants to be loved for "herself alone," rather than for her "yellow hair." In the first stanza the man tells her that her wish will not be granted. In the second stanza the woman remonstrates; she is unwilling to accept the man's judgment. In the third stanza, the man speaks again and explains that only God is capable of loving her for "herself alone." Hence, the relationship among the three stanzas is that of assertion, rejection of the assertion, reassertion with explanation.

Explaining the Relation of Structure and Meaning

Identifying the major divisions and determining how they are related are rather barren exercises unless they are used as a basis for explaining the functions of the structure, the ways in which the arrangement of the parts contributes to the meaning and effectiveness of the literary work. We must attempt to answer such questions as:

"Why does the author use this structure?"

"What does the author achieve through the structure he employs?"

"How does the structure reflect and reinforce meaning?"

"How does the structure contribute to the effectiveness of the work?"

Analysis of Structure—An Illustration

We can illustrate the process of answering these questions in terms of Leonard Cohen's poem, "Go By Brooks":

Go by brooks, love,
Where fish stare,
Go by brooks,
I will pass there,

> Go by rivers,
> Where eels throng,
> Rivers, love,
> I won't be long.
>
> Go by oceans,
> Where whales sail,
> Oceans, love,
> I will not fail.

Identifying the major parts   Note first the easy-to-see external form or pattern of the poem. The poet uses three short stanzas of four lines each. Each stanza has the same rhyming pattern: *xaxa, xaxa, xaxa*. The poet is speaking to his love and uses simple, very short sentences. The sentences are imperative; he is telling the woman he loves what to do. He is commanding her to take actions, one action in each stanza.

1. In the first line of each stanza, the poet instructs his love to go to a particular place.

2. In the second line of each stanza, he names a creature which inhabits that place.

3. In the third line of each stanza, he repeats the name of the place given in the first line (and in the last two stanzas, adds the word "love.")

4. In the fourth and final line of each stanza, he tells his love that she can find him there, at the place he has sent her to. The presence of the lover-poet (the "I") is common to the last line of each stanza.

Describing how the parts are related   We can perceive the arrangement and relation among the parts by analyzing the words used for their *arrangement* within the outer structure of four-line stanzas and for their *connotatively* similar meanings.

The first *place* the loved one is to go is by "brooks." The second *place* (second stanza) is a larger image, "rivers"; and the third and last stanza puts the love in the largest place of all, "oceans." Note that there is also a climactic order in the *depth* of each body of water, as well as in size. A brook is not as deep as a river, a river is not as deep as an ocean. We can see structure developing here in the three-stage movement from small size to larger to largest, from shallow depth to deeper to deepest.

Explaining the relation of structure and meaning   We can now begin to see the relationship between structure and meaning in the poem. Look at the second lines. The key nouns, in rising order of importance, are "fish," "eels," and "whales." Here again the progression is from smallest (fish) to larger (eels) to largest of all (whales). Look (still in the second lines) at the verbs associated with the water creatures mentioned. "Fish *stare*," "eels *throng*," "whales *sail*." The ordering principle here is not so obvious. There is no easy progression from smallest to largest. But there is a progression of intensity of feeling. "Stare" connotes a kind of looking without much emotional involvement; there is no immediacy of contact in a stare. "Throng" suggests a richness of contact, almost (especially when coupled with the image of eels) an overabundance of physical contact; "throng" suggests a kind of crowdedness, a togetherness with a vengeance. Then at last the verb *sail*—"Where whales *sail*." The last image suggests a powerful, purposeful, and calmly beautiful kind of love which parallels the climactic movement of the small to largest *sizes* of the water places and of their denizens.

In the last line of each stanza the poet again uses a climactic order that parallels the lover's deepening love. "I will pass there" suggests that the lover, like the "staring fish," may simply be looking, that his love may not be lasting or sure or deep. With the statement "I won't be long" the lover becomes more reassuring, more involved. "Wait for me," he suggests. "I will not merely pass you by. You can be *sure* I will come to you." Then: "I will not fail." The climactic last line of the third stanza and of the poem says in straightforward language what the *structure* of the poem has been saying all along: "I will not fail." Now I am *sure* of my love and you can be sure of it too. My love has grown from a shallow, small ("brooks"), casual ("stare") love to a deeper, growing ("rivers") more intimate and physical ("throng") love to the largest ("whale"), deepest, most encompassing ("ocean") love of all—to a love which is so confident that its movement is like sailing, in which the lovers can use the winds (of life, of passion, of change) to increase their love and to sail with assurance upon its deep waters. No failure of love is now possible. The last line makes that clear.

Plot Structure

All literature has structure; only fiction and drama have plot. Plot, then, is simply a certain kind of structure found in stories, novels, and plays.

In its barest form, *plot* can be defined as the causally related incidents and episodes which, in sum, make up the story. Thus, a plot summary is a summary of what happens. An analysis of *plot structure* is emphatically *not* the same as a plot summary. An analysis of plot structure should concentrate on how the major incidents are related to one another, and how the ordering of incidents functions in terms of meaning and effect.

This distinction between summarizing a plot and analyzing its structure requires clarification, for only the latter provides meaningful insight. We can illustrate the distinction in terms of John Steinbeck's short story "Flight" (pp. 11–26). A plot summary of the story might read:

> The short story "Flight" is about a young man named Pepé. He is sent into town on an errand, where he kills a man. He then returns home, tells his mother what he did, and flees on horseback into the mountains. He is fol-

lowed, and eventually his horse is shot from under him. A short time later he is wounded in the arm. The wound becomes infected and Pepé grows weaker. Finally, he can flee no further and is shot to death.

A plot summary of this sort is useful if you have to answer a quiz question such as, "What happens to Pepé at the end of 'Flight?,'" and haven't read the story, but that's about all it's good for. An analysis of the story's *plot structure* would read quite differently, its focus not on *what* but on *why* and *to what effect*. A sample first paragraph for a paper analyzing the story's plot structure points up the difference:

> In "Flight" there are three major plot elements: the initial home scene, which ends with Pepé's riding off to town; the second home scene, in which he prepares for flight; and the flight episode itself, by far the longest of the story's three sections. Each of these three major parts serves important functions.

Notice the shift in emphasis. Instead of presenting a running, undifferentiated summary of what happens, the writer identifies the major "blocks" or parts in the plot and then goes on to make an assertion about them—that each serves a major function. The remainder of the paper would be devoted to identifying and explaining these functions.

Summary

Analyzing structure in literature is a three-stage process in which one identifies the major parts, determines how the parts are related, and perceives the ways in which the structure complements meaning and heightens effectiveness. Effective and integral structure in literature almost never reveals itself fully on first reading. To perceive and analyze structure requires careful rereading of a literary work, often several careful rereadings.

Matthew Arnold's famous poem is a case in point. Although you have probably read the poem before, reread it now with an eye to its structure.

DOVER BEACH

Matthew Arnold

The sea is calm to-night,
The tide is full, the moon lies fair
Upon the Straits;—on the French coast, the light
Gleams, and is gone; the cliffs of England stand,
Glimmering and vast, out in the tranquil bay.   5
Come to the window, sweet is the night air!
Only, from the long line of spray
Where the ebb meets the moon-blanched sand,
Listen! you hear the grating roar
Of pebbles which the waves suck back, and fling,   10
At their return, up the high strand,
Begin, and cease, and then again begin,
With tremulous cadence slow, and bring
The eternal note of sadness in.

Sophocles long ago   15
Heard it on the Ægean, and it brought
Into his mind the turbid ebb and flow
Of human misery; we
Find also in the sound a thought,
Hearing it by this distant northern sea.   20

The sea of faith
Was once, too, at the full, and round earth's shore
Lay like the folds of a bright girdle furled;
But now I only hear
Its melancholy, long, withdrawing roar,   25
Retreating to the breath
Of the night-wind down the vast edges drear
And naked shingles of the world.

> Ah, love, let us be true
> To one another! for the world, which seems   30
> To lie before us like a land of dreams,
> So various, so beautiful, so new,
> Hath really neither joy, nor love, nor light,
> Nor certitude, nor peace, nor help for pain;
> And we are here as on a darkling plain   35
> Swept with confused alarms of struggle and flight,
> Where ignorant armies clash by night.

Applications

Identifying the major parts Obviously, the four stanzas represent major structural divisions in Arnold's poem. But each individual stanza is also carefully structured. Can you identify two parts in each of the stanzas?

Describing how the parts are related How would you describe the relationship among the four stanzas in "Dover Beach"? How would you describe the relationship between the two major parts of each stanza?

Explaining the relation of structure and meaning What is the relation between the stanzas and the poem's meaning? How are the structural divisions within each stanza related to the poem's meaning?

ANALYZING AND WRITING ABOUT STRUCTURE

Analyzing Structure

1. Identify the major parts To identify the major parts you should make use of both "external" and "internal" evidence. External evidence is provided by the author in the form of chapters, scenes and acts, stanzas, and so forth. Internal evidence consists of individual speeches, unified, self-contained incidents, contrasting words, shifts in time, place, or mood, and the like. If you are analyzing structure in a short work—a short story, play, or poem—start with the external evidence; identify the big blocks first. Hence in Arnold's poem:

Stanza one describes the scene the speaker sees, and his reaction to the scene.

Stanza two states that the sound of pebbles thrown up and drawn back by the waves suggests a thought to the speaker, just as it suggested a thought, the "ebb and flow/Of human misery," to Sophocles.

In *stanza three* the speaker states the thought which the sound of pebbles suggests to *him*.

Stanza four is a direct statement by the speaker to his companion, the woman he loves.

We should now examine each stanza for *internal* evidence of divisions or parts in addition to those indicated by external means:

Stanza one falls into two major parts. Lines 1–6 are straight description; they describe a lovely romantic scene. The word "only," which begins line 7, signals a significant break. Like a treacherous undercurrent beneath an innocent-appearing surf, the sound of the pebbles being washed up and drawn back injects into the seemingly idyllic scene the "eternal note of sadness."

Stanza two also falls into two parts. The portion before the semicolon describes the "note of sadness" which the same sound that the speaker hears evoked in the mind of Sophocles. The portion of the stanza after the semicolon states that the sound evokes a thought in the speaker's mind also—but we are left in suspense as to what this thought is.

Stanza three constitutes the "thought" referred to in stanza two. It, too, falls into two parts. Lines 21–23 describe "what used to be"—a world in which religious faith encompassed the world and solaced us all. Lines 24–28 contrast the present, in which religious faith is ebbing, with this earlier, most comforting, time.

Like the others, *stanza four* can be divided into two parts. The first sentence, an exclamation, is the "conclusion," the emotional outcry to which the speaker has been led by his reflections in the first three stanzas. The remaining lines constitute an "explanation" of the outcry.

2. Determine how the parts are related   After you have identified the major parts, you should determine how each part is related to the part before and after it, and how each part functions in the overall structure of the work. To illustrate:

In "Dover Beach" the first portion of stanza one (11.1–6) describes a typical romantic scene. Even the speaker's reaction is typical—he asks his love to come to the window and view the scene with him; he exclaims how the night air is "sweet." The second portion of the first stanza (11.7–14) begins the turn to the melancholy which comes to dominate the poem. The turn is gradual and natural; as the speaker approaches closer to the window, or perhaps leans out to breathe the sweet night air, he hears the grating of the pebbles, which suggests to him "the eternal note of sadness."

The speaker's somber mood at the end of stanza one, and the introduction of the term "eternal" make plausible the allusion to Sophocles that constitutes the first part of the second stanza. The second part of this stanza shifts our focus back to the present and prepares us for the crucial third stanza. Furthermore, since both the first and second stanzas involve striking contrasts, we are prepared for the major contrast which dominates stanza three.

Stanza three expresses the "thought" foreshadowed in the second stanza. In this stanza the first three lines hark back to the mood of beauty and spiritual tranquility communicated in the first portion of stanza one. But, just as this mood has now deserted the speaker, so, he feels, has the comforting "sea of faith" ebbed from its former fullness, leaving mankind bereft of religious conviction.

The speaker's reflection on the ebb of religious faith in stanza three motivates his exclamation to his love with which the final stanza begins. Since there is no longer comfort or meaning or solace to be found in religious belief, we must seek to fulfill these human needs in the devotion and "steadfastness" of another person. The needs that were once met by faith in God must now be met by faith in a loved one. The second portion of the fourth stanza, lines 30–37, represents the *dénouement* of the poem. In these lines the speaker explains that appearance is not reality; he explains that a world, however beautiful in appearance, that is bereft of religious faith is, in reality, a nightmare world which, "Hath really neither joy, nor love, nor light,/Nor certitude, nor peace, nor help for pain."

3. Explain why and how the structure complements meaning and heightens the work's effectiveness In order to perceive the interpenetration of structure, meaning, and effectiveness, ask yourself how characteristics of the structure are related to the expressed content, to the major ideas in the work.

One major idea in "Dover Beach" is the *contrast* between the past and the present, between a former world "furled" in the embrace of religious faith and the present era in which religious certainty is no longer possible. The structure of the poem complements this aspect of "meaning." Stanza one falls into two parts which contrast two moods of the speaker; stanza two also falls into two parts which contrast Sophocles' thought in the past with the speaker's thought in the present.

Another major concept suggested by the poem is that there has been a gradual *transition* from an age of faith to an age of doubt, from an age of spiritual peace to an age of spiritual pain. The structure of the poem also complements this aspect of the poem's meaning. In stanza one, especially, there is a transition in the speaker's mood, a transition from joy to sadness that foreshadows and parallels the transition from religious faith to religious doubt with which the poem is principally concerned.

Writing About Structure

Formulating your thesis After you have analyzed the structure of a work from the three perspectives discussed, you will have plenty of ideas and insights to serve as a basis for your essay. In fact, you may find that you have too many. So, when you formulate your thesis, limit yourself to the *major* characteristic(s) and function(s) of structure.

When you write a paper on structure, there is always the danger of losing sight of the forest in a wild proliferation of trees. You need to keep the limits of your reader's patience and concentration in mind. By concentrating on major elements, you will produce a more focused paper, and one which your reader can comprehend. Hence, on the basis of our analysis of the structure of "Dover Beach," we might write a thesis statement such as this:

> The most significant aspect of the structure of "Dover Beach" is the internal division of each stanza into two distinct and, in the first three stanzas, contrasting parts. This structure parallels and subtly reinforces the meaning of Arnold's poem.

85

Developing the essay   As you develop the essay, explain and illustrate each point made in your thesis. The following sample theme exemplifies this process of development:

Structure in "Dover Beach"

The most significant aspect of the structure of "Dover Beach" is the internal division of each stanza into two distinct and, in the first three stanzas, contrasting parts. This structure parallels and subtly reinforces the meaning of Arnold's poem.

The first portion of stanza one (11.1–6) describes a conventionally romantic scene. Even the speaker's reaction is "typical"—he asks his love to come to the window and view the scene with him; he exclaims how the night air is "sweet." The second portion of the first stanza (11.7–14) begins the turn to the melancholy which comes to dominate the poem. The turn is gradual and natural; as the speaker approaches closer to the window, or perhaps leans out to breathe the "sweet" night air, he hears the grating of the pebbles, which suggests to him the "eternal note of sadness."

The speaker's somber mood at the end of stanza one and the introduction of the term "eternal" make plausible the allusion to Sophocles that constitutes the first part of the second stanza. The second part of this stanza shifts our focus back to the present and prepares us for the crucial third stanza. Furthermore, since both the first and second stanzas have involved striking contrasts, we are prepared for the major contrast which dominates stanza three.

Stanza three expresses the "thought" foreshadowed in the second stanza. In this stanza the first three lines hark back to the mood of beauty and spiritual tranquility communicated in the first portion of stanza one. But, just as this mood has now deserted the speaker, so, he feels, has the comforting "sea of faith" ebbed from its former fullness, leaving mankind bereft of religious conviction.

The speaker's reflection on the ebb of religious faith in stanza three motivates his exclamation to his love with which the final stanza begins. Since there is no longer comfort or meaning or solace to be found in religious belief, we must seek to fulfill these human needs in the devotion and "steadfastness" of another person. The needs that were once met by faith in God must now be met by faith in a loved one. The second portion of the fourth stanza, lines 30–37, represents the *dénouement* of the poem. In these lines the speaker explains that appearance is not reality; he explains that a world, however beautiful in appearance, that is bereft of religious faith is, in reality, a nightmare world which, "Hath really neither joy, nor love, nor light,/Nor certitude, nor peace, nor help for pain."

Note: The first four body paragraphs support and develop the thesis assertion that each stanza is divided into two distinct parts.

The structure of the poem, characterized as we have seen by a major contrast or division within each stanza, complements its meaning. On the level of theme the poem is centrally concerned with the *contrast* between the past and the present, between a former world "furled" in the embrace of religious faith and the present era in which religious certainty is no longer possible. Stanza one, contrasting as it does two moods, and stanza two, with its contrast between the thought of Sophocles and that of the speaker, prepare us for, and give added impact to, the thematically central contrast in stanza three.

Note: In this paragraph the writer takes up the second assertion in the thesis, that the structure "parallels and subtly reinforces the meaning of Arnold's poem."

Another major concept suggested by the poem is that there has been a gradual *transition* from an age of faith to an age of doubt, from an age of spiritual peace to an age of spiritual pain. The structure of the poem also complements this aspect of the poem's meaning. In stanza one, especially, there is a transition in the speaker's mood, a transition from joy to sadness that foreshadows and parallels the transition from religious faith to religious doubt with which the poem is principally concerned. And, of course, the overall transition from the mood and atmosphere of the poem's first five lines to that of its last five is dramatic indeed. Juxtaposed, the beginning and ending passages point up the full extent of the spiritual loss mankind has suffered through the waning of religious certainty.

Note: In this paragraph the writer explains a second way in which structure complements meaning.

Thus, in "Dover Beach," form parallels content. Though recognizing the structural divisions which we have discussed may not be a prerequisite to understanding the poem, their elucidation does allow the reader to perceive how the import and impact of the poem are complemented by the poet's careful crafting of structure.

Note: The final paragraph restates the main idea of the paper and concludes that understanding the structure of the poem can heighten our appreciation of it.

FIVE

TONE

UNDERSTANDING TONE

"You idiot! You fool! You creep!"—the meaning of these exclamations depends entirely on the *tone of voice* with which they are uttered. The first, for example, could be an expression of endearment if uttered with a smile, higher pitch, and light stress. But, if uttered with a glare, low pitch, and heavy stress it could mean anger or hate. Tone is everything. Both the *meaning* of the expression, and the *attitude* of the speaker toward the person being addressed are revealed by tone.

In literature, too, accurate interpretation often demands that the reader recognize tone and interpret its bearing on the meaning of the work. Tone, in literature, refers to those qualities of the work which, like pitch, stress, and intonation in speech, reveal the author's attitude.

Let's return to our "you idiot" example. Assume that a young woman addresses her lover with these words when, coming to his apartment for what she expects to be a simple dinner, she finds an elaborately prepared feast, a table set with crystal and silver, a bottle of vintage wine cooling in an icebucket, and her lover wearing a tuxedo—"You idiot!" she might exclaim. Here, her exclamation indicates her attitude toward the man—she loves him, she is pleased. Her exclamation also indicates her belief that the man, her "audience," will recognize her attitude. If he doesn't recognize the attitude behind her words, he will not respond in the way she expects him to; he will misinterpret the import of her remark and, instead of accurate communication, there will be misunderstanding. Similarly, tone in a work of literature implies the author's attitude toward the subject, and reflects the author's belief that the reader will interpret the work in the light of this attitude.

Hence, understanding tone is important because the tone of a literary work indicates how the author wants the work to be read. It indicates the author's attitude toward the characters and the action. At the same time that it reveals the author's own attitude, it helps create a similar attitude toward the characters, events, or subject on the part of the reader. Furthermore, tone controls the "aesthetic distance" of author and reader from the work; it controls the degree of involvement in or detachment from the characters, action and subject.

Identifying and Describing Tone

When you *identify* the tone of a work or portion of a work you use words that express the author's attitude: ironic, serious, detached, clinical, bitter, amused, reverent, mocking, impassioned, and so forth.

When you *describe* how this tone is established and communicated, you should do so by describing the qualities of style that reveal the author's attitude: elevated language, comic imagery, stilted syntax, incongruous rhythm, and so on. To illustrate:

> It was just a week to the day since Mr. Martin had decided to rub out Mrs. Ulgine Barrows. The term "rub out" pleased him because it suggested nothing more than the correction of an error—in this case an error of Mr. Fitweiler. Mr. Martin had spent each night of the past week working out his plan and examining it. As he walked home now he went over it again. For the hundredth time he resented the element of imprecision, the margin of guesswork that entered into the business. The project as he had worked it out was casual and bold, the risks were considerable. Something might go wrong anywhere along the line. And therein lay the cunning of his scheme. No one would ever see in it the cautious, painstaking hand of Erwin Martin, head of the filing department at F & S, of whom Mr. Fitweiler had once said, "Man is fallible but Martin isn't." No one would see his hand, that is, unless it were caught in the act.
>
> Sitting in his apartment, drinking a glass of milk, Mr. Martin reviewed his case against Mrs. Ulgine Barrows, as he had every night for seven nights. He began at the beginning. Her quacking voice and braying laugh had first profaned the halls of F & S on March 7, 1941 (Mr. Martin had a head for dates). Old Roberts, the personnel chief, had introduced her as the newly appointed special adviser to the president of the firm, Mr. Fitweiler. The woman had appalled Mr. Martin instantly, but he hadn't shown it. He had given her his dry hand, a look of studious concentration, and a faint smile. "Well," she had said, looking at the papers on his desk, "are you lifting the oxcart out of the ditch?" As Mr. Martin recalled that moment, over his milk, he squirmed slightly.
>
> —James Thurber, "The Catbird Seat"

The tone of this passage is *ironic*. In other words, there is a contrast between the way Martin views himself and his plan (seriously) and the way Thurber views him and his plan (with amusement). The tip-off comes in the last part of the first paragraph and, decisively and unmistakably, in the first sentence of the second paragraph. Martin's occupation and position, "head of the filing department," evokes a picture of a meticulous, ineffectual little man, scarcely a hardened killer. The obvious pride Martin takes in the praise of his boss and in his ability to always file documents in just the right drawer also make us suspect that something's up. Then, in the first line of the next paragraph, we find the merciless killer-to-be reviewing his victim's provocations while "drinking a glass of milk." The *incongruity* of this act, its sharp contrast with our expectations, tells us that Thurber is viewing his character with an amused smile.

Thus, if we wished to describe how the ironic tone of this passage is established and communicated, we would point to such qualities of Thurber's style as these:

1. Thurber gives his character an occupation and position that evoke a picture of an ineffectual, fussy little man.

2. Thurber has his character drink *milk* while reviewing the case against his intended victim. The associations "milk-toast," "milk-sop," and the contrast with our expectations—"mixed himself a double scotch"—tell us that Thurber regards his character, not seriously, but with amusement.

The tone of the poem "Do Not Go Gentle Into That Good Night" by Dylan Thomas is quite different:

> Do not go gentle into that good night,
> Old age should burn and rave at close of day;
> Rage, rage against the dying of the light.
>
> Though wise men at their end know dark is right,
> Because their words had forked no lightning they
> Do not go gentle into that good night.
>
> Good men, the last wave by, crying how bright
> Their frail deeds might have danced in a green bay,
> Rage, rage against the dying of the light.
>
> Wild men who caught and sang the sun in flight,
> And learn, too late, they grieved it on its way,
> Do not go gentle into that good night.
>
> Grave men, near death, who see with blinding sight
> Blind eyes could blaze like meteors and be gay,
> Rage, rage against the dying of the light.
>
> And you, my father, there on the sad height,
> Curse, bless, me now with your fierce tears, I pray.
> Do not go gentle into that good night.
> Rage, rage against the dying of the light.

The tone of this poem is *intense* and *impassioned*. Thomas is deeply involved, he is totally serious, he is emotionally committed. The tone is established and communicated by the rhythms, by the imperatives, by the repetition of the same commands, and by the language.

The rhythmic iambic pentameter that dominates gives the poem a sonorous cadence. The imperatives "Do not go gentle into that good night" and "Rage, rage against the dying of the light," coupled with their repetition throughout the poem, communicate Thomas' own rage, his own passion. And the powerful, intense diction—*rage, burn, rave, blinding, blaze, curse, bless, fierce*—reinforces the impassionately involved tone.

Summary

Tone refers to the qualities of a literary work that establish and communicate the author's attitude toward character, action, and subject. Recognizing tone is important because the author expects the reader to read and interpret the work in terms of the attitude implied. If the reader fails to recognize the tone, misinterpretation of the work may result.

Read the following short story with an eye to tone. What is Pirandello's attitude toward the characters he presents and the events he recounts? How do you know? What qualities and aspects of his style communicate this attitude? After you've read the story, we will discuss the related matters of analyzing and writing about tone.

THE CAT, A GOLDFINCH AND THE STARS

Luigi Pirandello

A stone. Another stone. Man passes and sees the two lying side by side. But what does the stone know of the one beside it? Or what does the water know of the drain in which it flows? Man sees the water and the drain; he sees the water running in the drain, and he comes to fancy that the water, as it goes, may be confiding to the drain—who knows what secrets?

Ah, what a starry night over the roofs of this little mountain hamlet! Looking up at the sky from these roofs, one would swear that those brightly shining orbs beheld nothing else.

Yet the stars do not even know there is an earth.

Those mountains? Is it possible that they are not aware of this little hamlet which has nestled between them since time immemorial? Their names are known: Monte Corno; Monte Moro; and yet, can it be, they do not even know they are mountains? And is it possible that that house over there, the oldest in the village, does not know that it came to be there on account of the road that runs by it, which is the oldest of all roads? Can it, really, be?

And supposing that *is* so?

Go ahead and believe, then, if you like, that the stars see nothing but the roofs of your little mountain hamlet.

I once knew an old couple who had a goldfinch. And the question, certainly, never occurred to them as to how their faces, its cage, the house with its old-fashioned furnishings might look to the goldfinch, or what the latter might think of all the care and caresses lavished upon it; for they were sure that, when the goldfinch came to alight upon one of their shoulders and began pecking at their wrinkled necks or the lobes of their ears—they were sure that it knew very well that this was a shoulder upon which it had alighted, and that the shoulder or the ear belonged to one of them and not to the other. Was it possible that it did not know them both very well, that it did not know that this was Grandpa and this Grandma?

Or that it was not very well aware that the reason they both loved it so was because it had been their little dead granddaughter's goldfinch, and it was she who had trained it so nicely to come perch upon her shoulder and peck at her ear, and to leave its cage and fly about the house?

For the goldfinch's cage, between the curtains, upon the window shelf, was its home only at night; by day, it spent but a few moments there, pecking at its millet seed or cunningly throwing back its head to swallow a tiny drop of water. The cage, in short, was its palace, while the house was its boundless realm. And oftentimes, it would alight upon the shade of the hanging lamp in the dining-room or upon the back of Grandfather's chair, and there it would sit and trill, or—well, you know what goldfinches are!

"Nasty thing!" the old lady would scold, when she caught sight of it doing this. And she would come running with the dustcloth, always ready to clean up after it, just as if there were a baby in the house that simply could not learn to do certain things in a certain time and place. And as she did so, the old lady would think of her granddaughter, little angel, and of how, for more than a year, she had given her this task to do, until——

"You remember, eh?"

And the old man—did he remember? He could still see her running through the house, such a tiny little mite! And he would shake his head, long and sadly.

The old couple had been left with this orphan on their hands, and she had grown up in the house with them. They had hoped that she might be the joy of their old age; but instead, when she was fifteen—But her memory had remained alive, in the trilling and the fluttering of that goldfinch. It was strange they had not thought of it sooner! But in the depths of despair into which they had fallen after their great grief, how were they ever to have thought of a goldfinch? Upon their bent shoulders, shaking with sobs, it, the goldfinch—yes, the goldfinch—had come to alight, moving its little head from side to side; and then it had stretched out its neck, and with its little beak, had pecked their ears, as if to say— yes, it was something of hers, something alive—something that was alive still, and which still had need of their care, need of the same love that they had shown her.

Ah, how the old lady had trembled as she took it in her hand and showed it to her aged husband, sobbing all the while! What kisses they had showered upon its little head, upon its beak! It did not like to be held a prisoner in the hand, but had struggled with its tiny feet and head, and had returned the old couple's kisses with sharp little pecks.

The old lady was as sure as could be that, when the goldfinch trilled, it was calling for its lost mistress, and that, when it flew here and there through the rooms of the house, it was searching for her, searching for her ceaselessly, and that it was inconsolable at not finding her; it was certain, too, that all those prolonged trills were for her,—questions that spoke plainer than words, questions repeated three and four times in succession, the bird waiting for an answer and displaying its anger at not receiving one.

What did this mean,, she would like to know, if not that the goldfinch knew all about death? But did the goldfinch really know whom it was calling, who it was from whom it awaited a response to those questions that spoke louder than words?

Ah, good heavens, it was a goldfinch after all! Now it called for her, now it wept for her. How, after all, could anyone doubt that, at this moment, for example, sitting there all huddled up on the perch of its cage, with its little head tucked in and its beak sticking up and its eyes half-closed—how could anyone doubt that it was thinking of her, the dead? At such times, it would let out a few submissive cheeps, which were obvious proof that it was thinking of her, weeping for her, lamenting her absence. They were a torture, those cheeps.

The old man did not contradict his wife. For he was as certain of it as she! He would get up on a chair as if to whisper a few words of comfort to this poor little distressed soul; and scarcely letting himself see what he did, he would open once more the door of the cage.

"There he goes! There he goes! the little rascal!" he would exclaim, turning upon the chair to watch it with a smile in his eyes, his two hands up in front of his face as if to ward it off. And then, Grandpa and Grandma would have a quarrel; for the reason that she, time and time again, had told him that he should leave it alone when it was like that, and not disturb it in its sorrow.

"It's singing," the old man would say.

"What do you mean, it's singing!" the old lady would snap back at him, with a shrug of her shoulders. "You are talking nonsense! It's fairly frantic!"

And she would come running up to soothe it. But how was she to soothe it? It would flutter away disdainfully, first in one direction and then in the other; and quite right it was in so doing, for it must have thought that they had no consideration for it whatsoever at such a time as that.

And lo, the old man not only took all these scoldings from his wife, without telling her that the cage door had been shut, and that it was, possibly, on account of this that the goldfinch had been cheeping so pitifully; but he even wept at her words—wept and shook his head:

"That's right, poor little thing! That's right, poor little thing! He feels that we aren't considerate!"

He knew what it meant, the old man did, not to have consideration shown one. For the old couple were the talk of their neighbors, who severely criticized them for living the way they did, all wrapped up in that goldfinch, and with their windows all the time closed. The old man no longer so much as stuck his nose out of the door; for after all, he was an old man; and so, he stayed at home crying like a baby. But all the same, there were no flies on him; and if anyone in the street should have had the bad taste to crack a joke about him, his life (but what did his life mean to him now?)—his life would not have meant anything to him—it would have meant nothing at all, had he felt that he was an object of ridicule. Yes, sir, on account of that goldfinch there, if anyone had had the bad taste to say anything—Three times, when he was a young fellow, he had been within a hair's breadth—give him liberty or give him death! Ah, it no longer meant much to him, if his blind old eyes went out!

Every once in a while, these violent impulses would boil up in the old man, and he would rise and go, often with the goldfinch on his shoulder, to gaze with truculent eyes through the windowpane at the windows of the house across the way.

Of the reality of those houses across the way, those windows with the fancy panes, those balustrades, those vases of flowers and everything, or of the reality of those roofs, tiles and chimneys up above, the old man could not doubt, since he knew well enough to whom they belonged, who lived there, and how they lived. But the sad part is, he never once put to himself the question what either his own house or those others opposite could mean to the goldfinch upon his shoulder; and then, there was that big white tabby-cat, crouching and sunning itself on the windowsill directly facing him. Windows? panes? roofs? tiles? my house? your house? What was my house, your house for that big white cat, sleeping there in the sun? All houses were its houses, all that it could enter. What houses? Wherever it could find something to filch, wherever it could doze comfortably, or pretend to doze.

Did the old couple believe that, by thus keeping their doors and windows always shut, a cat, if it wanted to, could not find some other means of getting in to eat their goldfinch?

Was it too much to assume that the cat knew all about that goldfinch, knew that it was the very breath of life to that old couple, for the reason that it had belonged to their little granddaughter who was dead, and who had trained it so nicely to come out of its cage and fly around the house? And who could have foretold that the old man, once having caught the cat peering intently through the closed panes at the goldfinch in its heedless flight about the room, would go to warn the cat's mistress that—woe, woe, if he caught that cat there another time? There? Where? How was that? The cat's mistress—the old couple—the window?—the goldfinch?

And so, one day, it did eat it—yes, ate that goldfinch which, for it, might very well have been another. Entering the old couple's house, no one could say from where or how, the cat proceeded to eat the goldfinch up. It was near evening, and all the old lady heard was a little anguished peep and a moan. The old man came running in and caught a glimpse of a white object scampering away through the kitchen and, on the floor, a few delicate little white feathers which, as he opened the door, fluttered over the carpet. What a scream he let out! Despite the old lady's attempts to restrain him, he seized a weapon and ran like a madman to the house across the way. No, it was not the neighbor woman, but the cat—it was the cat that the old man wanted to kill, there, under her very eyes; and so, he fired into the dining-room, for he had caught sight of the cat there, quietly perched on the cupboard; he fired one, two, three times, and there was a great crashing of pottery. Then the neighbors' son came running out; he was armed, too, and he fired on the old man.

A tragedy. Weeping and screaming, the old man was taken back to his own house, in a dying condition; he had been shot through the lungs, and they carried him home to his aged wife.

The neighbors' son fled the country. A catastrophe in two homes; the whole countryside in an uproar for a night.

As for the cat, it scarcely remembered, a moment later, having eaten the goldfinch, any goldfinch; and it is doubtful if it understood that the old man was firing at it. It had taken a quick and nimble leap and had escaped; and now—there it was, all white against the black roof, gazing up at the stars which, from the darkening depths of interplanetary space, saw—and of this we may be quite certain—nothing whatsoever of the humble roofs of this mountain hamlet; and yet, so brilliantly did they shine up there, one would have sworn that they beheld nothing else that night.

Applications

Identifying tone   What is Pirandello's attitude toward his subject? In other words, how does he regard the characters in the story, their emotions, their actions?

Describing tone   How is the tone of the story established? What are the qualities of the story that reveal Pirandello's attitude toward the characters and events?

Explaining the significance of tone   How does Pirandello's attitude toward the characters and events in the story shape the reader's interpretation of the story? How does the tone bear on the effect or impact of the story?

ANALYZING AND WRITING ABOUT TONE

Analyzing Tone

Analyzing tone is a three-step process:

   1. **Identify and interpret the qualities of the work that establish and communicate its tone**   Ask yourself such questions as these: Is the diction elevated or base? Is the level of diction appropriate to the characters, events, and subject, or is it incongruous? Does the imagery ennoble the characters or make them look little and foolish? Is the point-of-view character intelligent and sympathetic or unintelligent and unsympathetically presented? Is the syntax natural or awkward and pretentious? Does the way the author introduces and presents the characters and events indicate closeness to them or distance from them?

   2. **Infer from these qualities the author's attitude toward character and event**   Ask yourself: Does the author regard the characters seriously or humorously? Does the author regard the events of the story as important and significant or as unimportant and of little significance? Is there an ironic contrast between the author's apparent attitude toward character, event, or subject and the characters' own attitude toward themselves, the events, or the subject? Is the author's apparent attitude different from the common or typical attitude toward similar characters, events or subjects?

   3. **Determine how tone and the qualities of the work that create it shape the work's meaning and effect**   Ask yourself: Is the tone ironic and, if so, how does this tone condition the interpretation of meaning? How do the qualities or aspects of style that communicate the tone complement the meaning? How does the tone affect the impact or effect of the work on the reader?

   We can exemplify the process of analyzing tone in terms of Pirandello's short story, but first let's review the story's meaning. For tone is important not in and of itself but as it bears on interpretation and effect.

Explication

In "The Cat, a Goldfinch, and the Stars" Pirandello is poking fun at a common human foible: our tendency to attribute to inanimate objects or nonhuman creatures human characteristics, human qualities, human capacities for thought and emotion. He's mocking our tendency to "anthropomorphize" the universe, our tendency to project, sentimentally, our own characteristics onto objects and animals. In the first page of his story Pirandello sets forth the uncomfortable but nevertheless inescapable truth that the nonhuman world is just that, nonhuman. It has no emotions, no feelings, no concern whatsoever for man and his inane and insane antics. He tells us, in effect, "If you don't like this rather bleak vision of the way things really are, 'Go ahead and believe, then, if you like, that the stars see nothing but the roofs of your little mountain hamlet.'"

He then launches into a little tale, almost an exemplum, of an elderly couple who made just this mistake, who projected their own emotions onto, in this case, a lowly goldfinch. The elderly grandparents have their contemporary counterpart in those animal lovers who talk to their shaved poodle, who dress "Fido" in an overcoat, who are convinced that their little pet dog or pet cat or pet bird really "understands" what they say to it, really cares about them. Such people, to Pirandello, are simply ridiculous and absurd.

He gets us to share his view by showing the absurd attachment of Grandpa and Grandma for their dead granddaughter's little goldfinch. They think it cheeps pathetically because it's thinking of and longing for its dead mistress; Pirandello irreverently thinks that it's cheeping because it wants to be let out of its cage. They think that it shares their emotions of grief and remorse; Pirandello believes that the goldfinch has no capacity to grieve at all. Grandpa sees in the cat's action a malicious and malignant purpose; Pirandello sees in the cat's action nothing more than its instinctual behavior. The story ends in a crescendo of absurdity—Grandpa rushing heroically forth to do battle with the malignant cat which, to his mind, deliberately ate up his granddaughter's grieving goldfinch; his mad blazing away at the tabby-cat in the neighbor's dining room; the son's misinterpretation of his behavior and his shooting of the grandfather; "weeping and screaming." Pirandello's summarizing words are "A tragedy" but his meaning is "A farce." It's as if he were saying "See, this is the sort of absurdity, this is the sort of inanity that results when people project their own feelings and emotions onto the nonhuman world."

The *tone* of the story is instrumental in communicating Pirandello's attitude and in establishing this interpretation.

With this capsule explication in mind, we can turn to the process of analyzing tone:

1. Identify and interpret the qualities of the work that establish and communicate its tone In this story Pirandello speaks to the reader directly, as author, in his own voice. He refers to himself in the first person, he addresses the reader familiarly as "you." This tends to ally author and reader; it creates a conversational, almost intimate tone at the very beginning of the story. As a result, when Pirandello turns to the tale of "an old couple who had a goldfinch," the reader is inclined to view them as spectacle. The reader feels close to the author, not to the old couple.

This emotional detachment or distance from the characters and events of the story is sustained and even increased in the course of the narrative by Pirandello's treatment of the old couple, by his description of the goldfinch, and by explicit comments in his own voice. Though the couple's grief is undoubtedly genuine, we are never allowed to sympathize with them. Instead, they are presented as comic, even ridiculous, figures—Grandpa and Grandma showering kisses on the struggling goldfinch, foolishly attributing to it their own emotions of sorrow and grief, absurdly quarreling over whether it should be freed or left alone to mourn when it utters those little "cheeps."

Pirandello is careful to prevent the reader from romanticizing or sentimentalizing the goldfinch as the grandparents do. When it perches on the back of Grandfather's chair it is an even bet whether it will "sit and trill, or—well you know what goldfinches are!" When the old couple showers kisses upon its head, it returns their kisses with "sharp little pecks." And when the grandmother starts ascribing to the bird knowledge of death and other such distinctly human capacities Pirandello, out of patience, exclaims "Ah, good heavens, it was a goldfinch after all!"

2. Infer from these qualities the author's attitude toward character and event   Pirandello's attitude toward the characters and events of his story is obviously *ironic*. He regards Grandpa and Grandma as ridiculous comic figures. He regards the goldfinch not as a "distressed soul" but as just a goldfinch, a stupid little bird that leaves its droppings all over the furniture and floor. To him, the "tragic" events which end the story are not tragic but farcical.

3. Determine how tone and the qualities of the work that create it shape the work's meaning and effect   The ironic tone of "The Cat, a Goldfinch, and the Stars" determines our interpretation of the story and accounts for its particular effectiveness. The characters and events of the story, if viewed without regard to Pirandello's tone, represent a sentimental melodrama:

> —The heavy-lidded, evil cat is the villain. It wants to eat up the precious goldfinch that was the joy of the grandparents' lovely granddaughter. The grandparents strive heroically to save the goldfinch from the vile clutches of the "big white tabby-cat," but in the end the cat pounces. In his righteous rage the grandfather attempts to execute the murderer but is instead murdered himself. What a tragedy!—

But the tone of the story, established, as we have seen, by Pirandello's mocking attitude toward the old couple, by his realistic description of the goldfinch, and by his own impatient interjections, effectively rules out the possibility of interpreting the story in this "sentimental" fashion. Instead, everything is inverted. The goldfinch is just a dumb bird, the grandparents are damned fools, and the "tragedy" is a farce, an absurd comedy of errors and inanities. It is as if Pirandello is saying, "See. Here is the sort of thing that happens when one projects human emotions onto the outer nonhuman world of cats, goldfinches, and stars."

Writing About Tone

Before you attempt to write a critical essay on tone in a literary work, be sure that tone is significant in that particular work. Your analysis of tone should produce the sort of detailed and extensive comments that our analysis of tone in Pirandello's story has evoked.

After you have analyzed the nature and functions of tone, you can organize your essay along these lines:

1. Identify the author's attitude toward character, event, and subject. In other words, identify the tone of the work.

2. In the same paragraph, set forth your view of the *function* of tone in the work. Make an assertion about the way in which the tone affects the interpretation and impact of the work.

3. Support your opinion about the nature of the tone of the work by describing the qualities of the work that establish and communicate this tone. Convince the reader that the tone you have alleged really exists.

4. Support your opinion about the function of tone by explaining how the tone and the qualities of the work that establish it do indeed affect interpretation and impact in the way you have asserted.

These steps are exemplified in the following essay:

Tone as Meaning in "The Cat, a Goldfinch, and the Stars"

In his short story "The Cat, a Goldfinch, and the Stars" Luigi Pirandello employs sustained irony to convert a potential melodrama into an ironic commentary on an aspect of man's sentimentality, the tendency to attribute human characteristics and emotions to the nonhuman world. Pirandello's ironic, mocking tone conditions our interpretation of the story by forcing us to regard the characters as absurd and the events as farcical.

> *Note: The first paragraph embodies steps 1 and 2. The writer identifies the tone as ironic and asserts that this tone functions to condition our interpretation of the story "by forcing us to regard the characters as absurd and the events as farcical."*

Irony demands a certain emotional detachment, a certain objectivity. Pirandello forestalls the reader's tendency to identify or empathize with the characters in his story by speaking to the reader directly, as author, in his own voice. He refers to himself in the first person, he addresses the reader familiarly as "you." This tends to ally author and reader; it creates a conversational, almost intimate tone at the very beginning of the story. As a result, when Pirandello turns to the tale of "an old couple who had a goldfinch," the reader is inclined to view them as spectacle. The reader feels close to the author rather than to "Grandpa and Grandma."

This emotional detachment or distance from the characters and events of the story is sustained and even increased in the course of the narrative by Pirandello's treatment of the old couple, by his description of the goldfinch, and by explicit comments in his own voice. Though the couple's grief is undoubtedly genuine, we are never allowed to sympathize with them. Instead, they are presented as comic, even ridiculous figures—Grandpa and Grandma showering kisses on the struggling goldfinch, foolishly attributing to it their own emotions of sorrow and grief, absurdly quarreling over whether it should be freed or left alone to mourn when it utters those little "cheeps."

Pirandello is careful to prevent the reader from romanticizing or sentimentalizing the goldfinch as the grandparents do. When it perches on the back of Grandfather's chair it is an even bet whether it will "sit and trill, or—well you know what goldfinches are!" When the old couple showers kisses upon its head, it returns their kisses with "sharp little pecks." And when the grandmother starts ascribing to the bird knowledge of death and other such distinctly human capacities Pirandello, out of patience, exclaims "Ah, good heavens, it was a goldfinch after all!"

Note: The preceding three paragraphs support the assertion that the tone of the story is ironic by describing the qualities of the work that establish and communicate this tone.

The ironic tone of "The Cat, a Goldfinch, and the Stars" determines our interpretation of the story and accounts for its particular effectiveness. The characters and events of the story, if viewed without regard to Pirandello's tone, represent a sentimental melodrama:

—The heavy-lidded, evil cat is the villain. It wants to eat up the precious goldfinch that was the joy of the grandparents' lovely granddaughter. The grandparents strive heroically to save the goldfinch from the vile clutches of the "big white tabby-cat," but in the end the cat pounces. In his righteous rage the grandfather attempts to execute the murderer but is instead murdered himself. What a tragedy!—

But the tone of the story, established, as we have seen, by Pirandello's mocking attitude toward the old couple, by his realistic description of the goldfinch, and by his own impatient interjections, effectively rules out the possibility of interpreting the story in this sentimental fashion. Instead, everything is inverted. The goldfinch is just a dumb bird, the grandparents are damned fools, and the "tragedy" is a farce, an absurd comedy of errors and inanities. It is as if Pirandello is saying, "See. Here is the sort of thing that happens when one projects human emotions onto the outer, nonhuman world of cats, goldfinches, and stars."

> Note: The final paragraph supports the earlier assertion about the function of tone. It explains why and how "Pirandello's ironic, mocking tone conditions our interpretation of the story by forcing us to regard the characters as absurd and the events as farcical."

SIX

IMAGERY

UNDERSTANDING IMAGERY

An image is a picture, a *sense picture*. It may involve any or all of the five senses, not just the sense of sight. If you can see it, hear it, smell it, taste it, or feel it, it's an image. Hence, "leap" but not "love," "caw" but not "kind," "hoof" but not "hope."

An image may be purely descriptive, having no function or meaning beyond the sensory impression it communicates—the citing of eye and hair color on a person's driver's license, for instance. Such merely descriptive images also occur in literature. But imagery in literature often serves additional purposes. Through selective use of images, an author can suggest character, build atmosphere, emphasize an emotion, and communicate ideas.

Show, don't tell. Images show   There's an old creative writing course bromide that goes "Show, don't tell." Another way to say it is: "Imply, don't state." T. S. Eliot put it still differently when he tagged his poetic technique with the high-sounding phrase, "objective correlative." All of these imperatives for the writer mean essentially the same thing. For example, a good author doesn't often write of a character: "John was unhappy." What the author wants to do is to *show* the reader that John is unhappy. The author does this by using images, by presenting sensory details which show how unhappy John is. Not

John was unhappy

but

John walked to the window again, looked out at the gray skies, lit a cigarette, inhaled twice and threw it into the fireplace. He turned up the volume of the Janis Joplin record on his stereo, and almost immediately shut it off. Then, moving stiffly, he crossed the room and opened the desk drawer for the third time in the last ten minutes. But this time he took out the gun.

Nowhere in the second passage does the author *state* that John was unhappy. We get the idea of his unhappiness from the series of images.

Notice the sense-pictures in this short passage: "John" (sight) "walks" (sight) "window" (sight) "stared out" (sight) "gray skies" (sight) "lit a cigarette" (sight, touch, sound, taste, smell) "inhaled" (taste) "threw it" (sight) "into the fireplace" (sight) "moving stiffly" (sight) "stereo" (sight, sound), "gun" (sight, touch).

The next step is to interpret the images. John seems restless; he is hoping for help (the window) but does not really expect it; his usual comforts (cigarettes, fire, music) no longer comfort him; the atmosphere also seems to be conspiring against him (gray skies). He is contemplating suicide—or perhaps murder (the gun). *Ergo,* John is unhappy.

Interpreting nonliteral imagery   The imagery we have examined so far has been literal imagery; it means what it says, it is literally true. But, especially in poetry, you will encounter nonliteral or figurative uses of imagery. Nonliteral imagery means more than it says. Nonliteral imagery always involves a comparison, implied or explicit, between two unlike matters. This comparison is false on the literal level, the level of denotation, but true on the figurative level, the level of connotation.

In "Sailing to Byzantium" Yeats writes:

> An aged man is but a paltry thing,
> A tattered coat upon a stick, unless
> Soul clap its hands and sing,
>   and louder sing
> For every tatter in its mortal dress.

The second line compares an old man to a *"tattered coat* upon a *stick."* Obviously, the comparison is literally false. But the connotations, the emotional associations that the images evoke, are valid. When we picture a tattered coat on a stick we think of something worthless, of something ugly and worn out, of a scarecrow. These associations reflect Yeats' view of old men who have no spiritual or intellectual vitality. In the third line Yeats asserts that an aged man can have dignity only if soul "clap its hands and sing." Again, the comparison is literally false—one's "soul" has neither hands to clap nor voice to sing. But the associations which the image "clapping" evokes (appreciation of art or things artistic) and the connotations of "singing" (rejoicing, affirming, creating), these again are valid and reflect Yeats' view that an aged man can redeem himself from the body's deterioration by studying and rejoicing in art, by the creation of works of art.

Let's take another example. In "The Love Song of J. Alfred Prufrock," Prufrock exclaims in a moment of impassioned despair:

> I should have been a pair of ragged claws
> Scuttling across the floors of silent seas.

His wish makes no *literal* sense. If a fairy godmother suddenly appeared waving a wand, Prufrock would quickly recant. And, of course, no creature consisting only of a "pair of ragged claws" exists. The import of Prufrock's cry only emerges when we explore the connotations of the images. Such a "ragged claw" would be virtually mindless; it would just "scuttle" along doing its instinctual thing in a world of darkness and absolute silence. No one would torment it with a "tedious argument/Of insidious intent." It would have no "overwhelming question" to ask. It would not have to "prepare a face to meet the faces that you meet." It would, in short, be free of all the self-consciousness, trepidation, and indecision that blight Prufrock's life; and to be freed from his particular brand of the "burden of being" is Prufrock's most ardent longing.

I. A. Richards has provided us with a couple of high-sounding but, nonetheless, helpful terms that can be used to clarify the process of getting from the nonliteral image to its meaning or significance: *vehicle* and *tenor*. "Vehicle" is Richards' term for the image itself: *tattered coat, ragged claw*, and so forth. Vehicle is stated and concrete. "Tenor" is Richards' term for the meaning of the image, its significance, its import. Tenor is unstated and abstract.

The way to get from vehicle to tenor, from image to meaning, is through the connotations, in context, of the image. You should ask yourself, "What qualities of man, what human emotions, what aspects of life, what human characteristics, what concepts are suggested by the image?" These qualities constitute tenor, the meaning of the image.

The speaker in Robinson's poem "Luke Havergal" tells Luke,

> No, there is not a dawn in eastern skies
> To rift the fiery night that's in your eyes

Let's examine the double image, "fiery night." It's vehicle—stated, concrete. It's also a nonliteral image—there can be no literal fire, no actual night in Luke's eyes. The connotations of each word, however, suggest the tenor, the meaning and significance of the image. "Fiery," when used in reference to people, suggests anger (*fiery* temper), passion or strong emotion (*burning* passion), and perhaps hate or outrage (*smouldering* hatred). "Night," the other part of the image, suggests, in the human world, such emotions as despair and sadness (dark night of the soul). The connotations of the two words, taken together, reveal the emotion that Luke is feeling—an angry raging despair at the death of his beloved. This blend of emotions, anger and despair, is the tenor of the image, its "meaning" in the poem.

The process of interpreting nonliteral images, then, is the process of moving from the concrete, stated image to its connotations, and then applying these connotations to the human emotion, or aspect of life, or concept that the poet is concerned with.

Some Functions of Imagery
Imagery characterizes

The Swede domineered the whole feast, and he gave it the appearance of a cruel bacchanal. He seemed to have grown suddenly taller; he gazed, brutally disdainful, into every face. His voice rang through the room. Once when he jabbed harpoon-fashion with his fork to pinion a biscuit, the weapon nearly impaled the hand of the Easterner, which had been stretched out quietly for the same biscuit.

—Stephen Crane, "The Blue Hotel"

Note: In this passage Crane uses imagery to suggest the violence and dangerousness of the drunken man. The image "grown suddenly taller" implies the Swede's sudden metamorphosis from sober coward to drunken brute. Other images, such as "jabbed harpoon-fashion," "pinion," "weapon," and "impaled" connote violence, danger, and hostility.

Imagery creates atmosphere

The coach was a relic with a decaying interior of ancient red-plush seats, bald in spots, and peeling iodine-colored woodwork. An old-time copper lamp, attached to the ceiling, looked romantic and out of place. Gloomy dead smoke sailed the air; and the car's heated closeness accentuated the stale odor of discarded sandwiches, apple cores, and orange hulls; this garbage, including Lily cups, soda-pop bottles, and mangled newspapers, littered the long aisle. From a water cooler, embedded in the wall, a steady stream trickled to the floor.

—Truman Capote, *A Tree of Night*

Note: This paragraph uses imagery to create an atmosphere of desolation and despair. Capote skillfully uses all of the senses: sight, primarily and obviously; smell and taste in phrases like "dead smoke," "heated closeness," "stale odor"; touch in such words as "mangled" and "littered"; sound (with touch suggested also) in the word "trickled." The atmosphere created is one of desolation, decay, gloom, weariness, and despair. Some of these descriptive words are used in the passage but it is the accumulation of images which evokes the atmosphere described.

Imagery heightens emotional impact

The beast once dead, she separated the red body from the skin; but the sight of the blood she was touching and which covered her hands, of the warm blood which she felt cooling and coagulating, made her tremble from head to foot; and she kept seeing her big boy cut in two, and quite red also, like this still-palpitating animal.

—Guy de Maupassant, "La Mère Sauvage"

Note: The mother, the "she" in the passage above, has just received a letter telling of her son's death at the hands of the Germans. Her "German occupiers," whom she has thought of as "boys" like her son, bring her a rabbit which they kill before her in a matter-of-fact fashion. Suddenly she sees the connection—her son and the rabbit are, alike, victims of the German soldiers. The images "red body," "skin," "blood," "trembling," "red," "palpitating" force an emotional reaction from the reader.

Imagery communicates ideas by implication

About half way between West Egg and New York the motor road hastily joins the railroad and runs beside it for a quarter of a mile, so as to shrink away from a certain desolate area of land. This is a valley of ashes—a fantastic farm where ashes grow like wheat into ridges and hills and grotesque gardens; where ashes take the forms of houses and chimneys and rising smoke and, finally, with a transcendent effort, of ash-gray men who move dimly and already crumbling through the powdery air. . . . The only building in sight was a small block of yellow brick sitting on the edge of the waste land, a sort of compact Main Street ministering to it, and contiguous to absolutely nothing.

—F. Scott Fitzgerald, *The Great Gatsby*

Note: By the end of this passage, the meaning becomes unmistakably clear. And yet no bald "statement" of meaning has been made. Instead the author has implied, through his central imagery of "grayness" and "ashes," his idea that industrial America is a wasteland—a desert of unfulfilled dreams and wasted lives.

Summary

Imagery in poetry and fiction is like stage setting and lighting in drama. It imparts to literature a sensory quality; it evokes mood and meaning. But you the reader must cooperate with the writer by actively "sensing" the writer's images. Stroke the images with your hand and feel their shape and texture, linger over them with your eyes and picture their appearance; roll them over your tongue and find their flavor. Failure to understand imagery is often simply failure to sense it.

As you read the short story that follows, try to convert it into a motion picture. *Listen* to the sounds, *taste* the liquor, *see* the island of light holding back the encircling night.

A CLEAN, WELL-LIGHTED PLACE

Ernest Hemingway

It was late and every one had left the café except an old man who sat in the shadow the leaves of the tree made against the electric light. In the daytime the street was dusty, but at night the dew settled the dust and the old man liked to sit late because he was deaf and now at night it was quiet and he felt the difference. The two waiters inside the café knew that the old man was a little drunk, and while he was a good client they knew that if he became too drunk he would leave without paying, so they kept watch on him.

"Last week he tried to commit suicide," one waiter said.

"Why?"

"He was in despair."

"What about?"

"Nothing."

"How do you know it was nothing?"

"He has plenty of money."

They sat together at a table that was close against the wall near the door of the café and looked at the terrace where the tables were all empty except where the old man sat in the shadow of the leaves of the tree that moved slightly in the wind. A girl and a soldier went by in the street. The street light shone on the brass number on his collar. The girl wore no head covering and hurried beside him.

"The guard will pick him up," one waiter said.

"What does it matter if he gets what he's after?"

"He had better get off the street now. The guard will get him. They went by five minutes ago."

The old man sitting in the shadow rapped on his saucer with his glass. The younger waiter went over to him.

"What do you want?"

The old man looked at him. "Another brandy," he said.

"You'll be drunk," the waiter said. The old man looked at him. The waiter went away.

"He'll stay all night," he said to his colleague. "I'm sleepy now. I never get into bed before three o'clock. He should have killed himself last week."

The waiter took the brandy bottle and another saucer from the counter inside the café and marched out to the old man's table. He put down the saucer and poured the glass full of brandy.

"You should have killed yourself last week," he said to the deaf man. The old man motioned with his finger. "A little more," he said. The waiter poured on into the glass so that the brandy slopped over and ran down the stem into the top saucer of the pile. "Thank you," the old man said. The waiter took the bottle back inside the café. He sat down at the table with his colleague again.

"He's drunk now," he said.

"He's drunk every night."

"What did he want to kill himself for?"

"How should I know."

"How did he do it?"

"He hung himself with a rope."

"Who cut him down?"

"His niece."

"Why did they do it?"

"Fear for his soul."

"How much money has he got?"

"He's got plenty."

"He must be eighty years old."

"Anyway I should say he was eighty."

"I wish he would go home. I never get to bed before three o'clock. What kind of hour is that to go to bed?"

"He stays up because he likes it."

"He's lonely. I'm not lonely. I have a wife waiting in bed for me."

"He had a wife once too."

"A wife would be no good to him now."

"You can't tell. He might be better with a wife."

"His niece looks after him. You said she cut him down."

"I know."

"I wouldn't want to be that old. An old man is a nasty thing."

"Not always. This old man is clean. He drinks without spilling. Even now, drunk. Look at him."

"I don't want to look at him. I wish he would go home. He has no regard for those who must work."

The old man looked from his glass across the square, then over at the waiters.

"Another brandy," he said, pointing to his glass. The waiter who was in a hurry came over.

"Finished," he said, speaking with that omission of syntax stupid people employ when talking to drunken people or foreigners. "No more tonight. Close now."

"Another," said the old man.

"No. Finished." The waiter wiped the edge of the table with a towel and shook his head.

The old man stood up, slowly counted the saucers, took a leather coin purse from his pocket and paid for the drinks, leaving half a peseta tip.

The waiter watched him go down the street, a very old man walking unsteadily but with dignity.

"Why didn't you let him stay and drink?" the unhurried waiter asked. They were putting up the shutters. "It is not half-past two."

"I want to go home to bed."

"What is an hour?"

"More to me than to him."

"An hour is the same."

"You talk like an old man yourself. He can buy a bottle and drink at home."

"It's not the same."

"No, it is not," agreed the waiter with a wife. He did not wish to be unjust. He was only in a hurry.

"And you? You have no fear of going home before your usual hour?"

"Are you trying to insult me?"

"No, hombre, only to make a joke."

"No," the waiter who was in a hurry said, rising from pulling down the metal shutters. "I have confidence. I am all confidence."

"You have youth, confidence, and a job," the older waiter, said. "You have everything."

"And what do you lack?"

"Everything but work."

"You have everything I have."

"No. I have never had confidence and I am not young."

"Come on. Stop talking nonsense and lock up."

"I am of those who like to stay late at the café," the older waiter said. "With all those who do not want to go to bed. With all those who need a light for the night."

"I want to go home and into bed."

"We are of two different kinds," the older waiter said. He was now dressed to go home. "It is not only a question of youth and confidence although those things are very beautiful. Each night I am reluctant to close up because there may be some one who needs the café."

"Hombre, there are bodegas open all night long."

"You do not understand. This is a clean and pleasant café. It is well lighted. The light is very good and also, now, there are shadows of the leaves."

"Good night," said the younger waiter.

"Good night," the other said. Turning off the electric light he continued the conversation with himself. It is the light of course but it is necessary that the place be clean and pleasant. You do not want music. Certainly you do not want music. Nor can you stand before a bar with dignity although that is all that is provided for these hours. What did he fear? It was not fear or dread. It was a nothing that he knew too well. It was all a nothing and a man was nothing too. It was only that and light was all it needed and a certain cleanness and order. Some lived in it and never felt it but he knew it all was nada y pues nada y nada y pues nada. Our nada who art in nada, nada be thy name thy kingdom nada thy will be nada in nada as it is in nada. Give us this nada our daily nada and nada us our nada as we nada our nadas and nada us not into nada but deliver us from nada; pues nada. Hail nothing full of nothing, nothing is with thee. He smiled and stood before a bar with a shining steam pressure coffee machine.

"What's yours?" asked the barman.

"Nada."

"Otro loco mas," said the barman and turned away.

"A little cup," said the waiter.

The barman poured it for him.

"The light is very bright and pleasant but the bar is unpolished," the waiter said.

The barman looked at him but did not answer. It was too late at night for conversation.

"You want another copita?" the barman asked.

"No, thank you," said the waiter and went out. He disliked bars and bodegas. A clean, well-lighted café was a very different thing. Now, without thinking further, he would go home to his room. He would lie in the bed and finally, with daylight, he would go to sleep. After all, he said to himself, it is probably only insomnia. Many must have it.

Applications

Identifying imagery   What are the major clusters of images in Hemingway's story?

Explaining the significance of the imagery   What ideas are suggested by the major image clusters in Hemingway's story? How does the imagery heighten the story's impact? How does the imagery help communicate the story's meaning?

ANALYZING AND WRITING ABOUT IMAGERY

Analyzing Imagery

Identification   Before you can analyze imagery in a literary work, you must, of course, identify the major images or image clusters. If the work is a poem or short story, you can underline or circle the images and then sort them into clusters of related images. In longer works, such as novels, you would probably choose to analyze just one kind of imagery—sun and fire imagery in *Moby-Dick,* wasteland imagery in *The Great Gatsby,* for example.

In "A Clean, Well-Lighted Place" we can identify at least three major clusters of images:

1. Images of *drinking.* The word *drink* and its other forms such as *drank, drunk, drunken* recur throughout the story. Other words connoting drinking such as *glass, bottle, brandy,* and *bar* reinforce this image, which involves all five of the senses: taste, smell, sight, touch, and even sound.

2. Images of *darkness* or *night.* The words *night* and *tonight* are repeated, and are reinforced by such related images as *shadow, bed, sleep* and other terms associated with the darkness of night.

3. Images of *light.* The words *light, well-lighted, street light, electric light, shining, shone, bright* and *daylight* make up an image cluster that contrasts with the imagery of night and darkness.

Significance   The next step is to explore the *significance* of the imagery by asking such questions as:

1. To what extent does the imagery help portray character?

2. To what extent does the imagery create or heighten atmosphere?

3. To what extent does the imagery increase the work's total emotional impact or effect?

4. To what extent does the imagery complement or help communicate meaning?

As you apply each of these questions to the major image clusters you have identified, you will often find that one or two of these image clusters are "richer" in significance than the others. If so, good. This is the time to *limit*. Concentrate on the image cluster or clusters that seem to do the most, for these are the most significant. Limiting in this way will allow you to go into greater detail, to probe more deeply, to write an "in-depth" report rather than a surface survey.

Hence, in Hemingway's story, you might well limit your investigation to the two contrasting, yet complementary, image clusters—the imagery of light and the imagery of night.

Writing About Imagery

Once you have identified the essential images, have sorted them into clusters, and have determined how these image clusters are related to character, meaning, effect, and other aspects of the work, you are ready to begin writing.

1. State your view about the function(s) of imagery in the work you are discussing.

2. Limit your attention to one or two image clusters.

3. Identify these image clusters for the reader.

4. Explain, amplify, and illustrate your assertion about the function(s) of imagery in the work.

This four-step process is exemplified in the essay that follows:

The Imagery of Light and Night in "A Clean, Well-Lighted Place"

In "A Clean, Well-Lighted Place," imagery and theme are inextricably interwoven. Hemingway does allow his central character, the older waiter, to make one unmistakable statement of idea in the *Nada y nada y pues nada* speech. However, the totality of the theme—Hemingway's view that life, though ultimately meaningless *(nada)*, can be lived out with the stoic virtues of compassion, endurance and dignity—is communicated through the story's imagery of light and night.

> *Note: The first paragraph combines steps 1–3. The first part of sentence 3 sets forth the writer's thesis about the function of imagery in the story; the last part of the sentence limits the discussion and identifies the image clusters to be discussed.*

The images of light and the associations that, in this story, go with light—cleanness, order, quiet, pleasantness—are connected in the mind of the old waiter with compassion, dignity, and endurance. The images of light are also associated with the character of the older waiter himself. His behavior, for example, is in direct contrast with that of the younger waiter who makes a bad joke at the expense of the old and deaf customer when he tells him, " 'You should have killed yourself last week.' " The younger waiter also asks callously " 'How much money has he got?' " and finally tells the old man that he must leave. The younger waiter wants to go home to his bed and his wife. He refuses compassion (or even under-standing) to the old man: "'A wife would be no good to him now.'" He also speaks to the old man in a patronizing kind of baby-talk as he hurries him out of the café, not caring that he is forcing the old man back into his unbearable eighty-year-old world of darkness and night:

> "Finished," he said speaking with that omission of syntax stupid people employ when talking to drunken people or foreigners. "No more tonight. Close now."

The old waiter seems less callous. Hemmingway associates him with "light" and compassion: "'Each night I am reluctant to close up because there may be someone who needs the [clean, well-lighted] café.'" When the other waiter replies that there are bodegas (saloons) open all night long, the older waiter answers (and the imagery is very clear here):

> "You do not understand; this is a clean and pleasant café. It is well lighted. The light is very good . . . ."

After the "impatient younger waiter" has said good night and has gone home, the older waiter continues the "conversation with himself." "It is the light of course, but it is necessary that the place be clean and pleasant." Later, the older waiter leaves the lighted café for the dark streets of night and takes his reluctant walk home to his room. On the way, he stops at a "shining" coffee machine and asks for a little cup of coffee. He drinks it and goes to his bed, waiting (sleepless) for "daylight."

It seems apparent that both the "old man" who has failed in his attempted suicide and the "old waiter" possess the dignity which is another of the concepts that Hemingway evokes with his images of light. The older waiter, we are told, does not like bodegas, the dark and dingy bars which rob a man of his dignity: "Nor can you stand before a bar with dignity," thinks the old waiter.

Hemingway indicates the dignity of the old man by both implication and statement. He shows us that the old man says "thank you," and that he leaves a tip. And we're told that when he leaves the café, "the very old man [was] walking unsteadily but with dignity." This dignity, Heming-way seems to suggest, is possible only because there is "a clean, well-lighted place" where the old man can drink his brandy until his unhappi-ness becomes a bearable burden.

Note: The paragraphs above explain, amplify, and illustrate the significance of the first image cluster, the imagery of light.

The second image-cluster centers around the word *night*. Some of the words used besides *night* are *tonight, goodnight, shadow, sleep, bed, insomnia,* and *unpolished*. Associated with these images of darkness and night are the emotions of death, despair, loneliness, and nothingness *(nada)*. These are the emotions that assail both the old man and the older waiter, who understands his customer's suffering and need.

> *Note: In this paragraph, the writer turns to the significance of the second major image cluster, the imagery of* night.

The last paragraph of the story reveals the waiter in his room waiting out the sleepless *night*. But in the last images, Hemingway also allows the waiter the consolations and the promises of light: "and finally with *daylight* he would go to sleep." Thus, the story ends with an affirmation of the stoic value of endurance. The old waiter in his single room, alone in his bed at three o'clock in the morning (the darkest hour of the night) refuses self-pity. If he cannot sleep, there are many who share his insomnia: "Many must have it." The last images in the story are mixed: light and night.

> *Note: Here the writer "pulls it all together," explaining how the imagery of "night" is relieved by the promise of coming "light."*

In this short study of two central images, we can see that an author may temper or even alter his statement of meaning with the strength of his images. Though at first "A Clean, Well-Lighted Place" may seem to call for an unmixed reaction of sorrow and despair, Hemingway succeeds in making his reader feel both sorrow and a kind of joy. The joy is evoked almost entirely by the repeated images of light—which succeed in counterbalancing the contrary and despairing images of night.

> *Note: The final and concluding paragraph puts the discussion of imagery in "A Clean, Well-Lighted Place" in a broader context. The writer generalizes from specific discussion to a statement about the thematic significance of imagery in literature.*

SEVEN

SYMBOLISM

UNDERSTANDING SYMBOLISM

In a sense, it seems almost silly to speak of "understanding" symbolism, for in reading this sentence, you are demonstrating such understanding. Yet, ironically, it is this very expertise in language symbolism which all of us possess that sometimes makes the understanding of symbolism in literature difficult.

In mastering our language, we've all become, to a greater or lesser extent, symbolic literalists, linguistic fundamentalists. We have learned that rain refers to water droplets falling from the sky—not to death; that a woman's "yellow hair" refers to the color of her tresses—not to her physicality.

Yet, in order to understand literary symbolism, all we need to do is utilize the same technique by which we learned language in the first place—receptivity to meaning in context. For a literary symbol is simply an image which stands for something else, that means *more than* its literal, "dictionary" meaning. Notice how, in the haiku below, "rose" comes to mean *more than* just a flower:

> I pick a rose,
> Its petals soft, sweet-smelling.
> The thorns tear my cheek.

"Love" is not explicitly mentioned. Yet we can scarcely miss the point that the poet is using the image of a rose as a symbol of love. What makes a rose especially effective as a symbol here is that it has some of the same complexity as "my love." It is beautiful, desirable, pleasure giving, but it is also capable of "tearing my cheek"; it has thorns which can bring blood, pain, suffering. A flower (and especially a rose) is also an appropriate symbol for romantic love because the rose lasts such a short time. It is lovely; it changes from a bud to a full bloom of beauty; and then its petals droop and fall and there is left only the thorny stem.

Obvious and Subtle Symbolism

Many writers use symbols quite consciously and obviously. For example, when Nathaniel Hawthorne, in his novel *The Scarlet Letter*, had Hester

Prynne embroider and wear the letter "A" on her bosom, he knew quite well that the reader and Hester herself realized that "A" symbolized "Adulteress." And when he named her illegitimate daughter "Pearl," he knew his melodrama-loving readers would buy the symbol. Today's writers are less likely to use symbolism so obviously.

The most significant characteristic of a symbol is that it means more than what it says. Sometimes if you overlook symbolic significance, you miss only a part of the author's meaning. Thus, in Hemingway's *A Farewell to Arms*, the mountains symbolize all that is pure, fine, and uncontaminated, while the plain symbolizes decay and corruption; rain in the novel symbolizes despair and death. Nevertheless, the mountains, plains, and rain are also "real." If we overlook their symbolic significance we miss much, but we do not necessarily misinterpret Hemingway's novel. We can say that, in this novel, symbolism *reinforces* or *adds to* meaning. In other instances, however, symbolism *carries* the meaning. That is, an image must be recognized as symbolic, and its meaning understood, if the work is to be correctly interpreted. "Cliff Klingenhagen" by Edwin Arlington Robinson is such a work:

> Cliff Klingenhagen had me in to dine
> With him one day; and after soup and meat,
> And all the other things there were to eat,
> Cliff took two glasses and filled one with wine
> And one with wormwood. Then, without a sign
> For me to choose at all, he took the draught
> Of bitterness himself, and lightly quaffed
> It off, and said the other one was mine.
> And when I asked him what the deuce he meant
> By doing that, he only looked at me
> And smiled, and said it was a way of his.
> And though I know the fellow, I have spent
> Long time a-wondering when I shall be
> As happy as Cliff Klingenhagen is.

If we do not perceive that the "wormwood" which Cliff lightly quaffs is a symbol of the bitterness, the sadness, the inevitable tragedy and suffering of life, we may judge Cliff to be some sort of masochistic madman who enjoys drinking, quite literally, wormwood. It is necessary to see Cliff Klingenhagen's act, and his drink, as symbolic if we are to accurately interpret the meaning of the poem: that men and women can only achieve happiness if they are willing to acknowledge the inevitability of sorrow and suffering and bitterness and accept these aspects of life as part of the human condition.

121

To reiterate: an image becomes symbolic when it embodies a distinct idea or concept *in addition to* its sensory representation. Thus, in "Cliff Klingenhagen," wormwood is an image; one can taste it, touch it, smell it. But it is *also*, as we have seen, a symbol; it stands for certain aspects of life. Similarly, in Shelley's "Ozymandias," the shattered statue is an image. But notice how, in the course of the poem, this image acquires symbolic meaning.

> I met a traveler from an antique land
> Who said: Two vast and trunkless legs of stone
> Stand in the desert . . . Near them, on the sand,
> Half sunk, a shattered visage lies, whose frown,
> And wrinkled lip, and sneer of cold command,
> Tell that its sculptor well those passions read
> Which yet survive, stamped on these lifeless things,
> The hand that mocked them, and the heart that fed:
> And on the pedestal these words appear:
> "My name is Ozymandias, King of Kings:
> Look on my works, ye Mighty, and despair!"
> Nothing beside remains. Round the decay
> Of that colossal wreck, boundless and bare
> The lone and level sands stretch far away.

When authors make subtle use of symbolism, they are presenting their readers a challenge to be alert and perceptive, to read between the lines, to harken to a little lower layer. The key questions we must ask are the reading-between-the-lines questions such as these closely related ones:

1. Is there more than meets the eye?

2. Does this object or character or action seem to mean more than it would ordinarily mean?

3. Does the object or character or action seem larger-than-life? In other words, does it stand for a larger, more universal meaning than its narrow, limited, and particular realistic meaning?

4. Is there emphasis on or repetition of certain words and phrases that suggests the author is signaling a generalized abstraction through a particularized concrete object, character, or action?

5. Does the reader feel an uneasy sense of "strangeness"?

6. Are there signs that the author is suggesting more (by indirection) than he or she comes right out with?

7. Does the story or poem seem slight, unimportant or pointless if it is read as straight realism?

Summary

We have observed that symbols communicate ideas other than, or in addition to, their literal denotative meaning. Hence, they must be first recognized and then "interpreted," a process that, at first difficult, becomes easier as one's range of reading broadens.

As you read Walter Van Tilburg Clark's highly symbolic story, try to answer these questions:

1. What are the objects, characters, and actions which seem to carry more weight than they would in a realistic story?

2. What are the abstract equivalents of these objects, characters, and actions? What are they symbols of?

3. When the symbols are put together, do they communicate a central idea which may be called the story's symbolic meaning?

THE PORTABLE PHONOGRAPH

Walter Van Tilburg Clark

The red sunset, with narrow black cloud strips like threats across it, lay on the curved horizon of the prairie. The air was still and cold, and in it settled the mute darkness and greater cold of night. High in the air there was wind, for through the veil of the dusk the clouds could be seen gliding rapidly south and changing shapes. A queer sensation of torment, of two-sided, unpredictable nature, arose from the stillness of the earth air beneath the violence of the upper air. Out of the sunset, through the dead, matted grass and isolated weed stalks of the prairie, crept the narrow and deeply rutted remains of a road. In the road, in places, there were crusts of shallow, brittle ice. There were little islands of an old oiled pavement in the road too, but most of it was mud, now frozen rigid. The frozen mud still bore the toothed impress of great tanks, and a wanderer on the neighboring undulations might have stumbled, in this light, into large, partially filled-in and weed-grown cavities, their banks channeled and beginning to spread into badlands. These pits were such as might have been made by falling meteors, but they were not. They were the scars of gigantic bombs, their rawness already made a little natural by rain, seed, and time. Along the road there were rakish remnants of fence. There was also, just visible, one portion of tangled and multiple barbed wire still erect, behind which was a shelving ditch with small caves, now very quiet and empty, at intervals in its back wall. Otherwise there was no structure or remnant of a structure visible over the dome of the darkling earth, but only, in sheltered hollows, the darker shadows of young trees trying again.

Under the wuthering arch of the high wind a V of wild geese fled south. The rush of their pinions sounded briefly, and the faint, plaintive notes of their expeditionary talk. Then they left a still greater vacancy. There was the smell and expectation of snow, as there is likely to be when the wild geese fly south. From the remote distance, towards the red sky, came faintly the protracted howl and quick yap-yap of a prairie wolf.

North of the road, perhaps a hundred yards, lay the parallel and deeply intrenched course of a small creek, lined with leafless alders and willows. The creek was already silent under ice. Into the bank above it was dug a sort of cell, with a single opening, like the mouth of a mine tunnel. Within the cell there was a little red of fire, which showed dully through the opening, like a reflection or a deception of the imagination. The light came from the chary burning of four blocks of poorly aged peat, which gave off a petty warmth and much acrid smoke. But the precious remnants of wood, old fenceposts and timbers from the long-deserted dugouts, had to be saved for the real cold, for the time when a man's breath blew white, the moisture in his nostrils stiffened at once when he stepped out, and the expansive blizzards paraded for days over the vast open, swirling and settling and thickening, till the dawn of the cleared day when the sky was thin blue-green and the terrible cold, in which a man could not live for three hours unwarmed, lay over the uniformly drifted swell of the plain.

Around the smoldering peat four men were seated crosslegged. Behind them, traversed by their shadows, was the earth bench, with two old and dirty army blankets, where the owner of the cell slept. In a niche in the opposite wall were a few tin utensils which caught the glint of the coals. The host was rewrapping in a piece of daubed burlap four fine, leather-bound books. He worked slowly and very carefully and at last tied the bundle securely with a piece of grass-woven cord. The other three looked intently upon the process, as if a great significance lay in it. As the host tied the cord he spoke. He was an old man, his long, matted beard and hair gray to nearly white. The shadows made his brows and cheekbones appear gnarled, his eyes and cheeks deeply sunken. His big hands, rough with frost and swollen by rheumatism, were awkward but gentle at their task. He was like a prehistoric priest performing a fateful ceremonial rite. Also his voice had in it a suitable quality of deep, reverent despair, yet perhaps at the moment a sharpness of selfish satisfaction.

"When I perceived what was happening," he said, "I told myself, 'It is the end. I cannot take much; I will take these.'"

"Perhaps I was impractical," he continued. "But for myself, I do not regret, and what do we know of those who will come after us? We are the doddering remnant of a race of mechanical fools. I have saved what I love; the soul of what was good in us is here; perhaps the new ones will make a strong enough beginning not to fall behind when they become clever."

He rose with slow pain and placed the wrapped volumes in the niche with his utensils. The others watched him with the same ritualistic gaze.

"Shakespeare, the Bible, *Moby Dick,* the *Divine Comedy*," one of them said softly. "You might have done worse, much worse."

"You will have a little soul left until you die," said another harshly. "That is more than is true of us. My brain becomes thick, like my hands."

125

He held the big, battered hands, with their black nails, in the glow to be seen.

"I want paper to write on," he said. "And there is none."

The fourth man said nothing. He sat in the shadow farthest from the fire, and sometimes his body jerked in its rags from the cold. Although he was still young, he was sick and coughed often. Writing implied a greater future than he now felt able to consider.

The old man seated himself laboriously and reached out, groaning at the movement, to put another block of peat on the fire. With bowed heads and averted eyes his three guests acknowledged his magnanimity.

"We thank you, Dr. Jenkins, for the reading," said the man who had named the books.

They seemed then to be waiting for something. Dr. Jenkins understood but was loath to comply. In an ordinary moment he would have said nothing. But the words of *The Tempest*, which he had been reading, and the religious attention of the three made this an unusual occasion.

"You wish to hear the phonograph," he said grudgingly.

The two middle-aged men stared into the fire, unable to formulate and expose the enormity of their desire.

The young man, however, said anxiously, between suppressed coughs, "Oh, please," like an excited child.

The old man rose again in his difficult way and went to the back of the cell. He returned and placed tenderly upon the packed floor, where the firelight might fall upon it, an old portable phonograph in a black case. He smoothed the top with his hand and then opened it. The lovely green-felt-covered disk became visible.

"I have been using thorns as needles," he said. "But tonight, because we have a musician among us"—he bent his head to the young man, almost invisible in the shadow—"I will use a steel needle. There are only three left."

The two middle-aged men stared at him in speechless adoration. The one with the big hands, who wanted to write, moved his lips, but the whisper was not audible.

"Oh, don't!" cried the young man, as if he were hurt. "The thorns will do beautifully."

"No," the old man said. "I have become accustomed to the thorns, but they are not really good. For you, my young friend, we will have good music tonight."

"After all," he added generously, and beginning to wind the phonograph, which creaked, "they can't last forever."

"No, nor we," the man who needed to write said harshly. "The needle, by all means."

126

"Oh, thanks," said the young man. "Thanks," he said again in a low, excited voice, and then stifled his coughing with a bowed head.

"The records, though," said the old man when he had finished winding, "are a different matter. Already they are very worn. I do not play them more than once a week. One, once a week, that is what I allow myself.

"More than a week I cannot stand it; not to hear them," he apologized.

"No, how could you?" cried the young man. "And with them here like this."

"A man can stand anything," said the man who wanted to write, in his harsh, antagonistic voice.

"Please, the music," said the young man.

"Only the one," said the old man. "In the long run, we will remember more that way."

He had a dozen records with luxuriant gold and red seals. Even in that light the others could see that the threads of the records were becoming worn. Slowly he read out the titles and the tremendous, dead names of the composers and the artists and the orchestras. The three worked upon the names in their minds, carefully. It was difficult to select from such a wealth what they would at once most like to remember. Finally the man who wanted to write named Gershwin's "New York."

"Oh, no!" cried the sick young man, and then could say nothing more because he had to cough. The others understood him, and the harsh man withdrew his selection and waited for the musician to choose.

The musician begged Dr. Jenkins to read the titles again, very slowly, so that he could remember the sounds. While they were read he lay back against the wall, his eyes closed, his thin, horny hand pulling at his light beard, and listened to the voices and the orchestras and the single instruments in his mind.

When the reading was done he spoke despairingly. "I have forgotten," he complained. "I cannot hear them clearly."

"There are things missing," he explained.

"I know," said Dr. Jenkins. "I thought that I knew all of Shelley by heart. I should have brought Shelley.

"That's more soul than we can use," said the harsh man. *Moby Dick* is better.

"By God, we can understand that," he emphasized.

The Doctor nodded.

"Still," said the man who had admired the books, "we need the absolute if we are to keep a grasp on anything.

"Anything but these sticks and peat clods and rabbit snares," he said bitterly.

127

"Shelley desired an ultimate absolute," said the harsh man. "It's too much," he said. "It's no good; no earthly good."

The musician selected a Debussy nocturne. The others considered and approved. They rose to their knees to watch the Doctor prepare for the playing, so that they appeared to be actually in an attitude of worship. The peat glow showed the thinness of their bearded faces, and the deep lines in them, and revealed the condition of their garments. The other two continued to kneel as the old man carefully lowered the needle onto the spinning disk, but the musician suddenly drew back against the wall again, with his knees up, and buried his face in his hands.

At the first notes of the piano the listeners were startled. They stared at each other. Even the musician lifted his head in amazement but then quickly bowed it again, strainingly, as if he were suffering from a pain he might not be able to endure. They were all listening deeply, without movement. The wet, blue-green notes tinkled forth from the old machine and were individual, delectable presences in the cell. The individual, delectable presences swept into a sudden tide of unbearably beautiful dissonance and then continued fully the swelling and ebbing of that tide, the dissonant inpourings, and the resolutions, and the diminishments, and the little, quiet wavelets of interlude lapping between. Every sound was piercing and singularly sweet. In all the men except the musician there occurred rapid sequences of tragically heightened recollection. He heard nothing but what was there. At the final, whispering disappearance, but moving quietly so that the others would not hear him and look at him, he let his head fall back in agony, as if it were drawn there by the hair, and clenched the fingers of one hand over his teeth. He sat that way while the others were silent and until they began to breathe again normally. His drawn-up legs were trembling violently.

Quickly Dr. Jenkins lifted the needle off, to save it and not to spoil the recollection with scraping. When he had stopped the whirling of the sacred disk he courteously left the phonograph open and by the fire, in sight.

The others, however, understood. The musician rose last, but then abruptly, and went quickly out at the door without saying anything. The others stopped at the door and gave their thanks in low voices. The Doctor nodded magnificently.

"Come again," he invited, "in a week. We will have the 'New York.'"

When the two had gone together, out towards the rimed road, he stood in the entrance, peering and listening. At first there was only the resonant boom of the wind overhead, and then far over the dome of the dead, dark plain the wolf cry lamenting. In the rifts of clouds the Doctor saw four stars flying. It impressed the Doctor that one of them had just been obscured by the beginning of a flying cloud at the very moment he heard what he had been listening for, a sound of suppressed coughing. It was not near by, however. He believed that down against the pale alders he could see the moving shadow.

With nervous hands he lowered the piece of canvas which served as his door and pegged it at the bottom. Then quickly and quietly, looking at the piece of canvas frequently, he slipped the records into the case, snapped the lid shut, and carried the phonograph to his couch. There, pausing often to stare at the canvas and listen, he dug earth from the wall and disclosed a piece of board. Behind this there was a deep hole in the wall, into which he put the phonograph. After a moment's consideration he went over and reached down his bundle of books and inserted it also. Then, guardedly, he once more sealed up the hole with the board and the earth. He also changed his blankets and the grass-stuffed sack which served as a pillow, so that he could lie facing the entrance. After carefully placing two more blocks of peat upon the fire he stood for a long time watching the stretched canvas, but it seemed to billow naturally with the first gusts of a lowering wind. At last he prayed, and got in under his blankets, and closed his smoke-smarting eyes. On the inside of the bed, next the wall, he could feel with his hand the comfortable piece of lead pipe.

Applications

Identifying the major symbols What are the major symbols in Clark's story?

Interpreting the symbols What does each of the symbols you listed represent? (What does each stand for? What is the significance or "meaning" of each symbol?)

Explaining the functions of symbolism How does the symbolism help communicate Clark's ideas? How does the symbolism contribute to the story's meaning?

ANALYZING AND WRITING ABOUT SYMBOLISM

Analyzing Symbolism

Analyzing symbolism is a three-step process:

1. *Identify* the objects, characters and actions that seem to have more than literal "realistic" significance.

2. *Interpret* the symbolic significance of these objects, characters and actions. What are their abstract equivalents; what are they symbols of?

3. *Explain* how the symbols function to communicate the idea(s), which may be called the work's "symbolic meaning."

We can illustrate this process by analyzing symbolism in "The Portable Phonograph." You should realize, however, that our division of the process of analyzing symbolism into three distinct and separate stages is for the purpose of clarification only. In actual practice all three stages are intertwined—as soon as you "sense" that an object, character, or action is symbolic you should begin to interpret its significance and to relate it to the overall meaning of the literary work. So the stages of identification, interpretation, and relation to meaning are not really separate and distinct.

Step one: Identifying symbolic objects, characters, and actions   We can identify several *symbolic objects* in Clark's story:

1. The portable phonograph itself is the most obvious object, both because it is the title object of the story and because it occupies such a central position within the action of the story.

2. The four books are symbolic objects. Each of the books named adds to the richness of the symbolism.

3. Other symbolic objects are the "red sky," the wolf, the "four stars," and the "comfortable piece of lead pipe."

Each of the four men are *symbolic characters:* Dr. Jenkins, "The Musician," the harsh man (the "writer"), and the gentle, soft-voiced man.

At least three *symbolic actions* can be defined:

1. The careful wrapping and hiding of the old man's treasures.

130

2. The "staring and listening" of Dr. Jenkins near the end of the story.

3. Dr. Jenkins' feeling for the "piece of lead pipe" at the very end of the story.

Step two: Interpreting the symbols The portable phonograph is the central symbolic object. It seems to symbolize the "soul" of the dead past, the highest achievement of a dead humanity. The four books symbolize to a lesser degree the same thing as the phonograph. The books represent the best and most lasting ideas of civilization: Shakespeare, The Bible, *Moby-Dick,* the *Divine Comedy*—four books of humanity's wisdom rescued for the last four men on earth. The red sky and wolf are symbols of death; together with "the cold" and "the ice," they symbolically show that even these four last men are marked for extinction. The fire is a symbol of security and survival. It also suggests that mankind has returned to the rigors of a cave-man existence. But even this symbol of survival (the fire) is used to point towards death because it is made clear that there may be not enough wood to keep alive the fire and the men who tend it. The four stars, the four books, and the four men are paralleled. The four stars symbolize the indestructible universe. The stars are nature's eternal counterpoint to our ephemeral lives and fragile books. We can destroy ourselves and our civilization (including the transcendent arts of literature and music), but we cannot destroy the stars. The last of the symbolic objects is the "comfortable piece of lead pipe" which reassures the old doctor as he prepares to sleep among his salvaged treasures of the past. The piece of lead pipe symbolizes violence.

The four actual characters symbolize four *kinds* of people. They are the last remnants of humanity. When they are gone, there will be no one left to listen to the phonograph or to read the books:

1. Dr. Jenkins symbolizes the scholar-humanist-traditionalist. He is the central and most powerful of the symbolic characters. He is the custodian of our culture.

2. "The musician" symbolizes the "pure" artist—young, sensitive, aesthetic, and dying. Like the old doctor, he seems at first a sympathetic character. But his moral weakness appears later.

3. The "harsh"-voiced man (the writer with no paper to write on) symbolizes the Truth-seeker and Sayer. He might once have been important, but he has given up.

4. The gentler "soft"-voiced man symbolizes the ordinary good person. He is not special in any way except that he also yearns for the beauty of the past. He, like the "harsh" man, gives no indication that he will survive.

All three of the symbolic actions listed under "step one" point to the total symbolic meaning of the story. (There are other symbolic actions, of course, but these three are most significant.) The careful wrapping and hiding of the old man's treasures is an action which symbolizes selfishness, greed, and distrust. The "staring and listening" action symbolizes fear and suspicion. The old doctor's reaching with his hand to touch the "comfortable piece of lead pipe" is the final symbolic action of the story. That action symbolizes mankind's continued drive toward violence, destruction, and death.

Step three: Explaining how the symbols help communicate the central meaning All of these symbols (objects, characters, actions) act together to communicate the ideas which we may call the work's symbolic meaning. Only four men are left of all the masses of humanity. Two of them are middle-aged, one is young but ill, the fourth is very old. They are all in imminent danger of death (from the cold, the wolf, tuberculosis, old age, and each other). All are living in the desolated rubble of their dead civilization, destroyed by war; all are nostalgic for the comfort and meaning and beauty of their lost world. The phonograph, the records, and the books are their only valued possessions. The men consider these possessions as the "soul" of humanity. The old man thinks he is a magnanimous and humanitarian custodian of the last remnants of mankind's glorious past. But he is really, it becomes apparent, selfish, greedy, suspicious, and ready to kill to protect his "property." The young man thinks that he alone deserves to possess and listen to the phonograph and its music because he alone of the four is special and elite. As a musician, he feels that he can appreciate most fully the old man's carefully preserved artifact of their destroyed culture. But the young musician is really, like the old man, selfish and greedy for a last pleasure before he dies. He is a perpetuator of the same errors which destroyed the world he purports to have loved, for he is stealthy, envious, and ready for violence.

The lead pipe is the "ultimate weapon" now as the bomb was the ultimate weapon then. There is no hope for mankind because greed and selfishness remain even in these last survivors, these "highest types of men." The symbolic meaning of the story is unpalatable but unmistakable: Mankind is doomed. This world will end with both a bang and a whimper. The cold, the ice, the wild geese, and the wolves will inherit the earth.

We can use the words of the author to support our interpretation.

Notice that at the beginning of the story, Clark sets the scene with images which seem threatening to human life: "The red sunset" with "narrow black cloud strips like threats across it," "darkness," "greater cold of night," "torment," "stillness," "remains of a road," "scars of gigantic bombs." All of these images evoke an atmosphere of doom.

We first meet the characters in the dugout of the old doctor, who is "an old man" with hands "swollen by rheumatism." He is playing host to the other three men, the sole survivors of a global holocaust involving "gigantic bombs." He is "re-wrapping . . . four fine leather-bound books." He works carefully and finally ties the bundle "securely" with a cord. "He [is] like a prehistoric priest performing a fateful ceremonial rite." But notice that he also feels "a sharpness of selfish satisfaction." He speaks righteously of saving what he loves; "'the soul of what was good in us is here,'" as he says; and he has hope that there may be other people alive to receive and carry on that "soul." He calls these possible survivors "'the new ones.'" But the other men make no comment upon his hope.

The other major character, the sick young musician, speaks little. He is unable to consider "a greater future" than the few months or days he thinks he has left.

Dr. Jenkins, we now discover, is "loath to comply" with the wishes of the other men for the music of the portable phonograph. He "grudgingly" agrees to play one record. "'One. . . . Only the one,'" he insists. The other men must petition him to dispense the rites of his religion. The men kneel in "an attitude of worship" as the music begins. Only the young musician suddenly draws back and, at the end of the "concert," lets "his head fall back in agony." He alone of the guests departs without thanking the "rich" doctor for his hospitality, for his sharing of riches: "The musician . . . went quickly out the door without saying anything. The others stopped at the door and gave their thanks in low voices."

When the doctor is left alone with his hoarded remnants of the past he is suspicious, fearful, protective. He stands "peering and listening"; he thinks he sees a "moving shadow"; he pegs the canvas door with "nervous hands"; he hides his books and his precious phonograph and records in a concealed hole in the wall; he acts "guardedly." And his last action is to "feel with his hand the comfortable piece of lead pipe."

It seems clear that the author is telling us, through the story's symbolism, that we are doomed to repeat the sins of greed and selfishness and violence until we have erased ourselves from the face of the harsh and beautiful earth.

Writing About Symbolism

1. State your thesis The thesis statement should indicate your view of how symbolism functions to create, heighten, or add extra dimensions to meaning. Does it heighten the meaning or create the meaning? Does it add extra dimensions to the meaning or is it the meaning? Can the work be understood on both a literal and a symbolic level, or is the work only comprehensible if its symbolism is understood?

2. Identify what you believe to be the major symbol, symbols, or clusters of symbols in the work Beware of lapsing into a list. If there is one central symbol, fine. If there are two or three central symbols, still fine. But if there are lots of symbols, you will need to classify them into two or three clusters or groups, or else limit yourself to the two or three most important symbols.

3. Interpret the meaning of the objects, characters, or actions that you have identified as symbolic

4. Explain how the symbols which you have identified and interpreted do indeed have the effects or communicate the ideas that you assert in your thesis

This four-step process is exemplified in the following essay:

Symbolism in "The Portable Phonograph"

To read "The Portable Phonograph" as a sort of science fiction vision of life after the "final" war is to overlook its deeper and more serious meaning. This meaning is only revealed when the story's pervasive symbolism is recognized. For in this story Walter Van Tilburg Clark uses symbolism to state and underscore his belief that mankind and civilization are doomed to destruction by the innate human impulses of selfishness and greed and by the willingness to use violence to protect valued possessions.

> Note: The first paragraph works down to a statement of the writer's view of the relationship between the story's symbolism and its meaning.

The symbols in Clark's story fall into three major categories: symbolic objects, symbolic characters and symbolic actions. Among the symbolic objects are the portable phonograph itself, which is the central symbol; the four books; the lead pipe; and such details of setting as the "red sky," the wolf, and the "four stars." Each of the four characters symbolizes a certain type of person, and their actions, such as the careful wrapping and hiding of the old man's treasures, the "staring and listening" of Dr. Jenkins, and his feeling for the piece of lead pipe at the story's end, carry clear symbolic overtones.

> Note: The second paragraph classifies the symbols into three major categories, and identifies significant symbols in each category.

The portable phonograph is the central symbolic object. It seems to symbolize the "soul" of the dead past, the highest achievement of a dead humanity. The four books—Shakespeare, the Bible, *Moby-Dick*, the *Divine Comedy*—carry essentially the same symbolic meaning as the phonograph, though to a lesser degree. They represent humanity's best and most lasting ideas. The other symbolic objects are less comforting. The "red sky" and the wolf are threatening and carry suggestions of impending death. Together with "the cold" and "the ice" they symbolically show that even these last four men are marked for extinction. The four stars, the four books, and the four men are paralleled. The stars are nature's eternal and indestructible counterpoint to the ephemeral lives of men and their fragile books. Man can destroy himself and his civilization, including the transcendent arts of music and literature, but he cannot destroy the stars. The last of the major symbolic objects is the "comfortable piece of lead pipe" which reassures the old doctor as he prepares to sleep among his salvaged treasures from the past. The length of pipe seems to represent mankind's ineradicable drive to violence. It is the ultimate weapon "now" as the gigantic bombs were the ultimate weapon "then." And the doctor is prepared to use it.

Note: The third paragraph fully interprets the first cluster of symbols, the symbolic objects. The next two paragraphs of the essay do the same for the other categories of symbols—characters, and actions.

The four actual characters stand for four kinds of people. Together, they represent the human race. They are the last remnants of humanity; when they are gone, there will be no one left to listen to the phonograph or to read the books. Dr. Jenkins represents the scholar-humanist-traditionalist. He is the central and most powerful of the symbolic characters, for he is the custodian of our culture. The musician represents the "pure" artist—young, sensitive, aesthetic, and dying. Like the old doctor he seems at first a sympathetic character but, later, his moral weakness appears. The "harsh"-voiced man, the writer with no paper to write on, seems to represent the truth-seeker and "sayer"; but he has given up. Finally, there is the "soft"-voiced character who symbolizes the ordinary good person. He is not special in any way except that he too yearns for the beauty of the past. Scholar, artist, philosopher, average person—the four characters cover the spectrum of mankind. Symbolically, they are mankind.

Note: The writer could have chosen to go into much greater detail here, giving additional evidence for the interpretation of the symbolic meaning of each character. If the discussion were limited to "symbolic characters in "The Portable Phonograph,'" such additional detail would be necessary.

The actions of the characters also have symbolic significance. The old doctor's careful wrapping and hiding of his treasures suggests selfishness, greed, and distrust. Similarly, his "staring and listening" suggest man's fear and suspicion of his fellow man. And in the final action of the story, when the doctor puts his hand on the "comfortable piece of lead pipe," Clark sums it all up. Mankind's drive toward violence, destruction, and death is itself indestructible.

Note: Having identified and interpreted the major symbols, the writer can now explain how "Clark uses symbolism to state and underscore his belief that mankind and civilization are doomed to destruction by the innate human impulses of selfishness and greed and by the willingness to use violence to protect valued possessions."

As we have seen, the full significance of Clark's story only becomes apparent when the significance of its symbolism is understood. Man never learns. He is incapable of changing his ways. In the nightmarish doomed world that Clark presents, man is still ruled by selfish greed, he is still willing to use deadly violence to protect the things he values and enjoys. This being so, there can be no hope. Even the most valuable outgrowths of man's long journey towards civilization—his music and his literature—do not erase these vices. Man condemns himself to extinction despite, or perhaps even because of, his most noble and human achievements.

EIGHT

MEANING

UNDERSTANDING MEANING

When we ask ourselves "What does this story mean?" (or this poem or this play), we are really asking another question: "What does the writer believe?" We need to ask, "What does the writer believe?" because the theme or central idea of a work of literature is inextricably bound up with the author's view of life.

Some stories do not have a significant or probing theme. They are written merely to entertain us, to help us escape the problems (big and little) which plague us every day. Some critics reject all such literature as insignificant and trivial escape literature. Actually, all literature is in a sense "escape literature." Some stories let us escape out of life (which is sometimes necessary); some help us escape into life. Literature which gives us a sense of increased life, of an enriched life-experience, is the greatest and most long-lasting literature. And literature of meaning, literature that interprets life, is this kind of literature.

Meaning and Values

The writer's values   The meaning of a work is not revealed by a summary of what it is "about." The work may be "about" an old man who goes fishing and comes back with only the shark-mangled carcass of a big fish. That is a bare summary of the action in Hemingway's novel, *The Old Man and the Sea*. But the meaning of the story is not caught in that summary. The meaning emerges only when we understand that Hemingway was saying something about life as he saw it when he wrote the story. He was talking about an old Cuban fisherman, but he was also talking about all of us who are neither old, nor Cuban, nor fishermen. He was talking about the old man's failure to bring back his catch, but he was also talking about the failure of all of us to succeed in all we attempt. He was talking about the old fisherman's endurance, but he was also talking about endurance as a universal human value. The major themes of the novel reflect Hemingway's view of life. And a view of life suggests a hierarchy of values. This is what meaning in literature is all about—an attitude toward life values.

What are "life values"? Here are some examples:

Goal Values	Character Values
Happiness	Gaiety
Peace	Endurance
Freedom	Persistance
Security	Creativity
Justice	Honesty
Mercy	Courage
Beauty	Compassion
Truth	Fairness
Status	Intelligence
Success	Sensitivity

These two columns are not meant to be parallel, and there are other ways to classify values and other values to classify. What's important is that our choice of values and the priority we give these values reveal our world-view, our philosophy of life, our ideas and feelings about ourselves, other people, our society, our universe. In the same way, authors reveal their ideas and their view of life by their choice and emphasis of certain values.

Most of us would affirm that all of the values listed above are legitimate ones. However, most of us (authors included) find one or two of these values more important than the rest. It is a question of priorities, as our politicians like to say. Some of us choose one priority value, others another, and none of us is really wrong. So it is with authors. Their works inevitably reflect their values, their world view. We can accept this view as legitimate without necessarily giving up on our own, perhaps different, philosophy.

The reader's values　We all come to literature with preconceptions. We come to an author with our own value system, with our own world-view, with our own priorities. There is nothing wrong with that. But we should resist the temptation to impose our own values on the author's work. We must remember to keep an open mind. It is sometimes very hard to acknowledge that a value counter to ours may be valid. Occasionally a reader will completely reject a work of literature because the author's central idea or meaning is opposed to the reader's own outlook on life. Even more often a reader will misread the author's meaning or world-view in such a way as to bring it into line with his or her own values, as illustrated in the following cartoon:

Robert Frost's poem "Design" provides us with a more serious example of this tendency:

> I found a dimpled spider, fat and white,
> On a white heal-all, holding up a moth
> Like a white piece of rigid satin cloth—
> Assorted characters of death and blight
> Mixed ready to begin the morning right,
> Like the ingredients of a witch's broth—
> A snow-drop spider, a flower like froth,
> And dead wings carried like a paper kite.
>
> What had that flower to do with being white,
> The wayside blue and innocent heal-all?
> What brought the kindred spider to that height,
> Then steered the white moth thither in the night?
> What but design of darkness to appall?—
> If design govern in a thing so small.

Some people, when they first read this poem, interpret it as a celebration of God's omnipresence, as a description of how God's loving hand is found directing even the littlest things. In doing so, they display selective perception, a defense mechanism which is, according to psychologists, a major means by which stereotypes and prejudices are protected. Such readers unconsciously ignore the disturbing images of death and blight, the equally disturbing question in the next-to-last line of the poem, and the crucial "If" in the final line. In short, they pass over aspects of the poem that would cause them to find in it a view of life and of God contrary to their own.

Preconceptions, inflexible attitudes, and closed-mind opinions can keep a reader from perceiving the writer's meaning. If we find nothing in literature except a confirmation of our own opinions and ideas, we are not opening ourselves up to the possibility of learning and growth. We should think of trying on new and even repugnant ideas as we'd try on a villain's costume for a play, or a clown's, or a knight's shining armor.

Trying on the idea (or the costume) will not change us except tempo-
rarily—unless we want to be changed. Acceptance of an author's meaning is not necessary. Consideration of it is.

The Moral and the Meaning

In literature the meaning or central idea easiest to discover, in fact almost
impossible to miss, is the "moral" or "lesson" meaning. Most often this
kind of meaning is found in ballads, in fables, in parables, and in stories
addressed to unsophisticated readers. A story with a moral is like a nutshell with a nut inside. You can extract the moral from the story as you
would extract the kernel from a nutshell. Crack the shell, pick out the nut
meat. *Voilà!* The moral.

But *meaning* is a larger concept and cannot be so simply extracted.
Meaning is like a perfume which permeates the whole. A story with a
meaning, rather than a moral, is like a room scented with flowers or
incense. We can remove the flowers but the fragrance remains. We cannot
carry out a cushion or a chair and say "Here is the perfume." If we want to
enjoy the scent of the room, we must enter it, we must wander through it,
we must recognize that the room and the scent are inseparable. Similarly,
the total meaning of a story can be described, just as the perfume can be
described, but it cannot really be separated and extracted from the story
itself.

We should not assume, however, that a story with a moral is necessarily inferior to a story with a meaning. Both have their place in literature;
both are valuable; both are needed. The intentions of the authors are
different, that's all—and often their views of life. The writer who states
a moral or who makes it very clear and extractable wants to be sure that
the reader gets it. Such a writer is also probably more of a "moralist" than
the writer who presents "meaning without moral"; the "moralist" is
probably less skeptical and more certain that there are simple answers to
life's problems. The writer who deals in meanings will give answers too,
but they will be more complex, more tentative, and may make lesser
claims to universality.

Writing a story with a moral is also likely to be an unappealing task
for the writer who sees life as multifaceted, or whose vision is different
from that of most people. A writer who rejects the stated moral is more
likely, too, to hold a world-view, a philosophy of life, not quite so palat-
able as that of the fable-maker or proverb-maker. Such a writer may avoid
happy endings, affirmations, and easy optimism.

Here are two examples of well-done "literature with morals":

The Man, the Boy, and the Donkey

A man and his son were once going with their Donkey to market. As they
were walking along by its side, a countryman passed them and said "You
fools, what is a Donkey for but to ride on?"

141

So the Man put the Boy on the Donkey and they went their way. But soon they passed a group of men, one of whom said: "See that lazy youngster, he lets his father walk while he rides."

So the Man ordered his Boy to get off, and got on himself. But they hadn't gone far when they passed two women, one of whom said to the other: "Shame on that lazy lout to let his poor little son trudge along."

Well, the Man didn't know what to do, but at last he took his Boy up before him on the Donkey. By this time they had come to the town, and the passersby began to jeer and point at them. The Man stopped and asked what they were scoffing at. The men said: "Aren't you ashamed of yourself for overloading that poor Donkey of yours—you and your hulking son?"

The Man and the Boy got off and tried to think what to do. They thought and thought, till at last they cut down a pole, tied the Donkey's feet to it, and raised the pole and the Donkey to their shoulders. They went along amid the laughter of all who met them till they came to the Market Bridge, when the Donkey, getting one of his feet loose, kicked out and caused the Boy to drop his end of the pole. In the struggle, the Donkey fell over the bridge, and his forefeet being tied together, he was drowned, "That will teach you," said an old man who had followed them: "Please all, and you please none."

The Bear Who Let It Alone

In the woods of the Far West there once lived a brown bear who could take it or let it alone. He would go into a bar where they sold mead, a fermented drink made of honey, and he would have just two drinks. Then he would put some money on the bar and say, "See what the bears in the back room will have," and he would go home. But finally he took to drinking by himself most of the day. He would reel home at night, kick over the umbrella stand, knock down the bridge lamps, and ram his elbows through the windows. Then he would collapse on the floor and lie there until he went to sleep. His wife was greatly distressed and his children were very frightened.

At length the bear saw the error of his ways and began to reform. In the end he became a famous teetotaller and a persistent temperance lecturer. He would tell everybody that came to his house about the awful effects of drink, and he would boast about how strong and well he had become since he gave up touching the stuff. To demonstrate this, he would stand on his head and on his hands and he would turn cartwheels in the house, kicking over the umbrella stand, knocking down the bridge lamps, and ramming his elbows through the windows. Then he would lie down on the floor, tired by his healthful exercise, and go to sleep. His wife was greatly distressed and his children were very frightened. Moral: You might as well fall flat on your face as lean over too far backward.

—James Thurber

Because finding a tag line or moral in some literature is so easy, we are sometimes tempted to try it with all. With an author who rejects clichés of thought, feeling, and meaning, the danger in this approach is obvious. The author's complicated exploration and interpretation of an aspect of life is reduced to a platitude, and the complexity and richness of meaning which the work presents is destroyed.

You probably know the story of Shakespeare's *Othello* even if you have not read the play. But if you "tagged" the meaning as "Love is blind" or "Jealousy destroys," you would hardly be describing all that Shakespeare is saying. That is part of what he is saying, but not the whole of it. Some critics have tagged Shakespeare's play *Macbeth* as a "tragedy of ambition." So it is—but it is much more than that. It presents characters living in a world in which the forces of good and evil are often almost indistinguishable, in which one is never sure whether what one sees is real or hallucination, in which good men do evil deeds and in which disaster overtakes good and bad alike. Such is one incomplete way to state the meaning of *Macbeth*. Although such a statement does not exhaust the meaning of the play, it comes closer to communicating Shakespeare's view of life, as presented in *Macbeth*, than a questionable statement of a moral such as "Excessive ambition is evil and must be punished."

Morals are generally true statements, but they are insufficient or inadequate truths. They are too easy, too simple, too trite. Significant works of literature, literature that attempts to interpret life in all its complexity and ambiguity, cannot be reduced to such clichés.

From Subject to Significance

Research scientists, attempting to solve a problem, construct a working hypothesis. That is, they postulate a certain theory and then try to determine whether the theory or hypothesis is substantiated by their research findings. If it is not, they construct a different working hypothesis and begin anew. We can construct such a working hypothesis for the understanding of meaning in literature. The hypothesis is this:

No matter what the subject of a work, the author is writing about some problem, concern, or characteristic of man that has universal significance.

When we read serious literature, we should try to perceive how the author uses the *subject* to communicate certain ideas about *man* (in the

143

generic sense, *mankind, men and women*) and to suggest certain ideas of *universal* truth: **Subject → Man → Universal.**

In Faulkner's "The Bear," after failing to shoot Old Ben, Ike speaks to his older cousin, McCaslin. McCaslin tries to explain Ike's refusal to shoot the bear by reading "Ode on a Grecian Urn" by John Keats:

> Thou still unravished bride of quietness,
>   Thou foster-child of silence and slow time,
> Sylvan historian, who canst thus express
>   A flowery tale more sweetly than our rhyme:
> What leaf-fringed legend haunts about thy shape
>   Of deities or mortals, or of both,
>   In Tempe or the dales of Arcady?
> What men or gods are these? What maidens loth?
>   What mad pursuit? What struggle to escape?
>   What pipes and timbrels? What wild ecstasy?
>
> Heard melodies are sweet, but those unheard
>   Are sweeter; therefore, ye soft pipes, play on;
> Not to the sensual ear, but, more endeared,
>   Pipe to the spirit ditties of no tone:
> Fair youth, beneath the trees, thou canst not leave
>   Thy song, nor ever can those trees be bare;
>   Bold Lover, never, never canst thou kiss.
> Though winning near the goal—yet, do not grieve;
>   She cannot fade, though thou hast not thy bliss,
>   For ever wilt thou love, and she be fair!
>
> Ah, happy, happy boughs! that cannot shed
>   Your leaves, nor ever bid the spring adieu;
> And, happy melodist, unwearied,
>   For ever piping songs for ever new;
> More happy love! more happy, happy love!
>   For ever warm and still to be enjoyed,
>   For ever panting, and for ever young;
> All breathing human passion far above,
>   That leaves a heart high-sorrowful and cloyed,
>   A burning forehead, and a parching tongue.
>
> Who are these coming to the sacrifice?
>   To what green altar, O mysterious priest,
> Lead'st thou that heifer lowing at the skies,
>   And all her silken flanks with garlands dressed?
> What little town by river or sea shore,
>   Or mountain-built with peaceful citadel,
>   Is emptied of this folk, this pious morn?

And, little town, thy streets for evermore
   Will silent be; and not a soul to tell
      Why thou art desolate, can e'er return.

O Attic shape! Fair attitude! with brede
   Of marble men and maidens overwrought,
With forest branches and the trodden weed;
   Thou, silent form, dost tease us out of thought
As doth eternity: Cold Pastoral!
   When old age shall this generation waste,
      Thou shalt remain, in midst of other woe
Than ours, a friend to man, to whom thou say'st,
   "Beauty is truth, truth beauty,"—that is all
      Ye know on earth, and all ye need to know.

Faulkner describes the scene in these words:

> He [McCaslin] read the five stanzas aloud and closed the book on his finger and looked up. "All right," he said. "Listen," and read again, but only one stanza this time and closed the book and laid it on the table, "She cannot fade, though thou hast not thy bliss," McCaslin said: "Forever wilt thou love and she be fair."
> "He's talking about a girl," Ike said.
> "He had to talk about something," McCaslin said. Then he said, "He was talking about truth. Truth is one. It doesn't change. It covers all things which touch the heart—honor and pride and pity and justice and courage and love. Do you see now?"

The boy, Ike, can't get beyond Keats' subject—"'He's talking about a girl.'" But, as McCaslin says, "'He had to talk about something.'" Authors use their subject—a scene painted on a Grecian urn, a man and his horse stopping by woods on a snowy evening, a cat that eats a goldfinch, or whatever—to communicate their ideas about people and life.

Conclusion

Literature that attempts more than entertainment of the reader is often styled "interpretive" literature. Other terms are also used—*serious, meaningful, significant*—but *interpretive* is probably the most descriptive. For most literature that endures interprets life. The interpretation of life or an aspect of life that a given work presents is the author's—the reader need not accept it. But, if the work is successful, the reader will acknowledge the author's interpretation as one which a reasonable person can hold, as, in the current jargon, a "viable alternative."

The work as a whole communicates the interpretation. In other words, the sequence of actions, the cast of characters, the pattern of images which "are" the work suggest the author's interpretation of aspects of life. And if the characters are convincing, the actions plausible, the images effective, the work also validates the interpretation, makes it credible and creditable.

The process of understanding meaning in literature is thus a process of inference. We must infer the aspect of life which the work interprets, and we must infer the nature of the interpretation, the ideas about this aspect of life that constitute the work's "meaning."

Try out your perceptiveness on "Gold Coast." We'll use this story to exemplify the process of analyzing and writing about meaning in literature.

GOLD COAST

James Alan McPherson

That spring, when I had a great deal of potential and no money at all, I took a job as a janitor. That was when I was still very young and spent money very freely, and when, almost every night, I drifted off to sleep lulled by sweet anticipation of that time when my potential would suddenly be realized and there would be capsule biographies of my life on dust jackets of many books, all proclaiming: ". . . He knew life on many levels. From shoeshine boy, free-lance waiter, 3rd cook, janitor, he rose to . . ." I had never been a janitor before, and I did not really have to be one, and that is why I did it. But now, much later, I think it might have been because it is possible to be a janitor without becoming one, and at parties or at mixers, when asked what it was I did for a living, it was pretty good to hook my thumbs in my vest pockets and say comfortably: "Why, I am an apprentice janitor." The hippies would think it degenerate and really dig me and people in Philosophy and Law and Business would feel uncomfortable trying to make me feel better about my station while wondering how the hell I had managed to crash the party.

"What's an apprentice janitor?" they would ask.

"I haven't got my card yet," I would reply. "Right now I'm just taking lessons. There's lots of complicated stuff you have to learn before you get your own card and your own building."

"What kind of stuff?"

"Human nature, for one thing. *Race* nature, for another."

"Why race?"

"Because," I would say in a low voice, looking around lest someone else should overhear, "you have to be able to spot Jews and Negroes who are passing."

"That's terrible," would surely be said then with a hint of indignation.

"It's an art," I would add masterfully.

After a good pause I would invariably be asked: "But you're a Negro yourself, how can you keep your own people out?"

At which point I would look terribly disappointed and say: "I don't keep them out. But if they get in it's my job to make their stay just as miserable as possible. Things are changing."

Now the speaker would just look at me in disbelief.

"It's Janitorial Objectivity," I would say to finish the thing as the speaker began to edge away. "Don't hate me," I would call after him to his considerable embarrassment. "Somebody has to do it."

It was an old building near Harvard Square. Conrad Aiken had once lived there, and in the days of the Gold Coast, before Harvard built its great houses, it had been a very fine haven for the rich; but that was a world ago, and this building was one of the few monuments of that era which had survived. The lobby had a high ceiling with thick redwood beams, and it was replete with marble floor, fancy ironwork, and an old-fashioned house telephone which no longer worked. Each apartment had a small fireplace, and even the large bathtubs and chain toilets, when I was having my touch of nature, made me wonder what prominent personage of the past had worn away all the newness. And, being there, I felt a certain affinity toward the rich.

It was a funny building, because the people who lived there made it old. Conveniently placed as it was between the Houses and Harvard Yard, I expected to find it occupied by a company of hippies, hopeful working girls, and assorted graduate students. Instead, there was a majority of old maids, dowagers, asexual middle-aged men, homosexual young men, a few married couples, and a teacher. No one was shacking up there, and walking through the quiet halls in the early evening, I sometimes had the urge to knock on a door and expose myself just to hear someone breathe hard for once.

It was a Cambridge spring: down by the Charles happy students were making love while sad-eyed middle-aged men watched them from the bridge. It was a time of activity: Law students were busy sublimating, Business School people were making records of the money they would make, the Harvard Houses were clearing out, and in the Square bearded pot-pushers were setting up their restaurant tables in anticipation of the Summer School faithfuls. There was a change of season in the air, and to comply with its urgings, James Sullivan, the old superintendent, passed his three beaten garbage cans on to me with the charge that I should take up his daily rounds of the six floors, and with unflinching humility, gather whatever scraps the old-maid tenants had refused to husband.

I then became very rich, with my own apartment, a sensitive girl, a stereo, two speakers, one tattered chair, one fork, a job, and the urge to acquire. Having all this and youth besides made me pity Sullivan: he had been in that building thirty years and had its whole history recorded in the little folds of his mind, as his own life was recorded in the wrinkles of his face. All he had to show for his time there was a berserk dog, a wife almost as mad as the dog, three cats, bursitis, acute myopia, and a drinking problem. He was well over seventy and could hardly walk, and his weekly check of twenty-two dollars from the company that managed the building would not support anything. So, out of compromise, he was retired to superintendent of my labor.

My first day as janitor, while I skillfully lugged my three overflowing cans of garbage out of the building, he sat on his bench in the lobby, faded and old and smoking, in patched, loose blue pants. He watched me. He was a chain smoker, and I noticed right away that he very carefully dropped all of the ashes and butts on the floor and crushed them under his feet until there was a yellow and gray smear. Then he laboriously pushed the mess under the bench with his shoe, all the while eyeing me like a cat in silence as I hauled the many cans of muck out to the big disposal unit next to the building. When I had finished, he gave me two old plates to help stock my kitchen and his first piece of advice.

"Sit down, for Chrisake, and take a load off your feet," he told me.

I sat down on the red bench next to him and accepted the wilted cigarette he offered me from the crushed package he kept in his sweater pocket.

"Now, I'll tell you something to help you get along in the building," he said.

I listened attentively.

"If any of these sons of bitches ever ask you to do something extra, be sure to charge them for it."

I assured him that I absolutely would.

"If they can afford to live here, they can afford to pay. The bastards."

"Undoubtedly," I assured him again.

"And another thing," he added. "Don't let any of these girls shove any cat shit under your nose. That ain't your job. You tell them to put it in a bag and take it out themselves."

I reminded him that I knew very well my station in life, and that I was not about to haul cat shit or anything of that nature. He looked at me through his thick-lensed glasses for a long time. He looked like a cat himself. "That's right," he said at last. "And if they still try to sneak it in the trash be sure to make the bastards pay. They can afford it." He crushed his seventh butt on the floor and scattered the mess some more while he lit up another. "I never hauled out no cat shit in the thirty years I been hear, and you don't do it either."

"I'm going up to wash my hands," I said.

"Remember," he called after me, "don't take no shit from any of them."

I protested once more that, upon my life, I would never, never do it, not even for the prettiest girl in the building. Going up in the elevator, I felt comfortably resolved that I would never do it. There were no pretty girls in the building.

I never found out what he had done before he came there, but I do know that being a janitor in that building was as high as he ever got in life. He had watched two generations of the rich pass the building on their way to the Yard, and he had seen many governors ride white horses into that same Yard to send sons and daughters of the rich out into life to produce, to acquire, to procreate, and to send back sons and daughters so that the cycle would continue. He had watched the cycle from when he had been able to haul the cans out for himself, and now he could not, and he was bitter.

He was Irish, of course, and he took pride in Irish accomplishments when he could have none of his own. He had known Frank O'Connor when that writer had been at Harvard. He told me on many occasions how O'Connor had stopped to talk every day on his way to the Yard. He had also known James Michael Curley, and his most colorful memory of the man was a long-ago day when he and James Curley sat in a Boston bar and one of Curley's runners had come in and said: "Hey, Jim, Sol Bernstein the Jew wants to see you." And Curley, in his deep, memorial voice, had said to James Sullivan: "Let us go forth and meet this Israelite Prince." These were his memories, and I would obediently put aside my garbage cans and laugh with him over the hundred or so colorful, insignificant little details which made up a whole lifetime of living in the basement of Harvard. And although they were of little value to me then, I knew that they were the reflections of a lifetime and the happiest moments he would ever have, being sold to me cheap, as youthful time is cheap, for as little time and interest as I wanted to spend. It was a buyer's market.

In those days I believed myself gifted with a boundless perception and attacked my daily garbage route with a gusto superenforced by the happy knowledge that behind each of the fifty or so doors in our building lived a story which could, if I chose to grace it with the magic of my pen, become immortal. I watched my tenants fanatically, noting their perversions, their visitors, and their eating habits. So intense was my search for material that I had to restrain myself from going through their refuse scrap by scrap; but at the topmost layers of muck, without too much hand soiling in the process, I set my perception to work. By late June, however, I had discovered only enough to put together a skimpy, rather naive Henry Miller novel, the most colorful discoveries being:

1. The lady in #24 was an alumnus of Paducah College.

2. The couple in #55 made love at least 500 times a week, and the wife had not yet discovered the pill.

3. The old lady in #36 was still having monthly inconvenience.

4. The two fatsos in #56 consumed nightly an extraordinary amount of chili.

5. The fat man in #54 had two dogs that were married to each other, but he was not married to anyone at all.

6. The middle-aged single man in #63 threw out an awful lot of flowers.

Disturbed by the snail's progress I was making, I confessed my futility to James one day as he sat on his bench chain-smoking and smearing butts on my newly waxed lobby floor. "So you want to know about the tenants?" he said, his cat's eyes flickering over me.

I nodded.

"Well, the first thing to notice is how many Jews there are."

"I haven't noticed any Jews," I said.

He eyed me in amazement.

"Well, a few," I said quickly to prevent my treasured perception from being dulled any further.

"A few, hell," he said. "There's more Jews here than anybody."

"How can you tell?"

He gave me that undecided look again. "Where do you think all that garbage comes from?" He nodded feebly toward my bulging cans. I looked just in time to prevent a stray noodle from slipping over the brim. "That's right," he continued. "Jews are the biggest eaters in the world. They eat the best too."

I confessed then that I was of the chicken-soup generation and believed that Jews ate only enough to muster strength for their daily trips to the bank.

"Not so!" he replied emphatically. "You never heard the expression: 'Let's get to the restaurant before the Jews get there'?"

I shook my head sadly.

"You don't know that in certain restaurants they take the free onions and pickles off the tables when they see Jews coming?"

I held my head down in shame over the bounteous heap.

He trudged over to my can and began to turn back the leaves of noodles and crumpled tissues from #47 with his hand. After a few seconds of digging, he unmucked an empty paté can. "Look at that," he said triumphantly. "Gourmet stuff, no less."

"That's from #44." I said.

"What else?" he said, all-knowingly. "In 1946 a Swedish girl moved in up there and took a Jewish girl for her roommate. Then the Swedish girl moved out and there's been a Jewish Dynasty up there ever since."

I recalled that #44 was occupied by a couple that threw out a good number of S. S. Pierce cans, Chivas Regal bottles, assorted broken records, and back issues of *Evergreen* and the *Realist*.

"You're right," I said.

"Of course," he replied, as if there were never any doubt. "I can spot them anywhere, even when they think they're passing." He leaned closer and said in a you-and-me voice: "But don't ever say anything bad about them in public. The Anti-Defamation League will get you."

Just then his wife screamed for him from the second floor, and the dog joined her and beat against the door. He got into the elevator painfully and said: "Don't ever talk about them in public. You don't know who they are, and that Defamation League will take everything you got."

Sullivan did not really dislike Jews. He was just bitter toward anyone better off than himself. He lived with his wife on the second floor, and his apartment was very dirty because both of them were sick and old, and neither could move very well. His wife swept dirt out into the hall, and two hours after I had mopped and waxed their section of the floor, there was sure to be a layer of dirt, grease, and crushed-scattered tobacco from their door to the end of the hall. There was a smell of dogs and cats and age and death about their door, and I did not ever want to have to go in there for any reason because I feared something about it I cannot name.

Mrs. Sullivan, I found out, was from South Africa. She loved animals much more than people, and there was a great deal of pain in her face. She kept little cans of meat posted at strategic points about the building, and I often came across her in the early morning or late at night throwing scraps out of the second-floor window to stray cats. Once, when James was about to throttle a stray mouse in their apartment, she had screamed at him to give the mouse a sporting chance. Whenever she attempted to walk she had to balance herself against a wall or a rail, and she hated the building because it confined her. She also hated James and most of the tenants. On the other hand, she loved the "Johnny Carson Show," she loved to sit outside on the front steps (because she could go no further unassisted), and she loved to talk to anyone who would stop to listen. She never spoke coherently except when she was cursing James, and then she had a vocabulary like a drunken sailor. She had great, shrill lungs, and her screams, accompanied by the rabid barks of the dog, could be heard all over the building. She was never really clean, her teeth were bad, and the first most pathetic thing in the world was to see her sitting on the steps in the morning watching the world pass, in a stained smock and a fresh summer blue hat she kept just to wear downstairs, with no place in the world to go. James told me, on the many occasions of her screaming, that she was mentally disturbed and could not help herself. The admirable thing about him was that he never lost his temper with her, no matter how rough her curses became and no matter who heard them. And the second most pathetic thing in the world was to see them slowly making their way in Harvard Square, he supporting her, through the hurrying crowds of miniskirted summer girls, J-Pressed Ivy Leaguers, beatniks, and bused Japanese tourists, decked in cameras, who would take pictures of every inch of Harvard Square except them. Once a hippie had brushed past them and called back over his shoulder: "Don't break any track records, Mr. and Mrs. Speedy Molasses."

Also on the second floor lived Miss O'Hara, a spinster who hated Sullivan as only an old maid can hate an old man. Across from her lived a very nice, gentle celibate named Murphy, who had once served with Montgomery in North Africa and who was now spending the rest of his life cleaning his little apartment and gossiping with Miss O'Hara. It was an Irish floor.

I never found out just why Miss O'Hara hated the Sullivans with such a passion. Perhaps it was because they were so unkempt and she was so superciliously clean. Perhaps it was because Miss O'Hara had a great deal of Irish pride, and they were stereotyped Irish. Perhaps it was because she merely had no reason to like them. She was a fanatic about cleanliness and put out her little bit of garbage wrapped very neatly in yesterday's *Christian Science Monitor* and tied in a bow with a fresh piece of string. Collecting all those neat little packages, I would wonder where she got the string and imagined her at night breaking meat market locks with a hair-pin and hobbling off with yards and yards of white cord concealed under the gray sweater she always wore. I could even imagine her back in her little apartment chuckling and rolling the cord into a great white ball by candlelight. Then she would stash it away in her bread box. Miss O'Hara kept her door slightly open until late at night, and I suspected that she heard everything that went on in the building. I had the feeling that I should never dare to make love with gusto for fear that she would over-hear and write down all my happy-time phrases, to be maliciously re-counted to me if she were ever provoked.

She had been in the building longer than Sullivan, and I suppose that her greatest ambition in life was to outlive him and then attend his wake with a knitting ball and needle. She had been trying to get him fired for twenty-five years or so, and did not know when to quit. On summer nights when I painfully mopped the second floor, she would offer me root beer, apples, or cupcakes while trying to pump me for evidence against him.

"He's just a filthy old man, Robert," she would declare in a little-old-lady whisper. "And don't think you have to clean up those dirty old butts of his. Just report him to the Company."

"Oh, I don't mind," I would tell her, gulping the root beer as fast as possible.

"Well, they're both a couple of lushes, if you ask me. They haven't been sober a day in twenty-five years.

"Well, she's sick too, you know."

"Ha!" She would throw up her hands in disgust. "She's only sick when he doesn't give her the booze."

I fought to keep down a burp. "How long have *you* been here?"

She motioned for me to step out of the hall and into her dark apartment. "Don't tell him"—she nodded toward Sullivan's door—"but I've been here thirty-four years." She waited for me to be taken aback. Then she added: "And it was a better building before those two lushes came."

She then offered me an apple, asked five times if the dog's barking bothered me, forced me to take a fudge brownie, said that the cats had wet the floor again last night, got me to dust the top of a large chest too high for her to reach, had me pick up the minute specks of dust which fell from my dustcloth, pressed another root beer on me, and then showed me her family album. As an afterthought, she had me take down a big old picture of her great-grandfather, also too high for her to reach, so that I could dust that too. Then together we picked up the dust from it which might have fallen to the floor. "He's really a filthy old man, Robert," she said in closing, "and don't be afraid to report him to the Property Manager anytime you want."

I assured her that I would do it at the slightest provocation from Sullivan, finally accepted an apple but refused the money she offered, and escaped back to my mopping. Even then she watched me, smiling, from her half-opened door.

"Why does Miss O'Hara hate you?" I asked James once.

He lifted his cigaretted hand and let the long ash fall elegantly to the floor. "That old bitch has been an albatross around my neck ever since I got here," he said. "Don't trust her, Robert. It was her kind that sat around singing hymns and watching them burn saints in this state."

In those days I had forgotten that I was first of all a black and I had a very lovely girl who was not first of all a black. It is quite possible that my ancestors rowed her ancestors across on the *Mayflower*, and she was very rich in that alone. We were both very young and optimistic then, and she believed with me in my potential and liked me partly because of it; and I was happy because she belonged to me and not to the race, which made her special. It made me special too because I did not have to wear a beard or hate or be especially hip or ultra Ivy Leagueish. I did not have to smoke pot or supply her with it, or be for any cause at all except myself. I only had to be myself, which pleased me; and I only had to produce, which pleased both of us. Like many of the artistically inclined rich, she wanted to own in someone else what she could not own in herself. But this I did not mind, and I forgave her for it because she forgave me moods and the constant smell of garbage and a great deal of latent hostility. She only minded James Sullivan, and all the valuable time I was wasting listening to him rattle on and on. His conversations, she thought, were useless, repetitious, and promised nothing of value to me. She was accustomed to the old-rich, whose conversations meandered around a leitmotiv of how well off they were and how much they would leave behind very soon. She was not at all cold, but she had been taught how to tolerate the old-poor and perhaps toss them a greeting in passing. But nothing more.

Sullivan did not like her when I first introduced them because he saw that she was not a beatnik and could not be dismissed. It is in the nature of things that liberal people will tolerate two interracial beatniks more than they will an intelligent, serious-minded mixed couple. The former liaison is easy to dismiss as the dregs of both races, deserving of each other and the contempt of both races; but the latter poses a threat because there is no immediacy of overpowering sensuality or "you-pick-my-fleas-I'll-pick-yours" apparent on the surface of things, and people, even the most publicly liberal, cannot dismiss it so easily.

"That girl is Irish, isn't she?" he had asked one day in my apartment soon after I had introduced them.

"No," I said definitely.

"What's her name?"

"Judy Smith," I said, which was not her name at all.

"Well, I can spot it," he said. "She's got Irish blood all right."

"Everybody's got a little Irish blood," I told him.

He looked at me cattily and craftily from behind his thick lenses. "Well, she's from a good family, I suppose."

"I suppose," I said.

He paused to let some ashes fall to the rug. "They say the Colonel's Lady and Nelly O'Grady are sisters under the skin." Then he added: "Rudyard Kipling."

"That's true," I said with equal innuendo, "that's why you have to maintain a distinction by marrying the Colonel's Lady."

An understanding passed between us then, and we never spoke more on the subject.

Almost every night the cats wet the second floor while Meg Sullivan watched the "Johnny Carson Show" and the dog howled and clawed the door. During commercials Meg would curse James to get out and stop dropping ashes on the floor or to take the dog out or something else, totally unintelligible to those of us on the fourth, fifth, and sixth floors. Even after the Carson show she would still curse him to get out, until finally he would go down to the basement and put away a bottle or two of wine. There was a steady stench of cat functions in the basement, and with all the grease and dirt, discarded trunks, beer bottles, chairs, old tools, and the filthy sofa on which he sometimes slept, seeing him there made me want to cry. He drank the cheapest sherry, the wino kind, straight from the bottle: and on many nights that summer at 2:00 A.M. my phone would ring me out of bed.

"Rob? Jimmy Sullivan here. What are you doing?"

There was nothing suitable to say.

"Come on down to the basement for a drink."

"I have to be at work at 8:30," I would protest.

"Can't you have just one drink?" he would say pathetically.

I would carry down my own glass so that I would not have to drink out of the bottle. Looking at him on the sofa, I could not be mad because now I had many records for my stereo, a story that was going well, a girl who believed in me and who belonged to me and not to the race, a new set of dishes, and a tomorrow morning with younger people.

"I don't want to burden you unduly," he would always preface.

I would force myself not to look at my watch and say: "Of course not."

"My Meg is not in the best health, you know," he would say, handing the bottle to me.

"She's just old."

"The doctors say she should be in an institution."

"That's no place to be."

"I'm a sick man myself, Rob. I can't take much more. She's crazy."

"Anybody who loves animals can't be crazy."

He took another long draw from the bottle. "I won't live another year. I'll be dead in a year."

"You don't know that."

He looked at me closely, without his glasses, so that I could see the desperation in his eyes. "I just hope Meg goes before I do. I don't want them to put her in an institution after I'm gone."

At 2:00 A.M., with the cat stench in my nose and a glass of bad sherry standing still in my hand because I refuse in my mind to touch it, and all my dreams of greatness are above him and the basement and the building itself, and I did not know what to say. The only way I could keep from hating myself was to start him talking about the AMA or the Medicare program or beatniks. He was pure hell on all three. To him, the Medical Profession was "morally bankrupt," Medicare was a great farce which deprived oldsters like himself of their "rainy-day dollars," and beatniks were "dropouts from the human race." He could rage on and on in perfect phrases about all three of his major dislikes, and I had the feeling that because the sentences were so well constructed and well turned, he might have memorized them from something he had read. But then he was extremely well read, and it did not matter if he had borrowed a phrase or two from someone else. The ideas were still his own.

It would be 3:00 A.M. before I knew it, and then 3:30, and still he would go on. He hated politicians in general and liked to recount, at these times, his private catalog of political observations. By the time he got around to Civil Rights it would be 4:00 A.M., and I could not feel responsible for him at that hour. I would begin to yawn, and at first he would just ignore it. Then I would start to edge toward the door, and he would see that he could hold me no longer, not even by declaring that he wanted to be an honorary Negro because he loved the race so much.

"I hope I haven't burdened you unduly," he would say again.

"Of course not," I would say, because it was over then, and I could leave him and the smell of the cats there, and sometimes I would go out in the cool night and walk around the Yard and be thankful that I was only an assistant janitor, and a transient one at that. Walking in the early dawn and seeing the Summer School fellows sneak out of the girls' dormitories in the Yard gave me a good feeling, and I thought that tomorrow night it would be good to make love myself so that I could be busy when he called.

"Why don't you tell that old man your job doesn't include babysitting with him," Jean told me many times when she came over to visit during the day and found me sleeping.

I would look at her and think to myself about social forces and the pressures massing and poised, waiting to attack us. It was still July then. It was hot, and I was working good.

"He's just an old man," I said. "Who else would listen to him."

"You're too soft. As long as you do your work you don't have to be bothered with him."

"He could be a story if I listened long enough."

"There are too many stories about old people."

"No," I said, thinking about us again, "there are just too many people who have no stories."

Sometimes he would come up and she would be there, but I would let him come in anyway, and he would stand there looking dirty and uncomfortable, offering some invented reason for having intruded. At these times something silent would pass between them, something I cannot name, which would reduce him to exactly what he was: an old man, come out of his basement to intrude where he was not wanted. But all the time this was being communicated, there would be a surface, friendly conversation between them. And after five minutes or so of being unwelcome, he would apologize for having come, drop a few ashes on the rug, and back out the door. Downstairs we could hear his wife screaming.

We endured the aged and August was almost over. Inside the building the cats were still wetting, Meg was still screaming, the dog was getting madder, and Sullivan began to drink during the day. Outside it was hot and lush and green, and the Summer girls were wearing shorter miniskirts and no panties and the middle-aged men down by the Charles were going wild on their bridge. Everyone was restless for change, for August is the month when undone summer things must be finished or regretted all through the winter.

Being imaginative people, Jean and I played a number of original games. One of them we called "Social Forces," the object of which was to see which side could break us first. We played it with the unknown night riders who screamed obscenities from passing cars. And because that was her side I would look at her expectantly, but she would laugh and say: "No." We played it at parties with unaware blacks who attempted to enchant her with skillful dances and hip vocabularies, believing her to be community property. She would be polite and aloof, and much later, it then being my turn, she would look at me expectantly. And I would force a smile and say: "No." The last round was played while taking her home in a subway car, on a hot August night, when one side of the car was black and tense and hating and the other side was white and of the same mind. There was not enough room on either side for the two of us to sit and we would not separate; so we stood, holding on to a steel post through all the stops, feeling all of the eyes, between the two sides of the car and the two sides of the world. We aged. And getting off finally at the stop which was no longer ours, we looked at each other, again expectantly, and there was nothing left to say.

I began to avoid the old man, would not answer the door when I knew it was he who was knocking, and waited until very late at night, when he could not possibly be awake, to haul the trash down. I hated the building then; and I was really a janitor for the first time. I slept a lot and wrote very little. And I did not give a damn about Medicare, the AMA, the building, Meg, or the crazy dog. I began to consider moving out.

In that same week, Miss O'Hara finally succeeded in badgering Murphy, the celibate Irishman, and a few other tenants into signing a complaint about the dog. No doubt Murphy signed because he was a nice fellow and women like Miss O'Hara had always dominated him. He did not really mind the dog: he did not really mind anything. She called him "Frank Dear," and I had the feeling that when he came to that place, fresh from Montgomery's Campaign, he must have had a will of his own; but she had drained it all away, year by year, so that now he would do anything just to be agreeable.

One day soon after the complaint, the little chubby Property Manager came around to tell Sullivan that the dog had to be taken away. Miss O'Hara told me the good news later, when she finally got around to my door.

"Well, that crazy dog is gone now, Robert. Those two are enough."

"Where is the dog?" I asked.

"I don't know, but Albert Rustin made them get him out. You should have seen the old drunk's face," she said. "That dirty old useless man."

"You should be at peace now," I said.

"Almost," was her reply. "The best thing is to get rid of those two old boozers along with the dog."

I congratulated Miss O'Hara and went out. I knew that the old man would be drinking and would want to talk. But very late that evening he called on the telephone and caught me in.

"Rob?" he said. "James Sullivan here. Would you come down to my apartment like a good fellow? I want to ask you something important?"

I had never been in his apartment before and did not want to go then. But I went down anyway.

They had three rooms, all grimy from corner to corner. There was a peculiar odor in that place I did not ever want to smell again, and his wife was dragging herself around the room talking in mumbles. When she saw me come in the door, she said: "I can't clean it up. I just can't. Look at that window. I can't reach it. I can't keep it clean." She threw up both her hands and held her head down and to the side. "The whole place is dirty, and I can't clean it up."

"What do you want?" I said to Sullivan.

"Sit down." He motioned me to a kitchen chair. "Have you changed that bulb on the fifth floor?"

"It's done."

He was silent for a while, drinking from a bottle of sherry, and he gave me some and a dirty glass. "You're the first person who's been in here in years," he said. "We couldn't have company because of the dog."

Somewhere in my mind was a note that I should never go into his apartment. But the dog had never been the reason. "Well, he's gone now," I said, fingering the dirty glass of sherry.

He began to cry. "They took my dog away," he said. "It was all I had. How can they take a man's dog away from him?"

There was nothing I could say.

"I couldn't do nothing," he continued. After a while he added: "But I know who it was. It was that old bitch O'Hara. Don't ever trust her, Rob. She smiles in your face, but it was her kind that laughed when they burned Joan of Arc in this state."

Seeing him there, crying and making me feel unmanly because I wanted to touch him or say something warm, also made me eager to be far away and running hard.

"Everybody's got problems," I said. "I don't have a girl now."

He brightened immediately, and for a while he looked almost happy in his old cat's eyes. Then he staggered over to my chair and held out his hand. I did not touch it, and he finally pulled it back. "I know how you feel," he said. "I know just how you feel."

"Sure," I said.

"But you're a young man, you have a future. But not me. I'll be dead inside of a year."

Just then his wife dragged herself in to offer me a cigar. They were being hospitable, and I forced myself to drink a little of the sherry.

"They took my dog away today," she mumbled. "That's all I had in the world, my dog."

I looked at the old man. He was drinking from the bottle.

During the first week of September one of the middle-aged men down by the Charles got tired of looking and tried to take a necking girl away from her boyfriend. The police hauled him off to jail, and the girl pulled down her dress tearfully. A few days later another man exposed himself near the same spot. And that same week a dead body was found on the banks of the Charles.

The miniskirted brigade had moved out of the Yard, and it was quiet and green and peaceful there. In our building another Jewish couple moved into #44. They did not eat gourmet stuff, and on occasion, threw out pork-and-beans cans. But I had lost interest in perception. I now had many records for my stereo, loads of S. S. Pierce stuff, and a small bottle of Chivas Regal which I never opened. I was working good again, and I did not miss other things as much; or at least I told myself that.

The old man was coming up steadily now, at least three times a day, and I had resigned myself to it. If I refused to let him in, he would always come back later with a missing bulb on the fifth floor. We had taken to buying cases of beer together, and when he had finished his half, which was very frequently, he would come up to polish off mine. I began to enjoy talking politics, the AMA, Medicare, beatniks, and listening to him recite from books he had read. I discovered that he was very well read in history, philosophy, literature, and law. He was extraordinarily fond of saying: "I am really a cut above being a building superintendent. Circumstances made me what I am." And even though he was drunk and dirty and it was very late at night, I believed him and liked him anyway because having him there was much better than being alone. After he had gone I could sleep, and I was not lonely in sleep; and it did not really matter how late I was at work the next morning because when I thought about it all, I discovered that nothing really matters except not being old and being alive and having potential to dream about, and not being alone.

Applications

1. What is the character of Rob in the early part of the story?
2. In what ways is Rob's character different at the end of the story?
3. How do Rob's values change in the course of the story?
4. How does the girl function in the story; why is she there?
5. Does Sullivan's character change in the course of the story?
6. Does the reader's attitude toward Sullivan change in the course of the story? If so, how and why?
7. What does the point of view from which the story is narrated contribute to the story?
8. What is the tone of the story? Does the tone change, and if so, in what ways?

ANALYZING AND WRITING ABOUT MEANING

Analyzing Meaning

We have placed this chapter last because meaning in literature is communicated through all the aspects of literature we have discussed. Meaning is not a lesson to be learned; it is an experience to be shared. That experience is created by the totality of the work: setting, character, point of view, tone, imagery, and so forth.

The process of analyzing meaning is a process of explication, of interpretation and explanation. You start with subject and move to significance. "Gold Coast" is about a young black who has a temporary summer job as a janitor in a deteriorating apartment house. That is the subject of the story; but it tells us almost nothing. Significance lies elsewhere, not in "subject" *per se* but in the presentation of subject.

Step one: Identify the theme of the work   Recall our *subject →man → universal* progression. The first step in analyzing meaning, and the most crucial one, is to correctly identify the aspect of life that the author is writing about *through* his or her subject. That aspect of life is the *theme* of the literary work, its *central concern*. The theme will be an abstraction: the nature of manhood, in Steinbeck's "Flight"; the loss of religious certainty, in Arnold's "Dover Beach"; man's proclivity to possessiveness and violence, in Clark's "The Portable Phonograph."

In order to identify the theme ask yourself such questions as these:
1. What is the author's central concern?
2. What aspect of the human condition is the author focusing on?
3. What general problem that all people face is the author exploring?

Determining the theme of the work by answering these questions is the first step toward understanding meaning.

Step two: Answer the question "What does the writer believe?" in terms of the theme you have identified   When you have identified the theme of a work you have identified the major problem or concern or aspect of life that the work interprets. But a statement of the theme does not indicate the nature of that interpretation. The nature of the interpretation depends upon the individual author and the individual work. Some basic themes recur again and again in different works of literature:

The Love and Death Theme
The Appearance vs. Reality Theme
The Search for a Father or Telemachus Theme
The Initiation Theme
The Mutability Theme
The Journey or Pilgrimage Theme
The Oedipus Theme
The Generation-Gap Theme
The Individual vs. Society Theme

Yet a literary work embodying one of these themes can be entirely fresh because the author's interpretation of the theme is fresh, unique to that work.

Thus, analyzing meaning also entails inferring the author's ideas and views and beliefs concerning the theme. Ask yourself:

1. What is the author suggesting about the aspect of life that constitutes the theme?

2. What views does the author present through his or her treatment of the theme?

3. What is the author's attitude toward the problem or concern dealt with?

The answers to these questions cannot be divorced from the specific context of the literary work you are analyzing. Hence, when you discuss meaning in literature, you inevitably and necessarily discuss setting and character and tone, and so forth. It is a matter of focus. When your primary concern is meaning, your focus will be on the *ideas* communicated through the writer's craft.

The best approach to analyzing meaning is an oblique approach or, if you like, a "building block" approach. Start with the aspect of the work that strikes you as most important, and analyze that aspect thoroughly. Then examine the work from each of the other perspectives that we have discussed and determine whether one or more of these other aspects throws additional light on the work's meaning.

Writing About Meaning

Your analysis of the relation of the various aspects of the work to its meaning will provide plenty of material from which to write your essay. The important consideration now is limiting and focusing:

1. You can discuss the ways in which two or three aspects of the work function to communicate meaning. The focus of such a paper would be on *technique;* how the author uses, for example, setting, tone, and point

163

of view to communicate meaning. The major divisions of such a paper would correspond to the different techniques considered.

2. You can state and explain one *central idea* that the work embodies. The focus of such a paper would be on the idea itself rather than on the techniques by which the author communicates it. This approach is particularly suitable when you are dealing with a long work that develops numerous themes.

3. You can, if the work is a short story or a short poem, attempt a full *explication* of its meaning. This meaning may be essentially one idea, as in Robinson's "Cliff Klingenhagen," or it may encompass several closely related ideas, as in Arnold's "Dover Beach." If you take this approach, you should, however, be able to state and fully discuss all of the ideas in the work within the confines of your essay.

In the sample essay that follows we will use the second approach. We will identify McPherson's central idea or theme and explain his views concerning this theme.

When you write your essay on the central idea of a work, you can structure it along these lines:

First, explain what aspect of the human condition the author is concerned with, and support your view by specific reference to the work.

Second, explain what the author is saying about this aspect of life, and amplify and illustrate your view.

Third, explain how the author's ideas about this aspect of life suggest universal truths.

A Thematic Analysis of James Alan McPherson's "Gold Coast"

In "Gold Coast" McPherson shows us a young man maturing. The theme of initiation—of movement from self-deception to self-knowledge, from ignorance to insight, from boyhood to manhood—is an old one. In this story McPherson shows such character growth occurring in the apparently mundane context of a young man's summer job as a janitorial "apprentice" to an old, worn-out Irishman.

> Note: The first paragraph identifies the aspect of the human condition the author is concerned with, the general problem that all men and women face. In this case it is the process of maturing, initiation.

When Rob begins his brief stint as a janitor he is in several ways quite immature. He dreams of future success and fame, "lulled by sweet anticipation of that time when my potential would suddenly be realized." He fancies himself "gifted with a boundless perception" and egotistically believes that he could immortalize any one of the tenants with the "magic" of his pen, if he chose to do so.

But as the summer wears on, Rob matures. His growing perceptiveness and insight are revealed by the gradual change in his attitude toward Sullivan, a change apparently brought about by his own changing values. Early in the summer Rob's only feeling toward Sullivan is pity. Rob feels "rich" with his own apartment, "a sensitive girl, a stereo, two speakers, one tattered chair, one fork, a job, and the urge to acquire . . . all this and youth besides." He sees no common ground, no brotherhood between himself and the old man whose only possessions are "a berserk dog, a wife almost as mad as the dog, three cats, bursitis, acute myopia, and a drinking problem." But, by the end of the story, pity has changed to fondness, distate to enjoyment.

Rob's behavior, especially in regard to Sullivan, also reflects his increasing maturity. At first, Rob holds himself at a distance from Sullivan. Even when he joins Sullivan in the basement, he does so reluctantly and will not drink the sherry Sullivan pours for him. The turning point in their relationship appears to be Rob's visit to the Sullivans' apartment. Here he accepts some sherry in one of their glasses, rather than his own, and actually drinks a little. Finally, we find Rob and Sullivan drinking and talking and enjoying each other's company in Rob's apartment. From the neutral territory of the basement, to Sullivan's apartment, to Rob's own—the progression of acceptance is clear. At the end of the story Rob can accept Sullivan because he has abandoned the superficial *Playboy* notion of happiness as a girl, a pad, and a stereo. One can do without all these, if necessary. With Sullivan's fate before him, Rob has come to recognize that "nothing really matters except not being old and being alive and having potential to dream about, and not being alone."

Note: The three preceding paragraphs support the view expressed in the first paragraph, that McPherson's central concern is the process of maturing.

The point of view and tone of the story give further evidence of McPherson's central concern with the process of "growing up." The Rob who narrates the story is older than the Rob whose summer is described. The narrator is looking back on his younger and less knowledgeable self. And, especially in the first part of the story, when Rob is filled with vaingloriousness and self-satisfied superiority to Sullivan, the narrator is unsympathetic. His attitude toward this benighted fellow that he once was is ironic and mocking.

The narrator mocks the young Rob's dreams of instant success, his naïve belief in his "boundless perception," his self-deception in trying to ignore his race. The young Rob is addicted to fantasies of success which ignore hard and lengthy effort. He nightly drifts off to sleep "lulled by sweet anticipation" of future fame. And, as the narrator observes of his younger self, "In those days I had forgotten that I was first of all a black. . . ." But, as the story progresses and Rob matures, the irony fades

165

until, at the end of the story, the tone has become quite serious. Hence, point of view and tone help communicate the idea that the Rob at the beginning of the story is not the Rob at the story's end.

Note: The two preceding paragraphs give further evidence that the central theme of the short story is indeed initiation, significant character growth.

As we have seen, Rob's character growth is mirrored in his changing attitude toward and relation to Sullivan. The reader's attitude toward Sullivan also changes in the course of the story. At first, Sullivan seems a nasty old man, a total failure. He smears his cigarette butts on the floor, he gets stoned on cheap wine, he intrudes himself. But, gradually, he becomes more sympathetic. We begin to see him as a person rather than a type. Outward failure that he is, he is nevertheless kind and forbearing. He recognizes that his wife is not well, and despite her screaming and her curses, never loses his temper with her. Despite the hell his wife puts him through, he cares for her and hopes he will outlive her so she will not be put in an institution. And he is no fool—he turns out to be "very well read in history, philosophy, literature, and law."

Sullivan, Rob tells us, was fond of saying, " 'I am really a cut above being a building superintendent. Circumstances made me what I am.' " At the end of the story, Rob believes him, and so do we. Sullivan has become a person, an old man who might have achieved better things had circumstances been different. This, McPherson seems to suggest, is the essence of maturity—being able to recognize ourselves in others, being able to recognize that, "There, but for the grace of God, go I." For such a recognition dissipates vaingloriousness and self-congratulation and compels us to realize that "nothing really matters except not being old and being alive and having potential to dream about, and not being alone."

Note: The two paragraphs above explain "what the author believes" concerning his central theme. Maturity, the author's central concern, lies in accepting one's fellowship with others, whatever their outward situation in life. This belief has "universal application. It applies to all people, all places, all times.

A MINI-ANTHOLOGY

THE LIFE YOU SAVE MAY BE YOUR OWN

Flannery O'Connor

The old woman and her daughter were sitting on their porch when Mr. Shiftlet came up their road for the first time. The old woman slid to the edge of her chair and leaned forward, shading her eyes from the piercing sunset with her hand. The daughter could not see far in front of her and continued to play with her fingers. Although the old woman lived in this desolate spot with only her daughter and she had never seen Mr. Shiftlet before, she could tell, even from a distance, that he was a tramp and no one to be afraid of. His left coat sleeve was folded up to show there was only half an arm in it and his gaunt figure listed slightly to the side as if the breeze were pushing him. He had on a black town suit and a brown felt hat that was turned up in the front and down in the back and he carried a tin tool box by a handle. He came on, at an amble, up her road, his face turned toward the sun which appeared to be balancing itself on the peak of a small mountain.

The old woman didn't change her position until he was almost into her yard; then she rose with one hand fisted on her hip. The daughter, a large girl in a short blue organdy dress, saw him all at once and jumped up and began to stamp and point and make excited speechless sounds.

Mr. Shiftlet stopped just inside the yard and set his box on the ground and tipped his hat at her as if she were not in the least afflicted; then he turned toward the old woman and swung the hat all the way off. He had long black slick hair that hung flat from a part in the middle to beyond the tips of his ears on either side. His face descended in forehead for more than half its length and ended suddenly with his features just balanced over a jutting steel-trap jaw. He seemed to be a young man but he had a look of composed dissatisfaction as if he understood life thoroughly.

"Good evening," the old woman said. She was about the size of a cedar fence post and she had a man's gray hat pulled down low over her head.

The tramp stood looking at her and didn't answer. He turned his back and faced the sunset. He swung both his whole and his short arm up slowly so that they indicated an expanse of sky and his figure formed a crooked cross. The old woman watched him with her arms folded across her chest as if she were the owner of the sun, and the daughter watched, her head thrust forward and her fat helpless hands hanging at the wrists. She had long pink-gold hair and eyes as blue as a peacock's neck.

He held the pose for almost fifty seconds and then he picked up his box and came on to the porch and dropped down on the bottom step. "Lady," he said in a firm nasal voice, "I'd give a fortune to live where I could see me a sun do that every evening."

"Does it every evening," the old woman said and sat back down. The daughter sat down too and watched him with a cautious sly look as if he were a bird that had come up very close. He leaned to one side, rooting in his pants pocket, and in a second he brought out a package of chewing gum and offered her a piece. She took it and unpeeled it and began to chew without taking her eyes off him. He offered the old woman a piece but she only raised her upper lip to indicate she had no teeth.

Mr. Shiftlet's pale sharp glance had already passed over everything in the yard—the pump near the corner of the house and the big fig tree that three or four chickens were preparing to roost in—and had moved to a shed where he saw the square rusted back of an automobile. "You ladies drive?" he asked.

"That car ain't run in fifteen year," the old woman said. "The day my husband died, it quit running."

"Nothing is like it used to be, lady," he said. "The world is almost rotten."

"That's right," the old woman said. "You from around here?"

"Name Tom T. Shiftlet," he murmured, looking at the tires.

"I'm pleased to meet you," the old woman said. "Name Lucynell Crater and daughter Lucynell Crater. What you doing around here, Mr. Shiftlet?"

He judged the car to be about a 1928 or '29 Ford. "Lady," he said, and turned and gave her his full attention, "lemme tell you something. There's one of these doctors in Atlanta that's taken a knife and cut the human heart—the human heart," he repeated, leaning forward, "out of a man's chest and held it in his hand," and he held his hand out, palm up, as if it were slightly weighted with the human heart, "and studied it like it was a day-old chicken, and lady," he said, allowing a long significant pause in which his head slid forward and his clay-colored eyes brightened, "he don't know no more about it than you or me."

169

"That's right," the old woman said.

"Why, if he was to take that knife and cut into every corner of it, he still wouldn't know no more than you or me. What you want to bet?"

"Nothing," the old woman said wisely. "Where you come from, Mr. Shiftlet?"

He didn't answer. He reached into his pocket and brought out a sack of tobacco and a package of cigarette papers and rolled himself a cigarette, expertly with one hand, and attached it in a hanging position to his upper lip. Then he took a box of wooden matches from his pocket and struck one on his shoe. He held the burning match as if he were studying the mystery of flame while it traveled dangerously toward his skin. The daughter began to make loud noises and to point to his hand and shake her finger at him, but when the flame was just before touching him, he leaned down with his hand cupped over it as if he were going to set fire to his nose and lit the cigarette.

He flipped away the dead match and blew a stream of gray into the evening. A sly look came over his face. "Lady," he said, "nowadays people'll do anything anyways. I can tell you my name is Tom T. Shiftlet and I come from Tarwater, Tennessee, but you never have seen me before: how you know I ain't lying? How you know my name ain't Aaron Sparks, lady, and I come from Singleberry, Georgia, or how you know it's not George Speeds and I come from Lucy, Alabama, or how you know I ain't Thompson Bright from Toolafalls, Mississippi?"

"I don't know nothing about you," the old woman muttered, irked.

"Lady," he said, "people don't care how they lie. Maybe the best I can tell you is, I'm a man; but listen lady," he said and paused and made his tone more ominous still, "what is a man?"

The old woman began to gum a seed. "What you carry in that tin box, Mr. Shiftlet?" she asked.

"Tools," he said, put back. "I'm a carpenter."

"Well, if you come out here to work, I'll be able to feed you and give you a place to sleep but I can't pay. I'll tell you that before you begin," she said.

There was no answer at once and no particular expression on his face. He leaned back against the two-by-four that helped support the porch roof. "Lady," he said slowly, "there's some men that some things mean more to them than money." The old woman rocked without comment and the daughter watched the trigger that moved up and down in his neck. He told the old woman then that all most people were interested in was money, but he asked what a man was made for. He asked her if a man was made for money, or what. He asked her what she thought she was made for but she didn't answer, she only sat rocking and wondered if a one-armed man could put a new roof on her garden house. He asked a lot of questions that she didn't answer. He told her that he was twenty-eight years old and had lived a varied life. He had been a gospel singer, a foreman on the railroad, an assistant in an undertaking parlor, and he come over the radio for three months with Uncle Roy and his Red Creek Wranglers. He said he had fought and bled in the Arm Service of his country and visited every foreign land and that everywhere he had seen people that didn't care if they did a thing one way or another. He said he hadn't been raised thataway.

A fat yellow moon appeared in the branches of the fig tree as if it were going to roost there with the chickens. He said that a man had to escape to the country to see the world whole and that he wished he had lived in a desolate place like this where he could see the sun go down every evening like God made it to do.

"Are you married or are you single?" the old woman asked.

There was a long silence. "Lady," he asked finally, "where would you find you an innocent woman today? I wouldn't have any of this trash I could just pick up."

The daughter was leaning very far down, hanging her head almost between her knees, watching him through a triangular door she had made in her overturned hair; and she suddenly fell in a heap on the floor and began to whimper. Mr. Shiftlet straightened her out and helped her get back in the chair.

"Is she your baby girl?" he asked.

"My only," the old woman said, "and she's the sweetest girl in the world. I would give her up for nothing on earth. She's smart too. She can sweep the floor, cook, wash, feed the chickens, and hoe. I wouldn't give her up for a casket of jewels."

"No," he said kindly, "don't ever let any man take her away from you."

"Any man come after her," the old woman said, "'ll have to stay around the place."

Mr. Shiftlet's eye in the darkness was focused on a part of the automobile bumper that glittered in the distance. "Lady," he said, jerking his short arm up as if he could point with it to her house and yard and pump, "there ain't a broken thing on this plantation that I couldn't fix for you, one-arm jackleg or not. I'm a man," he said with a sullen dignity, "even if I ain't a whole one. I got," he said, tapping his knuckles on the floor to emphasize the immensity of what he was going to say, "a moral intelligence!" and his face pierced out of the darkness into a shaft of doorlight and he stared at her as if he were astonished himself at this impossible truth.

171

The old woman was not impressed with the phrase. "I told you you could hang around and work for food," she said, "if you don't mind sleeping in that car yonder."

"Why, listen, lady," he said with a grin of delight, "the monks of old slept in their coffins!"

"They wasn't as advanced as we are," the old woman said.

The next morning he began on the roof of the garden house while Lucynell, the daughter, sat on a rock and watched him work. He had not been around a week before the change he had made in the place was apparent. He had patched the front and back steps, built a new hog pen, restored a fence, and taught Lucynell, who was completely deaf and had never said a word in her life, to say the word "bird." The big rosy-faced girl followed him everywhere, saying "Burrttddt ddbirrrttdt," and clapping her hands. The old woman watched from a distance, secretly pleased. She was ravenous for a son-in-law.

Mr. Shiftlet slept on the hard narrow back seat of the car with his feet out the side window. He had his razor and a can of water on a crate that served him as a bedside table and he put up a piece of mirror against the back glass and kept his coat neatly on a hanger that he hung over one of the windows.

In the evenings he sat on the steps and talked while the old woman and Lucynell rocked violently in their chairs on either side of him. The old woman's three mountains were black against the dark blue sky and were visited off and on by various planets and by the moon after it had left the chickens. Mr. Shiftlet pointed out that the reason he had improved this plantation was because he had taken a personal interest in it. He said he was even going to make the automobile run.

He had raised the hood and studied the mechanism and he said he could tell that the car had been built in the days when cars were really built. You take now, he said, one man puts in one bolt and another man puts in another bolt and another man puts in another bolt so that it's a man for a bolt. That's why you have to pay so much for a car: you're paying all those men. Now if you didn't have to pay but one man, you could get you a cheaper car and one that had a personal interest taken in it, and it would be a better car. The old woman agreed with him that this was so.

Mr. Shiftlet said that the trouble with the world was that nobody cared, or stopped and took any trouble. He said he never would have been able to teach Lucynell to say a word if he hadn't cared and stopped long enough.

"Teach her to say something else," the old woman said.

"What you want her to say next?" Mr. Shiftlet asked.

The old woman's smile was broad and toothless and suggestive. "Teach her to say 'sugarpie,'" she said.

Mr. Shiftlet already knew what was on her mind.

The next day he began to tinker with the automobile and that evening he told her that if she would buy a fan belt, he would be able to make the car run.

The old woman said she would give him the money. "You see that girl yonder?" she asked, pointing to Lucynell who was sitting on the floor a foot away, watching him, her eyes blue even in the dark. "If it was ever a man wanted to take her away, I would say, 'No man on earth is going to take that sweet girl of mine away from me!' but if he was to say, 'Lady, I don't want to take her away, I want her right here,' I would say, 'Mister, I don't blame you none. I wouldn't pass up a chance to live in a permanent place and get the sweetest girl in the world myself. You ain't no fool,' I would say."

"How old is she?" Mr. Shiftlet asked casually.

"Fifteen, sixteen," the old woman said. The girl was nearly thirty but because of her innocence it was impossible to guess.

"It would be a good idea to paint it too," Mr. Shiftlet remarked. "You don't want it to rust out."

"We'll see about that later," the old woman said.

The next day he walked into town and returned with the parts he needed and a can of gasoline. Late in the afternoon, terrible noises issued from the shed and the old woman rushed out of the house, thinking Lucynell was somewhere having a fit. Lucynell was sitting on a chicken crate, stamping her feet and screaming, "Burrddttt! bddurrddtttt!" but her fuss was drowned out by the car. With a volley of blasts it emerged from the shed, moving in a fierce and stately way. Mr. Shiftlet was in the driver's seat, sitting very erect. He had an expression of serious modesty on his face as if he had just raised the dead.

That night, rocking on the porch, the old woman began her business at once. "You want you an innocent woman, don't you?" she asked sympathetically. "You don't want none of this trash."

"No'm, I don't," Mr. Shiftlet said.

"One that can't talk," she continued, "can't sass you back or use foul language. That's the kind for you to have. Right there," and she pointed to Lucynell sitting cross-legged in her chair, holding both feet in her hands.

"That's right," he admitted. "She wouldn't give me any trouble."

"Saturday," the old woman said, "you and her and me can drive into town and get married."

Mr. Shiftlet eased his position on the steps.

"I can't get married right now," he said. "Everything you want to do takes money and I ain't got any."

"What you need with money?" she asked.

"It takes money," he said. "Some people'll do anything anyhow these days, but the way I think, I wouldn't marry no woman that I couldn't take on a trip like she was somebody. I mean take her to a hotel and treat her. I wouldn't marry the Duchesser Windsor," he said firmly, "unless I could take her to a hotel and giver something good to eat.

"I was raised thataway and there ain't a thing I can do about it. My old mother taught me how to do."

"Lucynell don't even know what a hotel is," the old woman muttered. "Listen here, Mr. Shiftlet," she said, sliding forward in her chair, "you'd be getting a permanent home and a deep well and the most innocent girl in the world. You don't need no money. Lemme tell you something; there ain't any place in the world for a poor disabled friendless drifting man."

The ugly words settled in Mr. Shiftlet's head like a group of buzzards in the top of a tree. He didn't answer at once. He rolled himself a cigarette and lit it and then he said in an even voice, "Lady, a man is divided into parts, body and spirit."

The old woman clamped her gums together.

"A body and a spirit," he repeated. "The body, lady, is like a house: it don't go anywhere; but the spirit, lady, is like a automobile: always on the move, always . . ."

"Listen, Mr. Shiftlet," she said, "my well never goes dry and my house is always warm in the winter and there's no mortgage on a thing about this place. You can go to the courthouse and see for yourself. And yonder under that shed is a fine automobile." She laid the bait carefully. "You can have it painted by Saturday. I'll pay for the paint."

In the darkness, Mr. Shiftlet's smile stretched like a weary snake waking up by a fire. After a second he recalled himself and said, "I'm only saying a man's spirit means more to him than anything else. I would have to take my wife off for the week end without no regard at all for cost. I got to follow where my spirit says to go."

"I'll give you fifteen dollars for a week-end trip," the old woman said in a crabbed voice. "That's the best I can do."

"That wouldn't hardly pay for more than the gas and the hotel," he said, "It wouldn't feed her."

"Seventeen-fifty," the old woman said. "That's all I got so it isn't any use you trying to milk me. You can take a lunch."

Mr. Shiftlet was deeply hurt by the word "milk." He didn't doubt that she had more money sewed up in her mattress but he had already told her he was not interested in her money. "I'll make that do," he said and rose and walked off without treating with her further.

On Saturday the three of them drove into town in the car that the paint had barely dried on and Mr. Shiftlet and Lucynell were married in the Ordinary's office while the old woman witnessed. As they came out of the courthouse, Mr. Shiftlet began twisting his neck in his collar. He looked morose and bitter as if he had been insulted while someone held him. "That didn't satisfy me none," he said. "That was just something a woman in an office did, nothing but paper work and blood tests. What do they know about my blood? If they was to take my heart and cut it out," he said, "they wouldn't know a thing about me. It didn't satisfy me at all."

"It satisfied the law," the old woman said sharply.

"The law," Mr. Shiftlet said and spit. "It's the law that don't satisfy me."

He had painted the car dark green with a yellow band around it just under the windows. The three of them climbed in the front seat and the old woman said, "Don't Lucynell look pretty? Looks like a baby doll." Lucynell was dressed up in a white dress that her mother had uprooted from a trunk and there was a Panama hat on her head with a bunch of red wooden cherries on the brim. Every now and then her placid expression was changed by a sly isolated little thought like a shoot of green in the desert. "You got a prize!" the old woman said.

Mr. Shiftlet didn't even look at her.

They drove back to the house to let the old woman off and pick up the lunch. When they were ready to leave, she stood staring in the window of the car, with her fingers clenched around the glass. Tears began to seep sideways out of her eyes and run along the dirty creases in her face. "I ain't ever been parted with her for two days before," she said.

Mr. Shiftlet started the motor.

"And I wouldn't let no man have her but you because I seen you would do right. Good-by, Sugarbaby," she said, clutching at the sleeve of the white dress. Lucynell looked straight at her and didn't seem to see her there at all. Mr. Shiftlet eased the car forward so that she had to move her hands.

The early afternoon was clear and open and surrounded by pale blue sky. Although the car would go only thirty miles an hour, Mr. Shiftlet imagined a terrific climb and dip and swerve that went entirely to his head so that he forgot his morning bitterness. He had always wanted an automobile but he had never been able to afford one before. He drove very fast because he wanted to make Mobile by nightfall.

Occasionally he stopped his thoughts long enough to look at Lucynell in the seat beside him. She had eaten the lunch as soon as they were out of the yard and now she was pulling the cherries off the hat one by one and throwing them out the window. He became depressed in spite of the car. He had driven about a hundred miles when he decided that she must be hungry again and at the next small town they came to, he stopped in front of an aluminum-painted eating place called The Hot Spot and took her in and ordered her a plate of ham and grits. The ride had made her sleepy and as soon as she got up on the stool, she rested her head on the counter and shut her eyes. There was no one in The Hot Spot but Mr. Shiftlet and the boy behind the counter, a pale youth with a greasy rag hung over his shoulder. Before he could dish up the food, she was snoring gently.

"Give it to her when she wakes up," Mr. Shiftlet said. "I'll pay for it now."

The boy bent over her and stared at the long pink-gold hair and the half-shut sleeping eyes. Then he looked up and stared at Mr. Shiftlet. "She looks like an angel of Gawd," he murmured.

"Hitch-hiker," Mr. Shiftlet explained. "I can't wait. I got to make Tuscaloosa."

The boy bent over again and very carefully touched his finger to a strand of the golden hair and Mr. Shiftlet left.

He was more depressed than ever as he drove on by himself. The late afternoon had grown hot and sultry and the country had flattened out. Deep in the sky a storm was preparing very slowly and without thunder as if meant to drain every drop of air from the earth before it broke. There were times when Mr. Shiftlet preferred not to be alone. He felt too that a man with a car had a responsibility to others and he kept his eye out for a hitchhiker. Occasionally he saw a sign that warned: "Drive carefully. The life you save may be your own."

The narrow road dropped off on either side into dry fields and here and there a shack or a filling station stood in a clearing. The sun began to set directly in front of the automobile. It was a reddening ball that through his windshield was slightly flat on the bottom and top. He saw a boy in overalls and a gray hat standing on the edge of the road and he slowed the car and stopped in front of him. The boy didn't have his hand raised to thumb the ride, he was only standing there, but he had a small cardboard suitcase and his hat was set on his head in a way to indicate that he had left somewhere for good. "Son," Mr. Shiftlet said, "I see you want a ride."

The boy didn't say he did or he didn't but he opened the door of the car and got in, and Mr. Shiftlet started driving again. The child held the suitcase on his lap and folded his arms on top of it. He turned his head and looked out the window away from Mr. Shiftlet. Mr. Shiftlet felt oppressed. "Son," he said after a minute, "I got the best old mother in the world so I reckon you only got the second best."

The boy gave him a quick dark glance and then turned his face back out the window.

"It's nothing so sweet," Mr. Shiftlet continued, "as a boy's mother. She taught him his first prayers at her knee, she give him love when no other would, she told him what was right and what was wasn't, and she seen that he done the right thing. Son," he said, "I never rued a day in my life like the one I rued when I left that old mother of mine."

The boy shifted in his seat but he didn't look at Mr. Shiftlet. He unfolded his arms and put one hand on the door handle.

"My mother was a angel of Gawd," Mr. Shiftlet said in a very strained voice. "He took her from heaven and giver to me and I left her." His eyes were instantly clouded over with a mist of tears. The car was barely moving.

The boy turned angrily in the seat. "You go to the devil!" he cried. "My old woman is a flea bag and yours is a stinking pole cat!" and with that he flung the door open and jumped out with his suitcase into the ditch.

Mr. Shiftlet was so shocked that for about a hundred feet he drove along slowly with the door still open. A cloud, the exact color of the boy's hat and shaped like a turnip, had descended over the sun, and another, worse looking, crouched behind the car. Mr. Shiftlet felt that the rottenness of the world was about to engulf him. He raised his arm and let it fall again to his breast. "Oh Lord!" he prayed. "Break forth and wash the slime from this earth!"

The turnip continued slowly to descend. After a few minutes there was a guffawing peal of thunder from behind and fantastic raindrops, like tin-can tops, crashed over the rear of Mr. Shiftlet's car. Very quickly he stepped on the gas and with his stump sticking out the window he raced the galloping shower into Mobile.

THE STONE BOY

Gina Berriault

Arnold drew his overalls and raveling gray sweater over his naked body. In the other narrow bed his brother Eugene went on sleeping, undisturbed by the alarm clock's rusty ring. Arnold, watching his brother sleeping, felt a peculiar dismay; he was nine, six years younger than Eugie, and in their waking hours it was he who was subordinate. To dispel emphatically his uneasy advantage over his sleeping brother, he threw himself on the hump of Eugie's body.

"Get up!" Get up!" he cried.

Arnold felt his brother twist away and saw the blankets lifted in a great wing, and, all in an instant, he was lying on his back under the covers with only his face showing, like a baby, and Eugie was sprawled on top of him.

"Whassa matter with you?" asked Eugie in sleepy anger, his face hanging close.

"Get up," Arnold repeated. "You said you'd pick peas with me."

Stupidly, Eugie gazed around the room to see if morning had come into it yet. Arnold began to laugh derisively, making soft, snorting noises, and was thrown off the bed. He got up from the floor and went down the stairs, the laughter continuing, like hiccups, against his will. But when he opened the staircase door and entered the parlor, he hunched up his shoulders and was quiet because his parents slept in the bedroom downstairs.

Arnold lifted his .22-caliber rifle from the rack on the kitchen wall. It was an old lever-action that his father had given him because nobody else used it anymore. On their way down to the garden he and Eugie would go by the lake, and if there were any ducks on it he'd take a shot at them. Standing on the stool before the cupboard, he searched on the top shelf in the confusion of medicines and ointments for man and beast and found a small yellow box of .22 cartridges. Then he sat down on the stool and began to load his gun.

It was cold in the kitchen so early, but later in the day, when his mother canned the peas, the heat from the wood stove would be almost unbearable. Yesterday she had finished preserving the huckleberries that the family had picked along the mountain, and before that she had canned all the cherries his father had brought from the warehouse in Cornith. Sometimes, on these summer days, Arnold would deliberately come out from the shade where he was playing and make himself as uncomfortable as his mother was in the kitchen by standing in the sun until the sweat ran down his body.

Eugie came clomping down the stairs and into the kitchen, his head drooping with sleepiness. From his perch on the stool Arnold watched Eugie slip on his green knit cap. Eugie didn't really need a cap; he hadn't had a haircut in a long time and his brown curls grew thick and matted, close around his ears and down his neck, tapering there to a small whorl. Eugie passed his left hand through his hair before he set his cap down with his right. The very way he slipped his cap on was an announcement of his status; almost everything he did was a reminder that he was eldest—first he, then Nora, then Arnold—and called attention to how tall he was, almost as tall as his father, how long his legs were, how small he was in the hips, and what a neat dip above his buttocks his thick-soled logger's boots gave him. Arnold never tired of watching Eugie offer silent praise unto himself. He wondered, as he sat enthralled, if when he got to be Eugie's age he would still be undersized and his hair still straight.

Eugie eyed the gun. "Don't you know this ain't duck season?" he asked gruffly, as if he were the sheriff.

"No, I don't know," Arnold said with a snigger.

Eugie picked up the tin washtub for the peas, unbolted the door with his free hand and kicked it open. Then, lifting the tub to his head, he went clomping down the back steps. Arnold followed, closing the door behind him.

The sky was faintly gray, almost white. The mountains behind the farm made the sun climb a long way to show itself. Several miles to the south, where the range opened up, hung an orange mist, but the valley in which the farm lay was still cold and colorless.

Eugie opened the gate to the yard and the boys passed between the barn and the row of chicken houses, their feet stirring up the carpet of brown feathers dropped by the molting chickens. They paused before going down the slope to the lake. A fluky morning wind ran among the shocks of wheat that covered the slope. It sent a shimmer northward across the lake, gently moving the rushes that formed an island in the center. Killdeer, their white markings flashing, skimmed the water, crying their shrill, sweet cry. And there at the south end of the lake were four wild ducks, swimming out from the willows into open water.

179

Arnold followed Eugie down the slope, stealing, as his brother did, from one shock of wheat to another. Eugie paused before climbing through the wire fence that divided the wheat field from the marshy pasture around the lake. They were screened from the ducks by the willows along the lake's edge.

"If you hit your duck, you want me to go in after it?" Eugie said.

"If you want," Arnold said.

Eugie lowered his eyelids, leaving slits of mocking blue. "You'd drown 'fore you got to it, them legs of yours are so puny," he said.

He shoved the tub under the fence and, pressing down the center wire, climbed through into the pasture.

Arnold pressed down the bottom wire, thrust a leg through and leaned forward to bring the other leg after. His rifle caught on the wire and he jerked at it. The air was rocked by the sound of the shot. Feeling foolish, he lifted his face, baring it to an expected shower of derision from his brother. But Eugie did not turn around. Instead, from his crouching position, he fell to his knees and then pitched forward onto his face. The ducks rose up crying from the lake, cleared the mountain background and beat away northward across the pale sky.

Arnold squatted beside his brother. Eugie seemed to be climbing the earth, as if the earth ran up and down, and when he found he couldn't scale it he lay still.

"Eugie?"

Then Arnold saw it, under the tendril of hair at the nape of the neck—a slow rising of bright blood. It had an obnoxious movement, like that of a parasite.

"Hey, Eugie," he said again. He was feeling the same discomfort he had felt when he had watched Eugie sleeping; his brother didn't know that he was lying face down in the pasture.

Again he said, "Hey, Eugie," an anxious nudge in his voice. But Eugie was as still as the morning around them.

Arnold set his rifle on the ground and stood up. He picked up the tub and, dragging it behind him, walked along by the willows to the garden fence and climbed through. He went down on his knees among the tangled vines. The pods were cold with the night, but his hands were strange to him, and not until some time had passed did he realize that the pods were numbing his fingers. He picked from the top of the vine first, then lifted the vine to look underneath for pods, and moved on to the next.

It was a warmth on his back, like a large hand laid firmly there, that made him raise his head. Way up the slope the gray farmhouse was struck by the sun. While his head had been bent the land had grown bright around him.

When he got up his legs were so stiff that he had to go down on his knees again to ease the pain. Then, walking sideways, he dragged the tub, half full of peas, up the slope.

The kitchen was warm now; a fire was roaring in the stove with a closed-up, rushing sound. His mother was spooning eggs from a pot of boiling water and putting them into a bowl. Her short brown hair was uncombed and fell forward across her eyes as she bent her head. Nora was lifting a frying pan full of trout from the stove, holding the handle with a dish towel. His father had just come in from bringing the cows from the north pasture to the barn, and was sitting on the stool, unbuttoning his red plaid Mackinaw.

"Did you boys fill the tub?" his mother asked.

"They ought of by now," his father said. "They went out of the house an hour ago. Eugie woke me up comin' downstairs. I heard you shootin'—did you get a duck?"

"No," Arnold said. They would want to know why Eugie wasn't coming in for breakfast, he thought. "Eugie's dead," he told them.

They stared at him. The pitch crackled in the stove.

"You kids playin' a joke?" his father asked.

"Where's Eugene?" his mother asked scoldingly. She wanted, Arnold knew, to see his eyes, and when he had glanced at her she put the bowl and spoon down on the stove and walked past him. His father stood up and went out the door after her. Nora followed them with little skipping steps, as if afraid to be left alone.

Arnold went into the barn, down along the foddering passage past the cows waiting to be milked, and climbed into the loft. After a few minutes he heard a terrifying sound coming toward the house. His parents and Nora were returning from the willows, and sounds sharp as knives were rising from his mother's breast and carrying over the sloping fields. In a short while he heard his father go down the back steps, slam the car door and drive away.

Arnold lay still as a fugitive, listening to the cows eating close by. If his parents never called him, he thought, he would say up in the loft forever, out of the way. In the night he would sneak down for a drink of water from the faucet over the trough and for whatever food they left for him by the barn.

The rattle of his father's car as it turned down the lane recalled him to the present. He heard the voices of his Uncle Andy and Aunt Alice as they and his father went past the barn to the lake. He could feel the morning growing heavier with sun. Someone, probably Nora, had let the chickens out of their coops and they were cackling in the yard.

After a while another car turned down the road off the highway. The car drew to a stop and he heard the voices of strange men. The men also went past the barn and down to the lake. The undertakers, whom his father must have phoned from Uncle Andy's house, had arrived from Corinth. Then he heard everybody come back and heard the car turn around and leave.

"Arnold!" It was his father calling from the yard.

He climbed down the ladder and went out into the sun, picking wisps of hay from his overalls.

Corinth, nine miles away, was the county seat. Arnold sat in the front seat of the old Ford between his father, who was driving, and Uncle Andy; no one spoke. Uncle Andy was his mother's brother, and he had been fond of Eugie because Eugie had resembled him. Andy had taken Eugie hunting and had given him a knife and a lot of things, and now Andy, his eyes narrowed, sat tall and stiff beside Arnold.

Arnold's father parked the car before the courthouse. It was a two-story brick building with a lamp on each side of the bottom step. They went up the wide stone steps, Arnold and his father going first, and entered the darkly paneled hallway. The shirt-sleeved man in the sheriff's office said that the sheriff was at Carlson's Parlor examining the Curwing boy.

Andy went off to get the sheriff while Arnold and his father waited on a bench in the corridor. Arnold felt his father watching him, and he lifted his eyes with painful casualness to the announcement, on the opposite wall, of the Corinth County Annual Rodeo, and then to the clock with its loudly clucking pendulum. After he had come down from the loft his father and Uncle Andy had stood in the yard with him and asked him to tell them everything, and he had explained to them how the gun had caught on the wire. But when they had asked him why he hadn't run back to the house to tell his parents, he had had no answer—all he could say was that he had gone down into the garden to pick the peas. His father had stared at him in a pale, puzzled way, and it was then that he had felt his father and the others set their cold, turbulent silence against him. Arnold shifted on the bench, his only feeling a small one of compunction imposed by his father's eyes.

At a quarter past nine Andy and the sheriff came in. They all went into the sheriff's private office, and Arnold was sent forward to sit in the chair by the sheriff's desk; his father and Andy sat down on the bench against the wall.

The sheriff lumped down into his swivel chair and swung toward Arnold. He was an old man with white hair like wheat stubble. His restless green eyes made him seem not to be in his office but to be hurrying and bobbing around somewhere else.

"What did you say your name was?" the sheriff asked.

"Arnold," he replied, but he could not remember telling the sheriff his name before.

"Curwing?"

"Yes."

"What were you doing with a .22, Arnold?"

"It's mine," he said.

"Okay. What were you going to shoot?"

"Some ducks," he replied.

"Out of season?"

He nodded.

"That's bad," said the sheriff. "Were you and your brother good friends?"

What did he mean—good friends? Eugie was his brother. That was different from a friend, Arnold thought. A best friend was your own age, but Eugie was almost a man. Eugie had had a way of looking at him, slyly and mockingly and yet confidentially, that had summed up how they both felt about being brothers. Arnold had wanted to be with Eugie more than with anybody else but he couldn't say they had been good friends.

"Did they ever quarrel?" the sheriff asked his father.

"Not that I know," his father replied. "It seemed to me that Arnold cared a lot for Eugie."

"Did you?" the sheriff asked Arnold.

If it seemed so to his father, then it was so. Arnold nodded.

"Were you mad at him this morning?"

"No."

"How did you happen to shoot him?"

"We was crawlin' through the fence."

"Yes?"

"An' the gun got caught on the wire."

"Seems the hammer must of caught," his father put in.

"All right, that's what happened," said the sheriff. "But what I want you to tell me is this. Why didn't you go back to the house and tell your father right away? Why did you go and pick peas for an hour?"

Arnold gazed over his shoulder at his father, expecting his father to have an answer for this also. But his father's eyes, larger and even lighter blue than usual, were fixed upon him curiously. Arnold picked at a callus in his right palm. It seemed odd now that he had not run back to the house and wakened his father, but he could not remember why he had not. They were all waiting for him to answer.

"I come down to pick peas," he said.

"Didn't you think," asked the sheriff, stepping carefully from word to word, "that it was more important for you to go tell your parents what had happened?"

"The sun was gonna come up," Arnold said.

"What's that got to do with it?"

"It's better to pick peas while they're cool."

The sheriff swung away from him, laid both hands flat on his desk. "Well, all I can say is," he said across to Arnold's father and Uncle Andy, "he's either a moron or he's so reasonable that he's way ahead of us." He gave a challenging snort. "It's come to my notice that the most reasonable guys are mean ones. They don't feel nothing."

For a moment the three men sat still. Then the sheriff lifted his hand like a man taking an oath. "Take him home," he said.

Andy uncrossed his legs. "You don't want him?"

"Not now," replied the sheriff. "Maybe in a few years."

Arnold's father stood up. He held his hat against his chest. "The gun ain't his no more," he said wanly.

Arnold went first through the hallway, hearing behind him the heels of his father and Uncle Andy striking the floorboards. He went down the steps ahead of them and climbed into the back seat of the car. Andy paused as he was getting into the front seat and gazed back at Arnold, and Arnold saw that his uncle's eyes had absorbed the knowingness from the sheriff's eyes. Andy and his father and the sheriff had discovered what made him go down into the garden. It was because he was cruel, the sheriff had said, and didn't care about his brother. Arnold lowered his eyelids meekly against his uncle's stare.

The rest of the day he did his tasks around the farm, keeping apart from the family. At evening, when he saw his father stomp tiredly into the house, Arnold did not put down his hammer and leave the chicken coop he was repairing. He was afraid that they did not want him to eat supper with them. But in a few minutes another fear that they would go to the trouble of calling him and that he would be made conspicuous by his tardiness made him follow his father into the house. As he went through the kitchen he saw the jars of peas standing in rows on the workbench, a reproach to him.

No one spoke at supper, and his mother, who sat next to him, leaned her head in her hand all through the meal, curving her fingers over her eyes so as not to see him. They were finishing their small, silent supper when the visitors began to arrive, knocking hard on the back door. The men were coming from their farms now that it was growing dark and they could not work anymore.

Old Man Matthews, gray and stocky, came first, with his two sons, Orion, the elder, and Clint, who was Eugie's age. As the callers entered the parlor where the family ate, Arnold sat down in a rocking chair. Even as he had been undecided before supper whether to remain outside or take his place at the table, he now thought that he should go upstairs, and yet he stayed to avoid being conspicuous by his absence. If he stayed, he thought, as he always stayed and listened when visitors came, they would see that he was only Arnold and not the person the sheriff thought he was. He sat with his arms crossed and his hands tucked into his armpits and did not lift his eyes.

The Matthews men had hardly settled down around the table, after Arnold's mother and Nora had cleared away the dishes, when another car rattled down the road and someone else rapped on the back door. This time it was Sullivan, a spare and sandy man, so nimble of gesture and expression that Arnold had never been able to catch more than a few of his meanings. Sullivan, in dusty jeans, sat down in another rocker, shot out his skinny legs and began to talk in his fast way, recalling everything that Eugene had ever said to him. The other men interrupted to tell of occasions they remembered, and after a time Clint's young voice, hoarse like Eugene's had been, broke in to tell about the time Eugene had beat him in a wrestling match.

Out in the kitchen the voices of Orion's wife and of Mrs. Sullivan mingled with Nora's voice but not, Arnold noticed, his mother's. Then dry little Mr. Cram came, leaving large Mrs. Cram in the kitchen, and there was no chair left for Mr. Cram to sit in. No one asked Arnold to get up and he was unable to rise. He knew that the story had got around to them during the day about how he had gone and picked peas after he had shot his brother, and he knew that although they were talking only about Eugie they were thinking about him and if he got up, if he moved even his foot, they would all be alerted. Then Uncle Andy arrived and leaned his tall lanky body against the doorjamb and there were two men standing.

Presently Arnold was aware that the talk had stopped. He knew without looking up that the men were watching him.

"Not a tear in his eye," said Andy, and Arnold knew that it was his uncle who had gestured the men to attention.

"He don't give a hoot, is that how it goes?" asked Sullivan, trippingly.

"He's a reasonable fellow," Andy explained, "That's what the sheriff said. It's us who ain't reasonable. If we'd of shot our brother, we'd of come runnin' back to the house, cryin' like a baby. Well, we'd of been unreasonable. What would of been the use of actin' like that? If your brother is shot dead, he's shot dead. What's the use of gettin' emotional about it? The thing to do is go down to the garden and pick peas. Am I right?"

The men around the room shifted their heavy, satisfying weight of unreasonableness.

Matthew's son Orion said: "If I'd of done what he done, Pa would've hung my pelt by the side of that big coyote's in the barn."

Arnold sat in the rocker until the last man had filed out. While his family was out in the kitchen bidding the callers good night and the cars were driving away down the dirt lane to the highway, he picked up one of the kerosene lamps and slipped quickly up the stairs. In his room he undressed by lamplight, although he and Eugie had always undressed in the dark, and not until he was lying in his bed did he blow out the flame. He felt nothing, not any grief. There was only the same immense silence and crawling inside of him; it was the way the house and fields felt under a merciless sun.

He awoke suddenly. He knew that his father was out in the yard, closing the doors of the chicken houses. The sound that had awakened him was the step of his father as he got up from the rocker and went down the back steps. And he knew that his mother was awake in her bed.

Throwing off the covers, he rose swiftly, went down the stairs and across the dark parlor to his parents' room. He rapped on the door.

"Mother?"

From the closed room her voice rose to him, a seeking and retreating voice. "Yes?"

"Mother?" he asked insistently. He had expected her to realize that he wanted to go down on his knees by her bed and tell her that Eugie was dead. She did not know it yet, nobody knew it, and yet she was sitting up in bed, waiting to be told, waiting for him to confirm her dread. He had expected her to tell him to come in, to allow him to dig his head into her blankets and tell her about the terror he had felt when he had knelt beside Eugie. He had come to clasp her in his arms and, in his terror, to pommel her breasts with his head. He put his hand upon the knob.

"Go back to bed, Arnold," she called sharply.

But he waited.

"Go back! Is night when you get afraid?"

At first he did not understand. Then, silently, he left the door and for a sticken moment stood by the rocker. Outside everything was still. The fences, the shocks of wheat seen through the window before him were so still it was as if they moved and breathed in the daytime and had fallen silent with the lateness of the hour. It was a silence that seemed to observe his father, a figure moving alone around the yard, his lantern casting a circle of light by his feet. In a few minutes his father would enter the dark house, the lantern still lighting his way.

Arnold was suddenly aware that he was naked. He had thrown off his blankets and come down the stairs to tell his mother how he felt about Eugie, but she had refused to listen to him and his nakedness had become unpardonable. At once he went back up the stairs, fleeing from his father's lantern.

At breakfast he kept his eyelids lowered as if to deny the humiliating night. Nora, sitting at his left, did not pass the pitcher of milk to him and he did not ask for it. He would never again, he vowed, ask them for anything, and he ate his fried eggs and potatoes only because everybody ate meals—the cattle ate, and the cats; it was customary for everybody to eat.

"Nora, you gonna keep that pitcher for yourself?" his father asked.

Nora lowered her head unsurely.

"Pass it on to Arnold," his father said.

Nora put her hands in her lap.

His father picked up the metal pitcher and set it down at Arnold's plate.

Arnold, pretending to be deaf to the discord, did not glance up, but relief rained over his shoulders at the thought that his parents recognized him again. They must have lain awake after his father had come in from the yard: had they realized together why he had come down the stairs and knocked at their door?

"Bessie's missin' this morning," his father called out to his mother, who had gone into the kitchen. "She went up to the mountain last night and had her calf, most likely. Somebody's got to go up and find her 'fore the coyotes get the calf."

That had been Eugie's job, Arnold thought. Eugie would climb the cattle trails in search of a newborn calf and come down the mountain carrying the calf across his back, with the cow running behind him, mooing in alarm.

Arnold ate the few more forkfuls of his breakfast, put his hands on the edge of the table and pushed back his chair. If he went for the calf he'd be away from the farm all morning. He could switch the cow down the mountain slowly, and the calf would run along at its mother's side.

When he passed through the kitchen his mother was setting a kettle of water on the stove. "Where you going?" she asked awkwardly.

"Up to get the calf," he replied, averting his face.

"Arnold?"

At the door he paused reluctantly, his back to her, knowing that she was seeking him out, as his father was doing, and he called upon his pride to protect him from them.

"Was you knocking at my door last night?"

He looked over his shoulder at her, his eyes narrow and dry.

"What'd you want?" she asked humbly.

"I didn't want nothing," he said flatly.

Then he went out the door and down the back steps, his legs trembling from the fright his answer gave him.

OLD MEN DREAM DREAMS, YOUNG MEN SEE VISIONS

John William Corrington

I tried to remember if I had ever felt better. No, I had not ever felt better. And I could remember. I was only fifteen. And I was driving alone in my father's 1941 Ford to pick up Helena.

It was the first time I had ever had the car alone. That was a victory. My mother had fenced, thrust, and parried with my father, who said I was too young, too wild, too inexperienced to take a girl out in a car. Later, he said. How much later, my mother asked. Be reasonable, my father said. That's right, my mother answered. Be reasonable. The girl expects him. In the car. Do you want to shame him? He can be degraded, humiliated and dishonored as far as I'm concerned, my father told her. My mother gave him a distant wintry smile, one of her specialties. Like an advocate cross-examining an unacknowledged embezzler or black marketeer. Be reasonable, she said with smooth earth-scouring irony.

—All right, my father shouted, turning to me at last, admitting that I was party to the contest—indeed, the plaintiff vindicated.—Take it. Take the goddamned thing. Go out. Wreck it. Cost me my job. Kill yourself.

And then he tossed me the keys.

I parked in front of Helena's. She lived off Creswell Avenue in a nice part of town with solid houses and large pleasant lawns. We had met at one of those teen-age dances sponsored by parents who took great stock in supervised activities. They were awful, except that you could meet girls. The day after, I had walked from Jesuit High over to the girls' school to catch her as classes finished in the afternoon. It was a long walk—no, it was a run, because she got out at the same time I did and they would expect her home within an hour. Her parents were very strict, she had told me at the dance.

So when she came upon me as she walked up Kings Highway, she smiled with delight, and wordlessly we walked past Fairfield, past Line Avenue and down the shallow hill that ran alongside Byrd High School, where the Protestants went, and where eventually I would go when the Jesuits determined that I was bound to end badly, indeed, already bore a bad name. We reached Creswell and slowed down. I took her hand. We stopped at the little bayou where the street dipped, where water stood several feet deep in the road after a heavy rain. We looked down at the brown water and she asked me what kind of fish might live in there. Before I could answer, she realized that we had walked a block past her house. She grinned and lowered her eyes as if admitting to an indiscretion. I shrugged and did not admit knowing all the time that we had passed that fatal street, ransoming ten precious minutes more by my pretense.

We met and walked so almost every day unless the weather was very bad and her mother drove to the school to pick her up. At last, one day, Helena asked me to come home with her to meet her mother. It was a beautifully furnished house, done in what I know now to have been good unobtrusive taste, though strongly feminine. Today I would put such a furnished house down as the work of a moderately talented interior decorator. But in 1949, I doubt that it was. People in Shreveport then had more substantial vices. They had not yet come to the contrefaction of sophistication.

As I waited for Helena to find her mother back in the unknown regions of the house, I stood caught up in a net of feelings that I had never experienced before. I saw Helena's round, bright, unremarkable face, her quick excited smile. I conjured her body, her slender legs and ankles. Sexuality was the least of it. That part was good and without complications because it was no more than an imagining, a vague aura that played around the person of every girl I met without settling into a realizable conception. Because then it seemed that an actual expression of unconcealed desire would surely smash itself and me against an invisible but real obstacle as unsettling as the sound barrier. No, it was something else that made me raise my arms and spread them as I smiled into a gold-framed mirror there in the foyer. I loved someone. It was a feeling composed and balanced between heights and depths that flared through me, leaving me exultant and ready for new things in the midst of a profound and indeterminate sadness. I looked at myself quizzically, arms akimbo, hair badly finger-combed. Was it the one or the other? Neither my own emotional history nor the mind that Jesuits had already forged in me had warned of ambivalence. It was disquieting and thrilling, somehow better than certainty. It was a victory taken from the flood of moments I lived but could not order. But even as I studied the physical shape of love in my face, I saw in the mirror, watching me from the parlor, a small face, serious, almost suffering, the face of a tiny Cassandra mute and miserable. For just an instant I thought insanely that it was Helena creeping up behind me on her knees. I was hot with embarrassment, chilled by something less personal, more sinister, as if a shard of some tomorrow had fallen inexplicably into the present. But the tiny disturbed copy of Helena's face vanished and I stood alone again fumbling a dog-eared Latin reader filled with the doings of Caesar.

Helena's mother was neat, attractive. The very picture of an efficient mother and housewife. Her eyes were dark, her face unlined in that metastatic poise of a woman who had passed forty by chronology but remains for months or a year as she must have been at thirty. She met me graciously, prepared Cokes for the three of us, and introduced me to Helena's small sister. I recognized the wraith in the foyer mirror. She did indeed look like Helena. Only without the smile, without the capacity to be excited and filled by a moment. I tousled her hair patronizingly, seeing in her eyes even as I did so a look that might have meant either *I know what you're really like*—or *help*.

It was a few days later that I asked Helena for a date. I had had a few dates before: humiliating affairs where my father drove me to the girl's house, took us to a movie, then came back and took us home afterward. But this would be different. This would be my first real date. And with someone I loved.

When I reached her house it was already dark. The air was chill. It was November, and the wind swept across my face as I opened the old car's door. Her porch light burned beyond the trees like an altar candle and I moved from the car toward it, key in my hand like power, into the circle of weak light close to Helena. When I rang, it was her mother who opened the door. Even entranced by the current of my triumphs and the size of coming pleasure, I noticed that her smile was forced. Had she had a tiring day? Or had she heard ill of me somewhere? That was possible. I had already the first stirrings of a bad name in certain Shreveport circles. But I forgot her expression as she introduced me to her husband, Helena's father.

He stood up heavily, a short red-faced man without charm or presence. He had reddish hair and that odd parti-colored complexion of certain redheaded farmers I knew who were most sensitive to the sun and yet obliged by their calling to work under it always. He looked at me as if I had come to clean the drains and was for some reason he could not fathom intruding into his parlor.

He shook hands with me perfunctorily and began at once to give me instructions as to where Helena and I might go, where we couldn't go. He brushed aside an attempt by his wife to make conversation and continued, making certain that I knew the time Helena was to be home. Eleven o'clock. He asked me to repeat the time back to him. I did so automatically, paying little attention because as he spoke I could make out the rank smell of whiskey on his breath, as if every word he uttered were being propelled up from his spreading shirtfront by the borrowed force of alcohol. As he went on talking, he looked not at me but past me toward the door, as if the effort of actually seeing me was more than he could bear. I stood silent, glancing at his wife. She was gnawing at the corner of her lip and looking down the hall toward the back of the house. At the edge of the dark hall I thought I could see, dim and distant, the face of Helena's little sister.

Then Helena came. She was dressed in a pale red woolen suit, high heels, a piece of gold jewelry like a bird of paradise on her shoulder. Her father turned from me, studied her, and said nothing. There was a flurry of last words and we were outside walking toward the car. As soon as the door closed, our hands met and clasped. We said nothing because both of us were back in the foyer of her house, the tension, her father and mother, vanished, annulled, decomposed by the look that had passed between us as we saw each other. We had sensed the whole garden of possibilities into which we were about to step. She came from her room assuming a schoolboy awaited her, only to find a slightly nervous young man in a sports jacket standing before her father armed with the key to an ancient car. I had been waiting for a girl but a young woman came to meet me. What joined us then, a current of our spirits, was all the stronger because neither of us had ever felt it flow forth to meet its counterpart before.

We reached the car. As I slid under the wheel, I turned to Helena. She was looking at me and her hand moved to meet mine again. We sat for a long moment until, embarrassed by the weight of our feeling, we drew apart and I started the car. Helena noticed that the inner door handle on her side was missing.

—That's to keep you in, I tried to joke, suddenly ashamed of my father's old car, seeing for the first time its shabbiness, the dusty dashboard, the stained head lining.

—I don't want to get out. Except with you, Helena said, her eyes large, the beginning of a smile on her lips.

For a while we drove, I headed in toward the city, driving up Highland Avenue past Causey's Music Shop, where I had learned the wherewithal of my bad name. I played trumpet every so often in a roadhouse across the Red River in Bossier Parish. It was called the Skyway Club and had bad name enough to splotch any number of fifteen-year-olds who could talk Earl Blessey, the band leader, into letting them limp through a chorus of "Blue Prelude" or "Georgia on my Mind." Before the Skyway Club and I were done with each other, I would have lost and gained things there enough to be worth any number of bad names.

We drove into downtown and looked at the marquees of the Don and Strand theaters.

—What would you like to see, I asked Helena.

—I don't think I want to go to the movies, she said.

—What would you like to do?

—Could we . . . just go somewhere? And talk?

—Sure, I said. We could go to the Ming Tree over in Bossier . . . No, your father . . .

—Why don't we just go out to the lake?

As I turned the car, I reached for her shoulder and drew her close to me. The lake was where people went when they had no reason to waste time with football games or movies. They went there to be alone, to construct within their cars apartments, palaces, to be solitary and share one another for a few hours.

Cross Lake was cold and motionless, a bright sheet under the autumn stars. Around us, trees rustled in the light breeze. But we were warm and I lit a cigarette and listened to Helena talk. She told me that she was sorry about her father. I said it was nothing. He was only thinking of her. He didn't know me. No, she said, he was thinking of himself. He drank at night. He sat drinking in the parlor, talking to himself, cursing his wife and the children sometimes. Sometimes it was worse than that. She said she wanted me to know. Because if I were to think less of her . . .

—That's crazy, I said, turning her to face me. And we kissed.

It would not surprise me to find that moment, that kiss, the final indelible sensation last to fade from my mind as I lie dying. Not because I am sentimental. I have used and misused kisses and promises, truths and lies, honor and fraud and violence as the years moved on. That world where I knew Helena recedes from me more rapidly each day, each year, shifting red with the sting of its velocity, but never vanishing, its mass increasing in my soul toward infinity as, one who has managed the world as it is better than well, I am subtle enough to recover those fragments from the past which at the moment of their transaction were free from plan or prophecy or the well-deep cynicism of one who recognizes the piquancy of an apparently innocent moment precisely because he knows not only that it will not, cannot last, but because he has long before taken that fragility, that ephemeral certainty, into account in order to enjoy his instant all the more.

And so I remember that kiss. It was well-done. Our lips fused, moving together as if contained in them was the sum of our bodies. Without the conscious thought of sex we achieved a degree of sensuality unmatched in all the embraces I had still to seek or to endure.

—I love you, I told her.

—You can't mean it, she said.

We kissed again and then sat looking at the water, each of us touched beyond speech. We held ourselves close and sent our happiness, our

193

exultation, out to move among the pines, over the water, toward the cold observant stars, keeping a time of their own. We sat that way for a long while.

In retrospect the appearances of banality are simple to determine. But the fact of it was not present between us that night. Banality presumes a certain self-consciousness, a kind of déjà vu, a realization explicit or implied that what one is doing has values other than those which seem. Or that certain values are missing. There must be a sly knowledge that the game in hand is not only not worth the candle, but hardly worth striking the match.

But Helena and I knew nothing then but each other and the shape of our victory. We were not repeating for the tenth or even the second time a ritual tarnished in its parts and lethally sure in its conclusion. We had for this moment conquered chance and youth, our fathers, the traps and distances laid for us. We were alone beside Cross Lake and no one on earth knew where we were. We belonged to ourselves, to each other. We did not know that neither of us, together or apart, would ever find this time and place, find each other like this again. It will always be exactly like this, we would have thought. Had we thought. It was not banal. The rest of our lives might be so, but not tonight.

Tonight we told each other of our troubles and our hopes. We said, each in a different way, that our fathers made us unhappy. That one day we would leave Shreveport, journey to London and Paris, to the farthest places we could imagine. Only now, after tonight, we would go together. We talked about much more, words cascading over each other as we exchanged all that we had been and done apart, all we planned and wished for together. Until, amidst a moment of silence, a pause for breath, Helena looked at her watch.

—Oh God, she gasped, her face stricken.

—It's . . .

We're going to be late . . . ?

—It's . . . almost four o'clock. In the morning.

We stared at each other. I lit a match and looked at her watch. It was eight minutes to four. I closed my eyes. We were supposed to be home by eleven. Even my father would be aroused, knowing that I wasn't at the Skyway Club with Earl. I tried not to think about Helena's father but his squat body, his nearly angry face, rose in my mind again and again like a looped strip of film.

—O God, I do love you, Helena said.

We kissed again, touched, embraced. Her nylon-covered legs rose and touched my body. My hand found her breasts. None of this had we intended. The fruit of the tree in that garden we entered was the knowledge of time, of duration: time past, time lost. Even then, in those hysterical seconds, we were trying not so much to hasten passage from recognition to fulfillment as to claim what we might before it was too late, before we were separated and everything died.

But we stopped. We were not brave enough. We were too wise. We could not bring ourselves to wager what we had found against the sullen covenant of all our fathers. We kissed one last time hastily and I started the car, the beginning of an anguish inside me even as my heart beat insanely from her touch.

I cut the engine and coasted up in front of Helena's house. It seemed as if I had not seen it in centuries. Inside, many lights were on and I could see that the front door was a little ajar. Helena turned to me and touched my arm. I could see that there were tears on her cheeks, and the anguish grew.

—Go on, she said. Don't come up to the house with me. He'll be awful, really . . .

—No, I said without thought. I'm going to take you to the door.

I was not frightened, only apprehensive. I had been in too many hassles to spook before the event. There was always time to flush, sometimes only a second or two but always time. Anyhow, I had that fifty-yard walk to make, I knew. My bad name did not include cowardice, at least not of the overt and measurable kind. More important, there would be nothing left if I drove away, left the field and Helena upon it to her father. Our triumph would dwindle to an absurdity. I was not yet old enough to weigh those things against reality. What we had found in each other was real, I thought. And I was not a boy any longer. What you do not defend, you cannot keep: the oldest of all rules.

We walked toward the lights. Out of our world back into theirs. We did not walk hand in hand and later I would wonder how much of the future had been bent around that smallest of omissions. As we reached the door we could hear Helena's father. He was now very drunk and he was cursing and bullying her mother.

. . . nice. Oh yes, Jesus son of God what do you reckon he's done . . . my baby. That little bastard. Telling her it's all right, taking off her . . . clothes . . .

I closed my eyes and blushed as if I were guilty of it all and more. Helena looked down at the concrete steps. Then she pushed open the door and stepped into the foyer to forestall any more of his raving.

—Hello, everybody, she said loudly, almost brightly, in that tone she used to greet me when we met after school each day.

Her father whirled about, his face red, thick, inarticulate with anger. Standing just behind Helena, I could not quite see the look that passed between them but it seemed to me that she nearly smiled, pale and upset as she was.

—Get to your room, her father spat out, swaying from side to side as he moved toward us. Toward me. No, don't say anything. I'll see to you later.

Helena's mother shook her head and signaled Helena to go, to leave it alone. But Helena wasn't ready.

—No, I want to say . . .

But her father pushed her out of the way roughly in order to face me. Her mother stepped forward behind him and took her from the foyer. She was beginning to cry.

—What did you do, he rasped. Where did you take her? What kind of dirt . . .

He clenched his fists in front of my face. I thought oddly that he could smash me to pieces easily. But for some reason the realization meant nothing.

—We talked, I said. —I'm sorry we . . .

—Talked? You liar . . . you . . .

Helena's mother, her face anxious, truly frightened, came back into the foyer. She touched her husband's arm. He shook her off. Now he was swaying, blinking.

—Nothing happened, I said, considering the immensity of that lie.

—I think you'd better go now, Bill, Helena's mother said, motioning me toward the door with her anxious eyes.

I started to say something more, but I could think of nothing more to say. Then I backed toward the door, too old by far in the ways of Caddo and Bossier Parishes to show my back to a drunk who held a score against me, a blood score. The occasions of my bad name had made me cautious. Before I reached the door, there in the gloom of the dark hallway I saw, dressed in a long nightgown, the figure of Helena's little sister. Her face was pinched and no larger than an orange, it seemed. Her eyes were wide with excitement and certainty.

As I stepped outside, Helena's father, who had followed me with his inflamed eyes, began to weep. He twisted his fists into his eyes, his shoulders quaking. He turned to his wife, who looked after me one last time and then gave her attention to her husband, who leaned against her like a child swallowed in the skirts of its mother. Behind, the little girl stood alone, one hand pressed against that duplicate of Helena's face.

—My little girl, her father sobbed, as if he knew Helena to be dead. —My baby . . .

I turned then and breathed deeply, walking slowly toward the black mass of my father's sequestered Ford. I stopped at the car door and looked back at Helena's house under two cedar trees, dwarfed by a sweep of sky pricked with distant stars. I breathed again, taking in the chill early-morning air like one who stares down from some great height at the place where his lover sleeps or the field where his enemy lies broken. Then, full of some large uncertain joy, I sat down in the old car and jammed the ignition key home.

HANDLING
QUOTATIONS

HANDLING QUOTATIONS

Integrating Quotations

A convincing essay on a literary work almost always makes extensive use of illustrative quotations. Such quotations—whether single words, phrases, clauses, sentences, or entire passages—constitute your "evidence"; they are the specific and concrete "facts" which you use to bolster and clarify your interpretation of the work. As such, it is essential that they be handled skillfully.

The basic principle governing the skillful handling of illustrative quotations is that they be smoothly *integrated* with your own sentences. The way to achieve such smooth integration is to think of an illustrative quotation as *part of a sentence you want to write.* A quotation should not be something separate, independent, unamalgamated. Rather, it should be fitted into and made an integral part of a sentence of your own composing.

You can achieve such smooth integration by employing one of the following structures:

1.   "_____quote_____"   _____your words_____ .

2.   _____your words_____ "_____quote_____ ."

3.   _____your words_____ "_____quote_____"   _____your words_____ .

4.   _____your words_____ :
        _____quote_____
        _____quote_____
        _____quote_____
        _____quote_____
        _____quote_____ .

The various sample essays in this book provide numerous examples of these four techniques for handling quoted material smoothly. We will illustrate each technique with representative examples and comment on the special features of each.

Technique 1: <u>"   quote   "   your words   .</u>

Example: " 'How extraordinary!' " Rosemary cries, as though abject poverty were a sort of diverting condition to be marvelled at, much like a curiously-designed ring or strange-looking hat.

Comment: This technique works best with relatively short quotations. Notice that Rosemary's exclamation, though punctuated as a complete sentence in the short story, is integrated into the sentence above; it is not allowed to stand separately.

Technique 2: <u>   your words   "   quote   ."</u>

Examples: When Pepé turns into the mountains, the country become "more rough and terrible and dry."

With Sullivan's fate before him, Rob has come to recognize that "nothing really matters except not being old and being alive and having potential to dream about, and not being alone."

Comment: This technique can be used to integrate longer quotations (up to four lines), since the quoted material completes the sentence smoothly and naturally.

Technique 3: <u>   your words   " quote "   your words   .</u>

Examples: Soon, however, this mood is shattered by a "hollow pounding" on the trail, and the horseman rides by.

The "wind of fear" generated by the galloping horseman may well have "bitten dead" the heights of Pepé's confidence and security.

Comment: This technique is especially useful for integrating one or more brief quotations—single words or short phrases.

Technique 4: <u>   your words   :</u>

<u>   quote   </u>
<u>   quote   </u>
<u>   quote   </u>
<u>   quote   </u>
<u>   quote   .</u>

Example: The landscape continues to deteriorate until, in the end, it is virtually lifeless:

Below him lay a deep canyon exactly like the last, waterless and desolate. There was no flat, no oak trees, not even heavy brush in the bottom of it. And on the other side a sharp ridge stood up, thinly brushed with starving sage, littered with broken granite. Strewn over the hill there were giant outcroppings, and on the top the granite teeth stood out against the sky.

Comment: Generally speaking, a prose quotation of five lines or more and a poetry quotation of three lines or more should be *extracted*, as in the example above. When you *extract* a quotation, you indent it and type it single spaced, keeping the punctuation exactly the same as in the original.

Unless your instructor indicates otherwise, you should feel free to extract shorter quotations (single lines of poetry, two or more lines of prose), if doing so will enhance clarity and readability.

Punctuating Quotations

Ellipses. An ellipsis is simply a mark (three spaced periods, ". . .") indicating omission of words or letters. The ellipsis mark should *not* be used before or after obvious fragments, such as single words and phrases. Nor is it needed if you are quoting one or more *complete* sentences. Instead, use the ellipsis mark to indicate omission of words from the middle of a quoted sentence and the omission of words at the beginning or end of a quoted sentence.

If you extract a poetry quotation, and omit one or more lines, use a row of spaced periods to indicate the omission:

> Go by brooks, love,
> . . . .
> I will pass there.   (See p. 77)

Single quotation marks When you quote a passage which has double quotation marks around it, you should reduce those original double marks to single quotation marks, unless you *extract* the quoted passage (see "Technique 4," above).

Original: He was extraordinarily fond of saying: "I am really a cut above being a building superintendent. Circumstances made me what I am."

Quoted: "He was extraordinarily fond of saying: 'I am really a cut above being a building superintendent. Circumstances made me what I am.'"

Brackets Square brackets (never parentheses) are used to enclose words that you add *within* a quoted passage. When typing, you can use two squared off slashes, /like this/ .

202

Original: He was extraordinarily fond of saying: "I am really a cut above being a building superintendent."

Quoted, with brackets: "He /¯James Sullivan¯/ was extraordinarily fond of saying: 'I am really a cut above being a building superintendent.'"

Slash marks A slash is used to separate lines of poetry when the lines are run into the text.

Original: Ah, love, let us be true
                To one another!

Quoted in text: "Ah, love, let us be true/To one another!"

End of quotation punctuation

1. Periods and commas are always placed *inside* the closing quotation mark.

2. Colons and semicolons are always placed *outside* the closing quotation mark.

3. A question mark is placed *inside* the closing quotation mark if the question mark is part of the quotation. If the question mark is not part of the quotation, it is placed *outside* the quotation mark.

A Note on Documentation

Documentation refers to the procedure by which writers cite the sources for ideas, information, and quotations not their own. You will notice that the illustrative quotations in the sample essays in this text are undocumented. Since the essays are meant to be read in conjunction with the work analyzed, we felt documentation was unnecessary. However, before writing your own critical essays, you should ask your instructor about the documentation system he or she would like for you to use.

GLOSSARY

GLOSSARY

Aesthetic Distance: A term applied by critics to describe the effect produced when an emotion or an experience, whether autobiographical or not, is so objectified by the proper use of form that it can be understood as being objectively realized and independent of the immediate personal experience of its maker. It is closely related to T. S. Eliot's OBJECTIVE CORRELATIVE.

Alliteration: The repetition of initial identical consonant sounds or any vowel sounds in successive or closely associated words or syllables. A good example of consonantal *alliteration* is Coleridge's lines:

> The fair breeze blew, the white foam flew,
> The furrow followed free.

Vowel *alliteration* is shown in the sentence: "Apt alliteration's artful aid is often an occasional ornament in prose." *Alliteration* of syllables within words appears in Tennyson's lines:

> The *m*oan of doves in *imm*em*m*orial el*m*s,
> And *m*ur*m*uring of innu*m*erable bees.

Old English versification rested in large measure on *alliteration*, as did much Middle English poetry. In modern times *alliteration* has usually been a secondary ornament in both verse and prose, although poets as unlike as Whitman, Swinburne, and W. H. Auden have made extensive and skillful use of it. In our time it has become the stock in trade of the sports writer and the advertising copy writer, in whose hands it often produces the ludicrous effects that Shakespeare mocked in Quince's "Prologue" in *A Midsummer Night's Dream:*

> Whereat, with blade, with bloody blameful blade,
> He bravely broach'd his boiling bloody breast.

Allusion: A rhetorical term applied to that figure of speech making casual reference to a famous historical or literary figure or event.

The definitions of critical terms that appear in this glossary are from *A Handbook to Literature* by William Field Thrall, Addison Hibbard and C. Hugh Holman, copyright © 1936, 1960, 1972 by the Odyssey Press, Inc., reprinted by permission of The Bobbs-Merrill Company, Inc. We recommend this excellent handbook to the serious student of literature.

> I know not where is that *Promethean heat*
> That can thy light relume.
>
> —Shakespeare

Biblical *allusions* are common in English literature, such as Shakespeare's "A Daniel come to judgment," in *The Merchant of Venice*. Complex literary *allusion* is characteristic of much modern poetry; a good example is T. S. Eliot's *The Waste Land* and the author's notes to the poem.

Ambiguity: The expression of an idea in language of such a nature as to give more than one meaning and to leave uncertainty as to the true significance of the statement. *Ambiguity* may be intentional, as when one wishes to evade a direct reply (see Juliet's replies to her mother in Act III, Scene 5, of Shakespeare's *Romeo and Juliet*). The chief causes of *ambiguity* are undue brevity and compression of statement, "cloudy" reference of pronoun, faulty or inverted (poetical) sequence, and the use of a word with two or more meanings.

However, in literature of the highest order may be found another aspect of *ambiguity* which results from the fact that language functions in art on other levels than that of communication, where *ambiguity* is a cardinal sin. In literature words demonstrate an astounding capacity for suggesting two or more equally suitable senses in a given context, for conveying a core meaning and accompanying it with overtones of great richness and complexity, and for operating with two or more meanings at the same time. One of the attributes of the finest poets is their ability to tap what I. A. Richards has called the "resourcefulness of language" and to supercharge words with great pressures of meaning. The kind of *ambiguity* which results from this capacity of words to stimulate simultaneously several different streams of thought all of which make sense is a genuine characteristic of the richness and concentration that makes great poetry.

William Empson, in *The Seven Types of Ambiguity*, in 1931 extended and enriched the meaning of the term to include these aspects of language. Although there have been those who feel that another word than *ambiguity* should be used for these characteristics of language functioning with artistic complexity, Empson's "seven types" of linguistic complexity "which adds some nuance to the direct statement of prose" have proved to be effective tools for the examination of literature. These "types of *ambiguity*" are (1) details of language which are effective in several ways at once; (2) alternative meanings that are ultimately resolved into the one meaning of the author; (3) two seemingly unconnected meanings that are given in one word; (4) alternative meanings that act together to clarify a complicated state of mind in the author; (5) a simile that refers imperfectly to two incompatible things and by this "fortunate confusion" shows the author discovering his idea as he writes; (6) a statement that is so contradictory or irrelevant that the reader is made to invent his own interpretation; and (7) a statement so fundamentally contradictory that it reveals a basic division in the author's mind.

207

Analogy: A comparison of two things, alike in certain respects; particularly a method of exposition by which one unfamiliar object or idea is explained by comparing it in certain of its similarities with other objects or ideas more familiar. In argumentation and logic *analogy* is also frequently used to establish contentions, it being argued, for instance, that since A works certain results, B, which is like A in vital respects, will also accomplish the same results. *Analogy*, however, is often a treacherous weapon since few *different* objects or ideas are essentially the *same* to more than a superficial observer or thinker.

Atmosphere: The prevailing tone or mood of a literary work, particularly—but not exclusively—when that mood is established in part by setting or landscape. It is, however, not simply setting but rather the emotional aura which the work bears and which establishes the reader's expectations and attitudes. Examples are the sombre mood established by the description of the prison door in the opening chapter of Hawthorne's *The Scarlet Letter*, the brooding sense of fatality engendered by the description of Egdon Heath at the beginning of Hardy's *The Return of the Native*, the sense of "something rotten in the state of Denmark" established by the scene on the battlements at the opening of *Hamlet*, or the more mechanical but still effective opening stanza of Poe's "The Raven."

Ballad: A form of verse adapted for singing or recitation and primarily characterized by its presentation in simple narrative form of a dramatic or exciting episode. A famous definition is that of F. B. Gummere who describes the *ballad* as "a poem meant for singing, quite impersonal in material, probably connected in its origins with the communal dance, but submitted to a process of oral tradition among people who are free from literary influences and fairly homogeneous in character." Though the *ballad* is a form still much written, the so-called "popular *ballad*" in most literatures properly belongs to the early periods before written literature was highly developed. They still develop, however, in isolated sections and among illiterate and semi-literate peoples. In America the folk of the southern Appalachian mountains have maintained a *ballad* tradition, as have the cowboys of the western plains, and people associated with labor movements, particularly when they were marked by violence. In Australia the "bush" *ballad* is still vigorous and popular. In the West Indies the "Calypso" singers produce something close to the *ballad* with their impromptu songs. Debate still rages as to whether the *ballad* originates with an individual composer or as a group or communal activity. Whatever the origin, it is true that the folk *ballad* is, in almost every country, one of the earliest forms of literature. Certain common characteristics of these early *ballads* should be noted: the supernatural is likely to play an important part in events, physical courage and love are frequent themes, the incidents are usually such as happen to common people (as opposed to the nobility) and often have to do with domestic episodes; slight attention is paid to characterization or description, transitions are abrupt, action is largely developed through dialogue, tragic situations are presented with the utmost simplicity, incremental repetition is common, imagination though not so common as in the art ballad nevertheless appears in brief flashes, a single episode of highly dramatic nature is presented, and, often enough, the *ballad* is brought to a close with some sort of summary STANZA. The greatest impetus to the study of *ballad* literature was given by the publication in 1765 of Bishop Percy's *Reliques of Ancient English Poetry*. The standard modern collection is *The English and Scottish Popular Ballads* edited by Francis James Child.

Characterization: In the lyric, the essay, and the autobiography, the author reveals aspects of his own character; in the biography and the history, he presents the characters of actual persons other than himself; and in fiction (the drama, the novel, the short story, and the narrative poem), he reveals the characters of imaginary persons. The creation of images of these imaginary persons so credible that they exist for the reader as real within the limits of the fiction is called *characterization*. The ability to characterize the people of his imagination successfully is one of the primary attributes of a good novelist, dramatist, or short-story writer.

There are three fundamental methods of *characterization* in fiction: (1) the explicit presentation by the author of the character through direct exposition, either in an introductory block or more often piece-meal throughout the work, illustrated by action; (2) the presentation of the character in action, with little or no explicit comment by the author, in the expectation that the reader will be able to deduce the attributes of the actor from the actions; and (3) the representation from within a character, without comment on the character by the author, of the impact of actions and emotions upon his inner self, with the expectation that the reader will come to a clear understanding of the attributes of the character.

It is difficult to distinguish among these methods of *characterization* without discussing them in terms of narrative POINT OF VIEW. Usually the explicit method results when the story is told by a first-person NARRATOR, such as Dickens' David Copperfield or Sterne's Tristram Shandy, or by an omniscient author, such as Fielding in *Tom Jones* or Thackeray in *Vanity Fair*. The success of the explicit method of *characterization* rests at least in part upon the personality of the NARRATOR or omniscient author. The presentation of characters through actions is essentially the dramatic method. It is the traditional way of establishing character in the drama; so much so, in fact, that only by changing some of the dramatic conventions, as in the use of a chorus, or Expressionism, or in plays like O'Neill's *Strange Interlude*, can other methods of *characterization* than this be used in the theater. We know Hamlet through what he says and does; the riddle of what Shakespeare intended his true character to be is eternally unanswerable. The novel and the short story in this century have frequently adopted the dramatic technique by making objective presentations of characters in action without authorial comment, to such an extent that the self-effacing author is today a fictional commonplace. Writers of the realistic novel, such as Bennett, Galsworthy, and Howells, usually

209

employ this method of character presentation. The presentation of the impact upon the PROTAGONIST's inner self of external events and emotions begins with the novels of Henry James, whose *The Ambassadors* is an excellent example, and continues into the stream of consciousness novel where, through interior monologues, the subconscious or unconscious mind of the character is revealed, as in Joyce's *Ulysses* or Faulkner's *The Sound and the Fury.*

But regardless of the method by which a character is presented, the author may concentrate upon a dominant trait to the exclusion of the other aspects of the character's personality or he may attempt to present a fully rounded personality. If the presentation of a single dominant trait is carried to an extreme, not a believable character but a caricature will result. If this method is handled with skill, it can produce two-dimensional characters that are striking and interesting but lack depth. Mr. Micawber in *David Copperfield* comes close to being such a two-dimensional character through the emphasis that Dickens puts upon a very small group of characteristics. Sometimes such characters are given descriptive names, such as Mr. Deuceace, the gambler in *Vanity Fair.* On the other hand the author may present us with so convincing a congeries of personality traits that a complex rather than a simple character emerges; such a character is three-dimensional or, in E. M. Forster's term, "round." As a rule, the major characters in a fiction need such three-dimensional treatment, while minor characters are often handled two-dimensionally.

Furthermore, a character may be either static or dynamic. A STATIC CHARACTER is one who changes little if at all in the progress of the narrative. Things happen *to* such a character, without things happening *within* him. The pattern of action reveals the character rather than showing the character changing in response to the actions. Sometimes a STATIC CHARACTER gives the appearance of changing simply because our picture of him is revealed bit by bit; this is true of Uncle Toby in *Tristram Shandy,* who does not change, although our view of him steadily changes. A dynamic character, on the other hand, is one who is modified by the actions through which he passes, and one of the objectives of the work in which he appears is to reveal the consequences of these actions upon him. Most great dramas and novels have dynamic characters as PROTAGONISTS. Short stories are more likely to reveal STATIC CHARACTERS through action than to show changes in characters resulting from actions.

Ultimately every successful character represents a fusion of the universal and the particular and becomes an example of the concrete universal. It is in this dramatic particularization of the typical and universal that one of the essences of the dramatic and of *characterization* is to be found. Our minds may delight in abstractions and ideas, but it is our emotions that ultimately give the aesthetic and dramatic response, and they respond to the personal, the particular, the concrete. This is why a novel speaks to us more permanently than an allegory, why Hamlet has an authority forever lacking the "Indecisive Man" in a seventeenth-century character.

Cliché: From the French word for a stereotype plate; a block for printing. Hence any expression so often used that its freshness and clearness have worn off is called a *cliché,* a stereotyped form. Some examples are: "bigger and better," "loomed on the horizon," "the light fantastic," "stood like a sentinel," "sadder but wiser."

Climax: In rhetoric a term used to indicate the arrangement of words, phrases, and clauses in sentences in such a way as to form a rising order of importance in the ideas expressed. Such an arrangement is called climactic and the item of greatest importance is called the *climax.* Originally the term meant such an arrangement of succeeding clauses that the last important word in one is repeated as the first important word in the next, each succeeding clause rising in intensity or importance.

In larger pieces of composition—the essay, the short story, the drama, or the novel—the *climax* is the point of highest interest, the point at which the reader makes his greatest emotional response. The term used in this sense is an index of emotional response in the reader or the spectator. However, in dramatic structure *climax* is a term used to designate the turning point in the action, the place at which the rising action reverses and becomes the falling action. In Freytag's five-part view of dramatic structure, the *climax* is the third part or third act. Both narrative fiction and drama have tended to move the *climax,* both in the sense of turning action and in that of highest response, nearer the end of the work and thus have produced structures less symmetrical than those that follow Freytag's pyramid. In speaking of dramatic structure, the term *climax* is synonymous with crisis. However, crisis is used exclusively in the sense of STRUCTURE, whereas *climax* is used as a synonym for crisis *and* as a description of the intensity of interest in the reader or spectator. In this latter sense *climax* sometimes occurs at other points than at the crisis.

Conflict: The struggle which grows out of the interplay of the two opposing forces in a PLOT. It is *conflict* which provides the elements of interest and suspense in any form of fiction, whether it be a drama, a novel, or a short story. At least one of the opposing forces is usually a person, or, if an animal or an inanimate object, is treated as though it were a person. This person, usually the PROTAGONIST, may be involved in *conflicts* of four different kinds: (1) he may struggle against the forces of nature, as in Jack London's "To Build a Fire"; (2) he may struggle against another person, usually the antagonist, as in Stevenson's *Treasure Island* and most melodrama; (3) he may struggle against society as a force, as in the novels of Dickens and George Eliot; or (4) two elements within him may struggle for mastery, as in the Restoration heroic drama or in *Macbeth.* A fifth possible kind of *conflict* is often cited, the struggle against Fate or destiny; however, except where the gods themselves actively appear, such a struggle is realized through the action of one or more of the four basic

211

conflicts. Seldom do we find a simple, single *conflict* in a PLOT, but rather a complex one partaking of two or even all the elements given above. For example, the basic *conflict* in *Hamlet* may be interpreted to be a struggle within Hamlet himself, but it is certainly also a struggle against his uncle as antagonist, and, if the Freudian interpretations of motive are accepted, even a struggle against nature. Dreiser's *Sister Carrie* records a girl's struggle against society, as represented by the city, and yet it is a struggle against her basic nature and even partly within herself. Even so seemingly simple a story as London's "To Build a Fire," in which the PROTAGONIST battles the cold unsuccessfully, is also the record of an inner *conflict.* The term *conflict* not only implies the struggle of a PROTAGONIST against someone or something, it also implies the existence of some motivation for the *conflict* or some goal to be achieved by it. *Conflict* is the raw material out of which PLOT is constructed. See PLOT, PROTAGONIST.

Connotation: The cluster of implications that words or phrases may carry with them, as distinguished from their denotative meanings. Connotations may be (1) private and personal, the result of individual experience, (2) group (national, linguistic, racial), or (3) general or universal, held by all or most men. The scientist and the philosopher attempt to hold words to their denotative meanings; the literary artist relies upon *connotation* to carry his deepest meanings. See DENOTATION, AMBIGUITY.

Denotation: The specific, exact meaning of a word, independent of its emotional coloration or associations. See CONNOTATION.

Dénouement: The final unraveling of the PLOT in drama or fiction; the solution of the mystery; the explanation or outcome. *Dénouement* implies an ingenious untying of the knot of an intrigue, involving not only a satisfactory outcome of the main situation but an explanation of all the secrets and misunderstandings connected with the plot complication. In drama *dénouement* may be applied to both TRAGEDY and comedy, though the common term for a tragic *dénouement* is catastrophe. The final scene of Shakespeare's *Cymbeline* is a striking example of how clever and involved a dramatic *dénouement* may be: exposure of villain, clearing up of mistaken identities and disguises, reuniting of father and children, of husband and wife, etc., etc. By some writers *dénouement* is used as a synonym for falling action.

Dialogue: Conversation of two or more people as reproduced in writing. Most common in fiction, particularly in dramas, novels, and short stories, *dialogue* is nevertheless used in general expository and philosophical writing (Plato). An analysis of *dialogue* as it has been employed by great writers shows that it embodies certain literary and stylistic values: (1) It advances the action in a definite way and is not used as mere ornamentation. (2) It is consistent with the character of the speakers, their social positions and special interests. It varies in tone and expression according to the nationalities, dialects, occupations, and social levels of the speakers. (3) It gives the *impression* of naturalness without being an actual, *verbatim* record of what may have been said, since fiction, as someone has explained, is concerned with "the semblance of reality," not with reality itself. (4) It presents the interplay of ideas and personalities among the people conversing; it sets forth a conversational give and take—not simply a series of remarks of alternating speakers. (5) It varies in diction, RHYTHM, phrasing, sentence length, etc., according to the various speakers participating. The best writers of *dialogue* know that rarely do two or more people of exactly the same cultural and character background meet and converse, and the *dialogue* they write notes these differences. (6) It serves, at the hands of some writers, to give relief from, and lightness of effect to, passages which are essentially serious or expository in nature.

It should be noted, however, that in the Elizabethan drama the convention of using blank verse and high rhetoric for noble or elevated characters and prose for underlings and comic characters modifies these rules, as did the doctrine of decorum in the seventeenth and eighteenth centuries. Furthermore, plays of wit, such as those by Oscar Wilde, and plays of idea, such as those by G. B. Shaw, unhesitatingly take liberties with the idea of appropriateness to station and character in *dialogue.*

The *dialogue* is also a specialized literary composition in which two or more characters debate or reason about an idea or a proposition. There are many notable examples in the world's literature, the best known being the *Dialogues* of Plato. Others include Lucian's *Dialogues of the Dead*, Dryden's *Essay on Dramatic Poesie*, and Landor's *Imaginary Conversations.* Richard Chase's commentary on American literature, *The Democratic Vista*, is cast in *dialogue* form.

Diction: The use of words in oral or written discourse. A simple list of words makes up a vocabulary; the accurate, careful *use* of these words in discourse makes good *diction*. The qualities of proper *diction* as illustrated by the work of standard authors are: (1) the apt selection of the word for the particular meaning to be conveyed, (2) the use of legitimate words accepted as good usage (excluding all solecisms, barbarisms, and improprieties) and (3) the use of words which are clear-cut and specific. The manner in which words are combined constitutes STYLE rather than *diction* since *diction* refers only to the selection of words employed in the discourse.

There are at least four levels of usage for words: the formal, the informal, the colloquial, and slang. Formal refers to the level of usage common in serious books and formal discourse; informal refers to the level of usage found in the relaxed but polite conversation of cultivated people; colloquial refers to the everyday usage of a group and it may include terms and constructions accepted in that group but not universally acceptable; and slang refers to a group of newly coined words which are not acceptable for polite usage as yet.

It should be noted that the accepted *diction* of one age often sounds unacceptable to another.

Dramatic Irony: The words or acts of a character in a play may carry a meaning unperceived by himself but understood by the audience. Usually the character's own interests are involved in a way he cannot understand. The IRONY resides in the contrast between the meaning intended by the speaker and the added significance seen by others. The term is occasionally applied also to nondramatic narrative, and is sometimes extended to include any situation (such as mistaken identity) in which some of the actors on the stage or some of the characters in a story are "blind" to facts known to the spectator or reader. So understood, *dramatic irony* is responsible for much of the interest in fiction and drama, because the reader or spectator enjoys being in on the secret. The complexity and the centrality of *dramatic irony* to a serious consideration of drama is shown in R. B. Sharpe's detailed *Irony in the Drama*.

Dramatic Monologue: A lyric poem which reveals "a soul in action" through the conversation of one character in a dramatic situation. The character is speaking to an identifiable but silent listener in a dramatic moment in the speaker's life. The circumstances surrounding the conversation, one side of which we "hear" as the *dramatic monologue,* are made clear by implication in the poem, and a deep insight into the character of the speaker is given. Although a quite old form, the *dramatic monologue* was brought to a very high level by Robert Browning, who is often credited with its creation. Tennyson used the form on occasion, and contemporary poets have found it congenial, as witness the work of Robert Frost, E. A. Robinson, Carl Sandburg, Allen Tate, and T. S. Eliot, whose "Love Song of J. Alfred Prufrock" is a distinguished twentieth century example of a *dramatic monologue.*

Dramatic Structure: The ancients compared the PLOT of a drama to the tying and untying of a knot. The principle of dramatic CONFLICT, though not mentioned as such in Aristotle's definition of drama, is implied in this figure. The technical structure of a serious play is determined by the necessities of developing this dramatic CONFLICT. Thus a well-built TRAGEDY will commonly show the following divisions, each of which represents a phase of the dramatic CONFLICT: introduction, rising action, CLIMAX or crisis (turning point), falling action, and catastrophe. The relation of these parts is sometimes represented graphically by the figure of a pyramid, called Freytag's pyramid, the rising slope suggesting the rising action or tying of the knot, the falling slope the falling action or resolution, the apex representing the CLIMAX.

The *introduction* (or exposition) creates the tone, gives the setting, introduces some of the characters, and supplies other facts necessary to the understanding of the play, such as events in the story supposed to have taken place before the part of the action included in the play, since a play, like an epic, is likely to plunge *in medias res,* "into the middle of things." In *Hamlet,* the bleak midnight scene on the castle platform, with the appearance of the ghost, sets the keynote of the TRAGEDY, while the conversation of the watchers, especially the words of Horatio, supply antecedent facts, such as the quarrel between the dead King Hamlet and the King of Norway. The ancients called this part the protasis.

The rising action, or complication, is set in motion by the exciting force (in *Hamlet* the ghost's revelation to Hamlet of the murder) and continues through successive stages of CONFLICT between the hero and the counterplayers up to the CLIMAX or turning point (in *Hamlet* the hesitating failure of the hero to kill Claudius at prayer). The ancients called this part the epitasis.

The downward or falling action stresses the activity of the forces opposing the hero and while some suspense must be maintained, the trend of the action must lead logically to the disaster with which the TRAGEDY is to close. The falling action, called by the ancients the catastasis, is often set in movement by a single event called the tragic force, closely related to the CLIMAX and bearing the same relation to the falling action as the exciting force does to the rising action. In *Macbeth* the tragic force is the escape of Fleance following the murder of Banquo. In *Hamlet* it is the "blind" stabbing of Polonius, which sends Hamlet away from the court just as he appears about to succeed in his plans. The latter part of the falling action is sometimes marked by an event which delays the catastrophe and seems to offer a way of escape for the hero (the apparent reconciliation of Hamlet and Laertes). This is called the "moment of final suspense" and aids in maintaining interest. The falling action is usually shorter than the rising action and often is attended by some lowering of interest (as in the case of the long conversation between Malcolm and MacDuff in *Macbeth*), since new forces must be introduced and an apparently inevitable end made to seem uncertain. Relief scenes are often resorted to in the falling action, partly to mark the passage of time, partly to provide emotional relaxation for the audience. The famous scene of the grave diggers in *Hamlet* is an example of how this relief scene may be justified through its inherent dramatic qualities and through its relation to the serious action.

The catastrophe, marking the tragic failure, usually the death, of the hero (and often of his opponents as well) comes as a natural outgrowth of the action. It satisfies, not by a gratification of the emotional sympathies of the spectator but by its logical conformity, and by a final presentation of the nobility of the succumbing hero. A "glimpse of restored order" often follows the catastrophe proper in a Shakespearean TRAGEDY, as when Hamlet gives his dying vote to Fortinbras as the new king.

This five-part *dramatic structure* was believed by Freytag to be reflected in a five-act structure for TRAGEDY. However, the imposing of a rigorous five-act structure upon Elizabethan TRAGEDY is questionable, since relatively few plays fall readily into the pattern of an act of exposition, an act of rising action, an act of CLIMAX, an act of falling action, and an act of catastrophe. It should be noted too that this structure based upon the analogy of the tying and untying of a knot is applicable to comedy, the novel, and the short story, with the adjustment of the use of the broader term DÉNOUEMENT for catastrophe in works that are not tragic, despite the fact that technically catastrophe and DÉNOUEMENT are synonymous.

During the nineteenth century conventional structure gave way to a newer technique. First, comedy, under the influence of French bourgeois comedy, the "well-made play" of Eugene Scribe and others, developed a set of technical conventions all its own; and as a result of the movement led by Ibsen, serious drama cast off the restrictions of five-act TRAGEDY and freed itself from conventional formality. By the end of the century the traditional five-act structure was to be found only in poetic or consciously archaic tragedy, whose connection with the stage was artificial and generally unsuccessful. However the fundamental elements of structure given here remained demonstrably present, though in modified form, in these newer types of plays. If at first glance it seems that Ibsen opens one of his domestic tragedies at or just before the tragic force, the exposition, the exciting force, and the rising action which brought about the situation with which he opens are still present and are communicated to the audience by implication and flashback. The fundamental *dramatic structure* seems timeless and impervious to basic change.

Fable: A brief tale, either in prose or verse, told to point a moral. The characters are most frequently animals, but they need not be so restricted since people and inanimate objects as well are sometimes the central figures. The subject matter of *fables* has to do with supernatural and unusual incidents and often draws its origin from folklore sources. By far the most famous *fables* are those accredited to Aesop, a Greek slave living about 600 B.C.; but almost equally popular are those of La Fontaine, a Frenchman writing in the seventeenth century, because of their distinctive humor and wit, their wisdom and sprightly satire. Other important fabulists are Gay (England), Lessing (Germany), Krylov (Russia). A *fable* in which the characters are animals is called a beast fable, a form that has been popular in almost every period of literary history, usually as a satiric device to point out the follies of mankind. The beast fable continues to be vigorous in such diverse works as Kipling's *Jungle Books* and *Just So Stories,* Joel Chandler Harris' Uncle Remus stories, and George Orwell's *Animal Farm.* Many critics, particularly in the neoclassic period, have used *fable* as a term for the PLOT of a fiction or a drama.

Farce: The word developed from Late Latin *farsus,* connected with a verb meaning "to stuff." Thus an expansion or amplification in the church liturgy was called a *farse.* Later, in France, *farce* meant any sort of extemporaneous addition in a play, especially comic jokes or "gags," the clownish actors speaking "more than was set down" for them. In the late seventeenth century *farce* was used in England to mean any short humorous play, as distinguished from regular five-act comedy. The development in these plays of certain elements of low comedy is responsible for the usual modern meaning of *farce:* a dramatic piece intended to excite laughter and depending less on PLOT and character than on exaggerated, improbable situations, the humor arising from gross incongruities, coarse wit, or horseplay, *Farce* merges into comedy, and the same play (e.g., Shakespeare's *The Taming of the Shrew*) may be called by some a *farce*, by others a comedy. *Life Below Stairs* (1759), with the production of which Garrick was connected, has been termed the "best farce" of the eighteenth century. In the American theatre, Brandon Thomas' *Charley's Aunt* (1892), dealing with the extravagant events resulting from a female impersonation, is the best known American *farce*, although *farce* has been the stock-in-trade of motion-picture comedians.

Figurative Language: Intentional departure from the normal order, construction, or meaning of words in order to gain strength and freshness of expression, to create a pictorial effect, to describe by ANALOGY, or to discover and illustrate similarities in otherwise dissimilar things. *Figurative language* is writing that embodies one or more of the various figures of speech, the most common of which are: antithesis, apostrophe, CLIMAX, hyperbole, IRONY, METAPHOR, metonymy, personification, SIMILE, synecdoche. These figures are often divided into two classes: tropes, literally meaning "turns," in which the words in the figure undergo a decided change in meaning, and "figures of thought," in which the words retain their literal meaning but their rhetorical pattern is changed. An apostrophe, for example, is a "figure of thought," and a METAPHOR is a trope.

Genre: A term used in literary criticism to designate the distinct types or categories into which literary works are grouped according to form or technique. The term comes from French, where it means "kind" or "type." In its customary application, it is used loosely, since the varieties of literary "kinds" and the principles on which they are made are numerous. The traditional *genres* include such "kinds" as TRAGEDY, comedy, epic, lyric, pastoral. Today a division of literature into *genres* would also include novel, short story, essay, and perhaps, radio or television play. The difficulty resulting from the loose use of the term is easily illustrated: novel designates a *genre*, but so does picaresque novel; lyric designates a *genre*, but so does sonnet, as do both elegy and pastoral elegy.

Genre classification implies that there are groups of formal or technical characteristics existing among works of the same "kind" regardless of time or place of composition, author, or subject matter; and that these characteristics, when they define a definite group of works, are of basic significance in talking about literary art. Prior to the Romantic Age in England, there was a tendency to assume that literary "kinds" had an ideal existence and obeyed "laws of kind," these laws being criteria by which works could be judged. In the Romantic Age, *genre* distinctions were often looked upon merely as restatements of conventions and were suspect. Today critics frequently regard *genre* distinctions as useful descriptive devices but rather arbitrary ones.

In painting the term *genre* is applied to works that depict ordinary, everyday life in realistic terms. By extension, the term is sometimes used in literary criticism to designate a poem that deals with commonplace or homely situations in subdued tones. By this usage, Whittier's "Snow-Bound" is often called "a *genre* study."

Northrop Frye's *Anatomy of Criticism* contains a detailed and provocative treatment of the theory of *genres*.

Image: Originally a sculptured, cast, or modeled representation of a person; even in its most sophisticated critical usage, this fundamental meaning is still present, in that an *image* is a literal and concrete representation of a sensory experience or of an object that can be known by one or more of the senses. It functions, as I. A. Richards has pointed out, by representing a sensation through the process of being a "relict" of an already known sensation. The *image* is one of the distinctive elements of the "language of art," the means by which experience in its richness and emotional complexity is communicated, as opposed to the simplifying and conceptualizing processes of science and philosophy. The *image* is, therefore, a portion of the essence of the meaning of the literary work, not ever properly a mere decoration.

Images may be either "tied" or "free," a "tied" *image* being one so employed that its meaning and associational value is the same or nearly the same for all readers; and a "free" *image* being one not so fixed by context that its possible meanings or associational values are limited; it is, therefore, capable of having various meanings or values for various people.

Images may also be either literal or figurative, a literal *image* being one that involves no necessary change or extension in the obvious meaning of the words, one in which the words call up a sensory representation of the literal object or sensation; and a figurative *image* being one that involves a "turn" on the literal meaning of the words. An example of a collection of literal *images* may be seen in Coleridge's "Kubla Khan":

> In Xanadu did Kubla Khan
> A stately pleasure-dome decree:
> Where Alph, the sacred river, ran
> Through caverns measureless to man
>   Down to a sunless sea.

These *images* apparently represent a literal scene. The literal *image* is one of the basic properties of prose fiction, as witness such different writers as Joseph Conrad and Ernest Hemingway, both of whose works are noted for the evocative power of their literal *images*. The opening lines of this Wordsworth sonnet show both kinds of *images*, literal and figurative:

> It is a beauteous evening, calm and free;
> The holy time is quiet as a Nun
> Breathless with adoration; the broad sun
> Is sinking down in its tranquillity.

The two middle lines are highly figurative, whereas the first and fourth lines are broadly literal, although there are figurative "turns" present by implication in "free" and "tranquillity."

218

The qualities usually found in *images* are particularity, concreteness, and an appeal to sensuous experience or memory. See IMAGERY, SYMBOL, METAPHOR, FIGURATIVE LANGUAGE.

Imagery: A term used widely in contemporary criticism, *imagery* has a great variety of meanings. In its literal sense it means the collection of IMAGES within a literary work or a unit of a literary work. In a broader sense it is used as synonymous with trope or figure of speech. Here the trope designates a special usage of words in which there is a change in their basic meanings. There are four major types of tropes: IMAGES, which are literal and sensory and properly should not be called tropes at all; SYMBOLS, which combine a literal and sensuous quality with an abstract or suggestive aspect; SIMILE, which describes by expressed ANALOGY; and METAPHOR, which describes by implied ANALOGY. Not only do these four types of tropes define the meaning of *imagery*, they also suggest the ranges of possible application that are to be found in the term.

Many contemporary critics are deeply concerned over the "structure of IMAGES," "the IMAGE-clusters," "IMAGE patterns," and "thematic *imagery*." Such patterns of *imagery*, often without the conscious knowledge of author or reader, are sometimes taken to be keys to the "deeper" meaning of a literary work or pointers to the unconscious motivations of its author. A few critics tend to see the "IMAGE patterns" as indeed being the basic meaning of the work and a sounder key to its values and interpretation than the explicit statements of the author or the more obvious events of PLOT or action. One of the notable contributions of the new critics has been their awareness of the importance of the relationships among IM-AGES to the nature and meaning of lyric poetry.

A study of the *imagery* of a literary work may center itself on the physical world which is presented through the language of the work; upon the rhetorical patterns and devices by which the tropes in the work are achieved; upon the psychological state which produced the work and gave it its special and often hidden meaning; upon the ways in which the pattern of its IMAGES reinforces (or on occasion contradicts) the ostensible meaning of statement, PLOT, and action in the work; or upon how the IMAGES strike responsively upon resonant points in the racial unconscious producing the emotive power of archetypes and myth. See IMAGE, METAPHOR, FIGURATIVE LANGUAGE.

Irony: A figure of speech in which the actual intent is expressed in words which carry the opposite meaning. *Irony* is likely to be confused with sarcasm but it differs from sarcasm in that it is usually lighter, less harsh in its working though in effect probably more cutting because of its indirectness. It bears, too, a close relationship to innuendo. The ability to recognize *irony* is one of the surest tests of intelligence and sophistication. Its presence is marked by a sort of grim humor, an "unemotional detachment" on the part of the writer, a coolness in expression at a time when the writer's emotions are really heated. Characteristically it speaks words of praise to imply blame and words of blame to imply praise, though its inherent critical quality makes the first type much more common than the second. The great effectiveness of *irony* as a literary device is the impression it gives of great restraint. The writer of *irony* has his tongue in his cheek; for this reason *irony* is more easily detected in speech than in writing since the voice can, through its intonation, so easily warn the listener of a double significance. One of the most famous ironic remarks in literature is Job's "No doubt but ye are the people, and wisdom shall die with you." Antony's insistence, in his oration over the dead Caesar, that "Brutus is an honorable man" bears the same ironic imprint. Goldsmith, Jane Austen, Thackeray—these authors have in one novel or another made frequent use of this form; Jonathan Swift is an arch-ironist; his "Modest Proposal" for saving a starving Ireland, by suggesting that the Irish sell their babies to the English landlords, is perhaps the most savagely sustained ironic writing in our literature. The novels of Thomas Hardy and Henry James are elaborate artistic expressions of the ironic spirit, for *irony* applies not only to statement but also to event, situation, and STRUCTURE. In drama, *irony* has a special meaning, referring to knowledge held by the audience but hidden from the relevant actors. In contemporary criticism, *irony* is used to describe a poet's "recognition of incongruities" and his controlled acceptance of them. Among the devices by which *irony* is achieved are hyperbole, understatement, and sarcasm.

Metaphor: An implied ANALOGY which imaginatively identifies one object with another and ascribes to the first one or more of the qualities of the second or invests the first with emotional or imaginative qualities associated with the second. It is one of the tropes; that is, one of the principal devices by which poetic "turns" on the meaning of words are achieved. I. A. Richards' distinction between the TENOR and the VEHICLE of a *metaphor* has been widely accepted and is very useful. The TENOR is the idea being expressed or the subject of the comparison; the VEHICLE is the IMAGE by which this idea is conveyed or the subject communicated. When Shakespeare writes

> That time of year thou mayst in me behold
> When yellow leaves, or none, or few, do hang
> Upon those boughs which shake against the cold,
> Bare ruined choirs, where late the sweet birds sang,

the TENOR is old age, the VEHICLE is the season of late fall or early winter, conveyed through a group of IMAGES unusually complex in their implications. The TENOR and VEHICLE taken together constitute the figure of speech, the trope, the "turn" in meaning which the *metaphor* conveys. The purposes for using *metaphors* can vary widely. At one extreme, the VEHICLE may merely be a means of decorating the TENOR; at the other extreme, the TENOR may merely be an excuse for having the VEHICLE. Allegory, for example, may be thought of as an elaborate and consistently constructed extended *metaphor* in which the TENOR is never expressed. In the simplest kinds of *metaphors* there is an obvious direct resemblance that exists objectively between the TENOR and the VEHICLE, and in some *metaphors*, particularly those which lend themselves to elaborate conceits, the relationship between TENOR and VEHICLE is in the mind of the maker of the *metaphor*. The first kind tends to be sensuous and the second witty.

Aristotle praised the *metaphor* as "the greatest thing by far" for the poet, and saw it as the product of his insight which permitted him to find the similarities in seemingly dissimilar things. Modern criticism follows Aristotle in placing a similarly high premium on the poet's abilities in the making of *metaphors*, and analytical criticism tends to find almost as much rich suggestiveness in the differences between the things compared as it does in the recognition of surprising but unsuspected similarities. Cleanth Brooks uses the term "functional *metaphor*" to describe the way in which the *metaphor* is able to have "referential" and "emotive" characteristics and to go beyond them and become a direct means in itself of representing a truth incommunicable by any other means. Clearly when a *metaphor* performs this function, it is behaving as a SYMBOL.

Metaphors may be simple, that is, may occur in the single isolated comparison, or a large *metaphor* may function as the controlling image of a whole work, or a series of VEHICLES may all be associated with a single TENOR, as in Hamlet's "To be or not to be" soliloquy. In this last kind of case, however, unless the IMAGES can harmoniously build the TENOR without impressing the reader with a sense of their incongruity, the danger of a mixed figure is grave.

The whole nature of our language is highly metaphorical. Most of our modern speech, which now seems prosaic enough, was once largely metaphorical. Our abstract terms are borrowed from physical objects. Natural objects and actions have passed over into abstractions because of some inherent metaphorical significance. Thus "transgression"—which today signifies a misdemeanor, an error, or mistake—formerly meant "to cross a line." The metaphorical significance has been lost—is said to be "dead"—and the former figure of speech now stands simply for an abstraction. (It is thus, in fact, that abstract terms possibly first came into language; early man was necessarily content simply to name the objects about him which he could see and feel and smell.)

Narrator: In the broadest sense, anyone who recounts a narrative, either in writing or orally. In fiction the term is used in a more technical sense, as the ostensible author or teller of a story. In fiction presented in the first person, the "I" who tells the story is the *narrator*; he may be in any of various relations to the events he describes, ranging from being their center (the PROTAGONIST) through various degrees of minor importance (minor characters) to being merely a witness. In fiction told from an omniscient-author point of view, the author himself acts self-consciously as *narrator*, recounting the story and freely commenting on it. A *narrator* is always present, at least by implication, in any work of fiction, except a story in which a self-effacing author relates events with apparent objectivity; yet even there the *narrator* exists in fact, although we and the author act as though he did not. See POINT OF VIEW.

221

Objective Correlative: A term first used by T. S. Eliot to describe a pattern of objects, actions, or events, or a situation which can serve effectively to awaken in the reader the emotional response which the author desires without being a direct statement of that emotion. It is an impersonal or objective means of communicating feeling. Eliot calls the *objective correlative* "the only way of expressing emotion in the form of art" and defines it as "a set of objects, a situation, a chain of events which shall be the formula of that *particular* emotion, such that when the external facts, which must terminate in sensory experience, are given, the emotion is immediately evoked." The term has had wide currency in this sense among contemporary critics. It had been used by Washington Allston in a lecture on art as early as 1850 to describe the process by which the external world produces pleasurable emotion, but Eliot's usage gave it new meaning and made of it a new term. See AESTHETIC DISTANCE.

Parable: An illustrative story answering a question or pointing a moral or lesson. A true *parable*, however, is much more than an anecdote since, implicitly at least, detail for detail in the *parable* is parallel with the situation which calls forth the *parable* for illustration. *Parables* are, in this sense, allegories. Naturally in Christian countries the most famous *parables* are those told by Christ, such for instance as the *parable* of the sower.

Plot: A planned series of interrelated actions progressing, because of the interplay of one force upon another, through a struggle of opposing forces to a climax and a *dénouement.* However, such abstract terms as the above mean little; it is perhaps more helpful to describe *plot* than to define it with generalities. The incidents which are part of a *plot* are, it has been said, (1) *planned;* they are preconceived by the author; they spring from his conscious thought; they are not simply taken over from life. No matter how realistic an author may be, he must arrange and select his incidents according to a *plot* purpose since life itself only rarely, if ever, unfolds according to the plans of a fiction *plot. Plot* is, too, (2) a *series of actions* moving from a beginning through a logically related sequence to a logical and natural outcome. One incident—an afternoon's cruise—does not make a *plot,* no matter how interesting the afternoon may have been. Several incidents—if the story is one of action—are essential. There must at least be a beginning, a middle, and an end in the interplay of the opposing forces and, most frequently, this means three or more episodes. And these incidents grow one upon another; incident two following by a causal relationship from incident one, and incident three following, by this same relationship, from two. The difference between a simple narrative and a story of *plot* is the difference between a calendar and a knitted scarf. In the calendar the pages follow one another over and under another. In a story with closely knit *plot* the removal of one incident would bring the whole structure down upon one's head much as though he had removed an important prop from the scaffolding for a building. In a story of mere unrelated incidents, the removal of one incident would leave, simply, a gap. (3) This interrelationship of action is the result, as has been said, of the *interplay of one force upon another*. Without CONFLICT, without opposition, *plot per se* does not exist. We must have a Claudius flouting a Hamlet, an Iago making jealous an Othello, if we are to have *plot*. These forces may be physical (or external), or they may be spiritual (or internal); but physical or spiritual they must afford an opposition. And this opposition it is, which knits one incident to another, which dictates the causal relationship, which develops the struggle. This struggle between the forces, moreover, comes to a head in some one incident—the crisis—which forms the turning-point of the story and which usually marks the point of greatest suspense. In this climactic episode the rising action comes to a termination, the falling action begins; and as a result of this incident some DÉNOUEMENT or catastrophe is bound to follow.

Plot is, in this sense, an artificial rather than a natural ordering of events. Its function is to simplify life by imposing order upon it. It would be possible, though most tedious, to recite *all* incidents, *all* events, *all* thoughts which pass through the minds of one or more characters during a period of, say, a week. And somewhere in this recital might be buried a story. But the demands of *plot* stipulate that the author *select* from this welter of event and reflection those items which have a certain unity, which point to a certain end, which have a common interrelationship, which represent not more than two or three threads of interest and activity. *Plot* brings order out of life; it selects only one or two emotions out of a dozen, one or two conflicts out of hundreds, only two or three people out of thousands, and a half-dozen episodes from possible millions. In this sense it focuses life.

And it usually focuses with one principal idea in mind—character. The most effective incidents are those which spring naturally from the given characters, the most effective *plot* presents struggle such as would engage these given characters, and the most effective emotion for the *plot* to present is that inherent in the quality of the given characters. The function of *plot*, from this point of view, is to translate character into action.

The use of a *deus ex machina* to solve a complication is now pretty generally condemned as a weakness in *plot* structure since it is now generally conceded that *plot* action should spring from the innate quality of the characters participant in the action. But *fate*, since it may be interpreted as working through character, is, with the development of the realistic method, still very popular. The one great weakness good writers of fiction avoid is the use of incident and episode which are extraneous to the essential purposes of the *plot* pattern. *Plot*, it need hardly be added, is an element common to various forms of fiction: the novel, the short story, the drama being the types of writing most frequently making use of the interest which springs from the suspense which *plots* develop. See CHARACTERIZATION.

Point of View: A term used in the analysis and criticism of fiction to describe the way in which the reader is presented with the materials of the story, or, viewed from another angle, the vantage point from which the author presents the actions of the story. If the author serves as an all-knowing maker, not restricted to time, place, or character, and free to move and to comment at will, the *point of view* is usually called omniscient. At the other extreme, a character within the story—major, minor, or merely a witness—may tell the story as he experienced it, saw it, heard it, and understood it. Such a character is usually called a first-person NAR-RATOR; if he does not comprehend the implications of what he is telling he is called a naïve or disingenuous NARRATOR. The author may tell the story in the third person and yet present it as it is seen and understood by a single character—major, minor, or merely witness—restricting information to what that character sees, hears, feels, and thinks; such a *point of view* is said to be limited to one character. The author may employ such a limited *point of view* and restrict the materials presented to the interior responses of the *point of view* character, resulting in the interior monologue. The author may present his material by a process of narrative exposition, in which actions and conversations are presented in summary rather than in detail; such a method is usually called *panoramic*. On the other hand, he may present actions and conversations in detail, as they occur, and objectively—without authorial comment; such a method is usually called *scenic*. If the scenic method is carried to the point where the author never speaks in his own person and does not ostensibly intrude himself into the scenes he presents, he is said to be a self-effacing author. In extended works of fiction authors frequently employ combinations of several of these methods. The concern with *point of view* in current criticism and the experimentation with *point of view* by many current novelists are both very great. Since Henry James's critical essays and Prefaces, *point of view* has often been considered the technical aspect of fiction which leads the critic most readily into the problems and the meanings of a novel or a short story. See NARRATOR.

Protagonist: The chief character in a play or story. When the PLOT involves conflict, the chief opponent or rival of the *protagonist* is called an antagonist. If the main PLOT centers about the career of a hero who overcomes a villain who tries to thwart his efforts, the hero would be called the *protagonist*, the villain the antagonist. If, however, the main interest lies in the career of a villain, whose plans are defeated by the appearance of a successful hero, the villain would be called the *protagonist*, and the hero the antagonist. In Shakespeare's *Hamlet*, Hamlet is himself the *protagonist*, as his fortunes are the chief interest in the play. King Claudius and Laertes are his antagonists. The sentence "The protagonists of Christopher Marlowe's tragedies are usually of the super-personality type" illustrates a usual use of the word. In a looser sense *protagonist* is sometimes used in the sense of champion or chief advocate of a cause or movement, as when Bryan is referred to as the *protagonist* of the free-silver movement in 1896. The word *protagonist* was originally applied to the first actor added to chorus and leader in early Greek drama; hence its continuing sense of "first" or chief player in the drama.

Rhythm: The passage of regular or approximately equivalent time intervals between definite events or the recurrence of specific sounds or kinds of sounds is called *rhythm*. Man has a seemingly basic need for such regularity of recurrence, or for the effect produced by it, as laboratory experiments in psychology have demonstrated and as one can see for himself by watching a crew of men digging a deep ditch or hammering a long stake or by listening to chanteys and work songs.

In both prose and poetry the presence of rhythmic patterns lends both pleasure and heightened emotional response to the listener or reader, for it establishes for him a pattern of expectations and rewards him with the pleasure of a series of fulfillments or gratifications of expectation. In poetry three different elements may function in a pattern of seemingly regular temporal occurrence: quantity, accent, and number of syllables. In English poetry, the rhythmic pattern is most often established by a combination of accent and number of syllables. This pattern of a fairly regular number of syllables with a relatively fixed sequence of stressed and unstressed syllables lends itself to certain kinds of basic rhythmic analysis in English versification. The *rhythm* may be "marching" or double—that is, involve one stressed and one unstressed syllable, as in iambs and trochees. Or it may be "dancing" or triple—that is, involve one stressed and two unstressed syllables, as in dactyls and anapests. It may be "rising"—that is, beginning with unstressed and ending with stressed syllables, as in iambs and anapests. Or it may be "falling"—that is, beginning with stressed and ending with unstressed syllables, as in trochees and dactyls. Other kinds of *rhythm* than these are, of course, possible (and even common) in English verse, as witness sprung rhythm and free verse, as well as the *rhythm* used in Old English versification or that used by Walt Whitman.

In prose, despite the absence of the formal regularity of pattern here described for verse, cadence is usually present and in impassioned prose it often establishes definite patterns of rhythmic recurrence.

Rime: Similarity or identity of sound existing between accented syllables occupying corresponding positions within two or more lines of verse. The correspondence of sound is based on the *vowels and succeeding consonants* of the accented syllables, which must, for a perfect *rime*, be preceded by different consonants. That is, "fan" and "ran" constitute perfect *rimes* because the vowel and succeeding consonant sounds are identical and the preceding consonants ("f" and "r") are different. *Rime,* in that it is based on this correspondence of sounds, is related to assonance and ALLITERA-TION, but is unlike these two forms both in construction and in the fact that it is commonly used at stipulated intervals, whereas assonance and ALLITERATION are pretty likely to range freely through various positions.

Rime is more than a mere ornament or device of versification. It performs certain valuable functions. To begin with, it affords pleasure through the sense impression it makes. The ear of the reader recognizes a sound already echoing in his consciousness and the accord the two similar sounds set up is likely, if the poet has deftly rimed, to bring the reader a real, sensuous gratification. Again, the recurrence of *rime* at regular intervals serves to establish the form of the STANZA. *Rime* serves to unify and distinguish divisions of the poem since it is likely that the *rime* sounds followed in one STANZA—the Spenserian for instance—will be changed when the next STANZA is started. This principle at once gives unity to the one STANZA and marks it off as separate from the next, affording a sense of movement and progress to the poem as a whole. The fact that these qualities as well as others reside in *rime* will be immediately granted when we recall how commonly folklore and the play of children—to take only two instances—resort to *rime* to make memorizing easy.

The types of *rime* are classified according to two schemes: (1) as to the position of the rimed syllables in the line, and (2) as to the number of syllables in which the identity of sound occurs.

On the basis of the position of the rime, we have:

1. *End rime,* much the most common type, which occurs at the end of the verse.

2. *Internal rime,* (sometimes called leonine rime), which occurs at some place after the beginning and before the closing syllables.

3. *Beginning rime,* which occurs in the first syllable (or syllables) of the verse.

On the basis of the number of syllables presenting similarity of sound, we have:

1. *Masculine rime,* where the correspondence of sound is restricted to the final accented syllable as "fan" and "ran." This type of *rime* is generally more forceful, more vigorous than those below.

2. *Feminine rime,* where the correspondence of sound lies in *two* consecutive syllables, as in "lighting" and "fighting." This is sometimes called *double rime.* *Feminine rime* is used for lightness and delicacy in movement.

3. *Triple rime,* where the correspondence of sound lies in *three* consecutive syllables, as in "glorious" and "victorious." Triple rime has been used for serious work—such as Thomas Hood's *Bridge of Sighs*—but much more frequently it is reserved for humorous, satirical verse, for the sort of use Byron makes of it in his satiric poems, and Ogden Nash in his comic ones.

While at one time or another most poets have been responsible for poor *rimes,* have violated consciously one or another of the riming customs, still these conventions persist. Some of them may be mentioned here:

1. Syllables which are spelled differently but which have the same pronunciation (such as "rite" and "right") do not make acceptable *rimes.*

2. A true *rime* is based on the correspondence of sound in *accented* syllables as opposed to unaccented syllables. "Stating" and "mating" thus make a good *rime,* and for the same reason, "rating" and "forming" make a bad *rime* since the correspondence is between unaccented syllables.

3. For a true *rime* all syllables *following* the accented syllable must *rime*, as is the case, for instance, with "fascinate" and "deracinate." According to this rule "fascinate" and "deracinating" would not be true *rime* because of the difference between the last syllables.

4. It is well to avoid repetition of the same vowel sounds in different *rimes* which occur near each other. For instance "stone" and "bone" are good rimes as are also "home" and "tome" but a quatrain composed of those four *rimes* would usually be condemned as weak because of the repetition of the long *o* throughout. Of course, like all rules, this may be violated when there is a special reason for doing so.

5. Conversely to 4 above, it should be noted that there should not be too great a separation between *rime*-sounds since such separation will result in a loss of effect. A *rime* occurring in the first line and the sixth line, for instance, is rather a strain on the reader's attention.

6. It is permissible, when not done too frequently, to allow a *rime* to fall on an unaccented syllable. There is a certain variety coming from the riming of "free" and "prosperity," for instance, which justifies its use occasionally.

Rime and the importance it enjoys in modern versification are comparatively modern developments. The ancient Greek and Latin poetry was not rimed; our earliest English verse (*Beowulf* is an example) was not based on *rime*. Historians of the subject generally credit the development of *rime* to ceremonials within the Catholic Church and suggest that the priests made use of *rime* as a device to aid the worshipers in their singing and memorizing of the ritualistic procedure. *Dies Irae* is an example of one of the earliest rimed songs of the Church.

Among contemporary poets a tendency to use imperfect *rimes*, substituting assonance, consonance, and dissonance for true *rimes*, is widespread; and most present-day poets take interesting liberties with the traditional "rules" for *rime* cited in this article.

Satire: A literary manner which blends a critical attitude with humor and wit to the end that human institutions or humanity may be improved. The true satirist is conscious of the frailty of institutions of man's devising and attempts through laughter not so much to tear them down as to inspire a remodeling. If the critic simply abuses he is writing invective; if he is personal and splenetic he is writing sarcasm; if he is sad and morose over the state of society he is writing IRONY or mere gloom. As a rule modern *satire* spares the individual and follows Addison's self-imposed rule: to "pass over a single foe to charge whole armies."

Satire existed in early classical literature of Greece and Rome. It is only necessary to name Aristophanes, Juvenal, Horace, Martial, and Petronius to recall the rich vein which ran at that time. Through the Middle Ages the manner persisted in the fabliau and beast-epic. In Spain the picaresque novel developed a strong element of *satire* to lend it interest; in France Molière and Le Sage proved themselves capable of handling the

227

manner deftly, and somewhat later Voltaire established himself as the arch-satirist of literature. In England, from the time of Gascoigne (*Steel Glass*—1576) and Lodge (*Fig for Momus*—1595) writers condemned the vices and follies of the age in verse and prose (Hall, Nash, Donne, Jonson). By the time of Charles I, however, interest in *satire* had declined, only to revive with the struggle between Cavaliers and Puritans. At the hands of Dryden the heroic couplet, already the favorite form with most English satirists, developed into the finest satiric verse form. The eighteenth century in England became a period of *satire;* poetry, drama, essays, criticism, all took on the satirical manner at the hands of such men as Dryden, Swift, Addison, Steele, Pope and Fielding,—a golden age of *satire,* which, great as are such later satirists as Byron and Thackeray, marks off the period as that in English literature most definitely satirical.

Early American *satire* naturally followed English in style. Before the Revolution, American *satire* dealt chiefly with the political struggle. Of the Hartford Wits Trumbull produced *M'Fingal,* a Hudibrastic *satire* on Tories. Freneau (*The British Prison Ship*) wrote the strongest and most original Revolutionary *satire.* Shortly after the Revolution, the *Anarchiad* (verse), by Trumbull, Barlow, Humphreys, and Hopkinson and *Modern Chivalry* (fiction) by Breckenridge, attacked domestic political difficulties and the crudities of our frontier. Irving's good-humored *satire* in *The Sketch Book* and *Knickerbocker's History,* Holmes' society verse, Lowell's dialect poems (*Biglow Papers*), and Mark Twain's prose represent the general trend of American *satire* up to the twentieth century.

In the twentieth century English writers like G. B. Shaw, Noel Coward, Evelyn Waugh, and Aldous Huxley have maintained the satiric spirit in the face of the gravity of naturalism and the earnestness of SYMBOLISM. In America, Eugene O'Neill (on occasion), Edith Wharton, Sinclair Lewis, Kaufman and Hart, and John P. Marquand have commented critically upon man and his institutions.

Satire is fundamentally of two types, named for their most distinguished classical practitioners: *Horatian satire* is gentle, urbane, smiling; it aims to correct by gentle and broadly sympathetic laughter; *Juvenalian satire* is biting, bitter, angry; it points with contempt and moral indignation to the corruption and evil of men and institutions. Addison is a *Horatian* satirist, Swift a *Juvenalian* one.

For centuries the word *satire,* which literally means "a dish filled with mixed fruits," was reserved for long poems, such as the pseudo-Homeric *Battle of the Frogs and Mice,* the poems of Juvenal and Horace, *The Vision of Piers Plowman,* Chaucer's "Nun's Priest's Tale," Butler's *Hudibras,* Pope's *The Rape of the Lock,* Lowell's *A Fable for Critics.* Almost from its origins, however, the drama has been suited to the satiric spirit, and from Aristophanes to Shaw and Noel Coward, it has commented with penetrating IRONY on human foibles. There was a notable concentration of its attention on Horatian *satire* in the comedy of manners of the Restoration Age. But it has been in the fictional narrative, particularly the novel, that *satire* has found its chief vehicle in the modern world. Cervantes, Rabelais,

Voltaire, Swift, Fielding, Jane Austen, Thackeray, H. H. Brackenridge *(Modern Chivalry)*, Mark Twain, Sinclair Lewis, Aldous Huxley, Evelyn Waugh, John P. Marquand—all have made extended fictional narratives the vehicles for a wide-ranging and powerfully effective satiric treatment of man and his institutions.

In England since 1841 *Punch* has maintained a high level of comic *satire*. In America, the *New Yorker* has demonstrated since 1925 the continuing appeal of sophisticated Horatian *satire*. The motion pictures, the plastic and graphic arts, and the newspaper comic strip and political cartoon have all been instruments of telling, satiric comment on human affairs.

Setting: The physical, and sometimes spiritual, background against which the action of a narrative (novel, drama, short story, etc.) takes place. The elements which go to make up a *setting* are: (1) the actual geographical location, its topography, scenery, and such physical arrangements as the location of the windows and doors in a room; (2) the occupations and daily manner of living of the characters; (3) the time or period in which the action takes place, e.g., epoch in history, season of the year, etc.; (4) the general environment of the characters, e.g., religious, mental, moral, social, and emotional conditions through which the people in the narrative move. From one point of view most fiction can be broken up into four elements: *setting,* incident (or PLOT), CHARACTERIZATION, and—added at Poe's insistence—effect. When *setting* dominates, or when a piece of fiction is written largely to present the manners and customs of a locality, the writing is often called a piece of local color writing or of regionalism. The term is also often applied to the stage *setting* of a play.

Simile: A figure of speech in which a similarity between two objects is directly expressed, as in Milton's

> A *dungeon horrible,* on all sides round,
> As one great furnace flamed;

Here the comparison between the dungeon (Hell) and the great furnace is directly expressed in the *as* which labels the comparison a *simile.* Most *similes* are introduced by *as* or *like.* In the illustration above, the similarity between Hell (the dungeon) and the furnace is based on the great heat of the two. So it is generally with this figure of speech: the comparison of two things essentially unlike, on the basis of a resemblance in one aspect, forms a *simile.* It is, however, no *simile* to say, "My house is like your house," although, of course, comparison does exist. Another way of expressing it is to say that in a *simile* both TENOR and VEHICLE are clearly expressed and are joined by an indicator of resemblance, "like" or "as." See METAPHOR.

Stanza: A recurrent grouping of two or more lines of a poem in terms of length, metrical form, and, often, rime-scheme. However, the division into *stanzas* is sometimes made according to *thought* as well as form, in

229

which case the *stanza* is a unit not unlike a paragraph of prose. Strophe is another term used for *stanza*, but one should avoid "verse" in this sense, since "verse" is properly reserved to indicate a single line of poetry. Some of the more common stanzaic forms are couplet, tercet, quatrain, rime royal, ottava rima, and the Spenserian stanza.

Static Character: A character in the novel, the short story, or the drama who changes little if at all in the progress of the action. Things happen to *static characters* without modifying their interior selves; the pattern of action reveals characters as they are without showing them in the process of development. See CHARACTERIZATION.

Structure: The planned framework of a piece of literature. Though such external matters as kind of language used (French or English, prose or verse, or kind of verse, or type of sentence) are sometimes referred to as "structural" features, the term usually is applied to the general plan or outline. Thus the scheme of topics (as revealed in a topical outline) determines the *structure* of a formal essay. The logical division of the action of a drama and also the mechanical division into acts and scenes are matters of *structure*. In a narrative the PLOT itself is the structural element. Groups of stories may be set in a larger structural plan such as the pilgrimage in Chaucer's *Canterbury Tales*. The *structure* of an Italian sonnet suggests first its division into octave and sestet, and more minutely the internal plan of each of these two parts. A Pindaric ode follows a special structural plan which determines not only the development of the theme but the sequence of stanzaic forms. Often the author advertises his *structure* as a means of securing clearness (as in some college textbooks), while at other times the artistic purpose of the author leads him to conceal his *structure* (as in narratives) or subordinate it altogether (as in some informal essays). In the novel, the short story, and the drama, the *structure* is generally regarded today as the most reliable as well as the most revealing key to the meaning of the work. In the contemporary criticism of poetry, too, *structure* is used to define not only verse form and formal arrangement but also the sequence of IMAGES and ideas which unite to convey the meaning of the poem.

Style: The arrangement of words in a manner which at once best expresses the individuality of the author and the idea and intent in his mind. The best *style*, for any given purpose, is that which most nearly approximates a perfect adaptation of one's language to one's ideas. In a perfect world, it is perhaps true that each speaker or writer would find expression in words which would exactly present the idea in his mind and would carry with them the exact personality of the author; but this side of paradise all that authors can do is to labor to achieve that end as closely as human limitations will permit.

Style, then, is a combination of two elements: the idea to be expressed, and the individuality of the author. It is, as Lowell said, "the establishment of a perfect mutual understanding between the worker and his material." From this point of view it is impossible to change the diction or to alter the phrasing of a statement and thus to say exactly the same thing; for what the reader receives from a statement is not alone what is said, but also certain connotations which affect his consciousness from the manner in which the statement is made. And from this it follows that, just as no two personalities are alike, no two *styles* are exactly alike.

There are, in fact, many *styles*. The critic is fond of categories and fixes a label to a Milton, a Lyly, a Pope; gives a name to a *style* and calls it ornamental, forceful, poetic, or what-not, in the conviction perhaps that he has described the *style* of a writer when all he has done has been to place him in a group with many others who have written ornate or forceful or poetic prose. A mere recital of some of these categories may, however, be suggestive of the infinite range of manners the one word *style* covers. We speak, for instance, of journalistic, scientific, or literary *styles*; we call the manners of other writers abstract or concrete, rhythmic or pedestrian, sincere or artificial, dignified or comic, original or imitative, dull or vivid, as though each of these was somehow a final category of its own. But, if we are actually to estimate a *style,* we need more delicate tests than these; we need terms which will be so final in their sensitiveness as ultimately to distinguish the work of each writer from that of all other writers, since, as has been said, in the last analysis no two *styles* are exactly comparable.

A study of *styles* for the purpose of analysis will include, in addition to the infinity of personal detail suggested above, such general qualities as: diction, sentence structure and variety, IMAGERY, RHYTHM, coherence, emphasis, and *arrangement of ideas.*

Symbol: On the most literal level, a *symbol* is something which is itself and yet stands for or suggests or means something else; as the letters *a p p l e* form a word which stands for a particular objective reality; or as a flag is a piece of colored cloth which stands for a nation. All language is symbolic in this sense, and many of the objects which we commonly use in daily life are.

In a literary sense, a *symbol* is a trope which combines a literal and sensuous quality with an abstract or suggestive aspect, a definition which also applies to the function of the flag as *symbol.* However, in criticism it is necessary to distinguish *symbol* from IMAGE, allegory, and METAPHOR. If we consider an IMAGE to have a concrete referent in the objective world and to function as IMAGE when it powerfully evokes that referent, then a *symbol* is like an IMAGE in doing the same thing but different from it in going beyond the evoking of the objective referent by making that referent suggest to the reader or audience a meaning beyond itself; in other words, a *symbol* is an IMAGE which evokes an objective, concrete reality and has that reality suggest another level of meaning. However, the *symbol* does not "stand for" the meaning; it evokes an object which suggests the meaning. As Coleridge said, "It partakes of the reality which it renders intelligible." *Symbol* differs from allegory in that in allegory the

231

objective referent evoked is without value until it is translated into the fixed meaning that it has in its own particular structure of ideas, whereas a *symbol* embodies the idea or the quality. As W. M. Urban said, "The metaphor becomes a symbol when by means of it we embody an ideal content not otherwise expressible."

Literary *symbols* are of two broad types: one includes those which embody within themselves universal suggestions of meaning, as the ocean and land suggest time and eternity, the voyage suggests life, and phallic *symbols* are universally recognized. Such *symbols* are used widely (and sometimes unconsciously) in the world's literature. The other type of *symbol* secures its suggestiveness not from qualities inherent in itself but from the way in which it is used in a given work. Thus in *Moby-Dick* the voyage, the land, the ocean—these objects are pregnant with meanings that seem almost independent of Melville's use of them in his story; on the other hand, the white whale is invested with meaning—and differing meanings for different crew members—through the handling of materials in the novel. Similarly, in Hemingway's *A Farewell to Arms*, rain, which is merely a physical fact in the opening chapter, is converted into a *symbol* of death through the uses to which it is put in the book. See IMAGE, IMAGERY, METAPHOR, SIMILE.

Symbolism: In its broad sense, *symbolism* is the use of one object to represent or suggest another; or, in literature, the use of SYMBOLS in writing, particularly the serious and extensive use of such SYMBOLS.

Symbolism is also the name given to a literary movement which originated in France in the last half of the nineteenth century, strongly influenced Irish and British writing around the turn of the century, and has been a dominant force in much British and American poetry in the twentieth century. This *symbolism* represents one of the romantic reactions to realism. It sees the immediate, unique, and personal emotional response as the proper subject of art, and its full expression as the ultimate aim of art. Since the emotions experienced by a poet in a given moment are unique to that person and that moment and are finally both fleeting and incommunicable, the poet is reduced to the use of a complex and highly private kind of symbolization in an effort to give expression to his ineffable feeling. The result is a kind of writing consisting of what Edmund Wilson has called "a medley of metaphor" in which SYMBOLS lacking apparent logical relation are put together in a pattern, one of whose characteristics is an indefiniteness as great as the indefiniteness of the experience itself and another of whose characteristics is the conscious effort to use words for their musical effect, without very much attention to precise meaning. As Baudelaire, one of the principal forerunners of the movement, said, man lives in a "forest of symbols" which results from the fact that the materiality and individuality of the physical world dissolves into the "dark and confused unity" of the unseen world. In this process synaesthesia takes place. Baudelaire and the later symbolists, particularly Mallarmé and Valéry, were greatly influenced by the theory and poetic practice of Edgar Allan Poe. Other important French writers in the movement were Rimbaud, Verlaine, Leforgue, Rémy de Gourmont, and Claudel, and Maeterlinck in the drama and Huysman in the novel. The Irish writers of this century, particularly Yeats in poetry, Synge in the drama, and Joyce in the novel, have been notably responsive to the movement. In Germany Rilke and Stefan George have functioned as symbolist poets. In America the imagist poets reflected the movement, as did Eugene O'Neill in the drama. Through its pervasive influence on T. S. Eliot, *symbolism* has affected much of the best British and American poetry in our time.

Tenor and **Vehicle:** Terms used by I. A. Richards for the two essential elements of a METAPHOR. The *tenor* is the discourse or subject which the *vehicle* illustrates or illuminates; or, stated another way, the *vehicle* is the figure that carries the weight of the comparison, while the *tenor* is the subject to which the *vehicle* refers. According to Richards' definition, a METAPHOR always involves two ideas—*tenor* and *vehicle*. If it is impossible to distinguish them, we are dealing with a literal statement; if we can distinguish them, even slightly, we are dealing with a metaphoric expression. Hamlet's question, "What should such fellows as I do crawling between earth and heaven?" is metaphoric. While Hamlet may literally crawl, there is, as Richards points out, "an unmistakable reference to other things that crawl . . . and this reference is the *vehicle* as Hamlet . . . is the *tenor*." See METAPHOR.

Theme: The central or dominating idea in a literary work. In nonfiction prose it may be thought of as the general topic of discussion, the subject of the discourse, the thesis. In poetry, fiction, and drama it is the abstract concept which is made concrete through its representation in person, action, and IMAGE in the work.

Tone (Tone Color): *Tone* is used in contemporary criticism, following I. A. Richards' example, as a term designating the attitudes toward the subject and toward the audience implied in a literary work. In such a usage, a work may have a *tone* that is formal, informal, intimate, solemn, sombre, playful, serious, ironic, condescending, or any of many other possible attitudes. Clearly, *tone* in this sense contributes in a major way to the effect and the effectiveness of a literary work.

In another sense, *tone* is used to designate the mood of the work itself and the various devices that are used to create that mood. In this sense, *tone* results from combinations and variations of such things as meter, RIME, ALLITERATION, assonance, consonance, diction, sentence structure, repetition, IMAGERY, SYMBOLISM, etc.

Tone or *tone color* is sometimes used to designate a musical quality in language which Sidney Lanier discussed in *The Science of English Verse*, where he asserts that the sounds of words have qualities equivalent to timbre in music. "When the ear exactly coordinates a series of sounds with primary reference to their *tone-color*, the result is a conception of (in music, flute-tone as distinct from violin-tone, and the like; in verse, rhyme as opposed to rhyme, vowel varied with vowel, phonetic syzygy, and the like), in general . . . *tone-color.*"

Tragedy: A drama, in prose or verse, which recounts an important and causally related series of events in the life of a person of significance, such events culminating in an unhappy catastrophe, the whole treated with great dignity and seriousness. According to Aristotle, whose definition in the *Poetics* is an inductive description of the Greek *tragedies*, the purpose of a *tragedy* is to arouse the emotions of pity and fear and thus to produce in the audience a catharsis of these emotions. Such a definition as this is broad enough to admit almost any drama that is serious and that ends with an unhappy catastrophe, although its various formulations have been interpreted from time to time in terms of the attitudes and conventions of the age in which the formulations have been made. The question of the nature of the significance of the tragic hero is answered in each age by the concept of significance that is held by that age. In a period of monarchy, Shakespeare's PROTAGONISTS were kings and rulers; in other ages they have been and will be other kinds of men. In a democratic nation, founded on an egalitarian concept of man, a tragic hero can be the archetypal common man—a shoe salesman, a policeman, a gangster, a New England farmer, a Negro servant. From time to time the basis of unity has been debated. With the classical writers of the Renaissance and in the Neo-Classic Period, the unities were observed with rigor. Yet ages which find unity in other aspects of drama than its technique, may wed the serious and the comic, may take liberties with time and place, may use multiple PLOTS, and still achieve a unified effect as the non-classic Renaissance writers did. What constitutes dignity and seriousness in presentation is also subject to the interpretation of the age in which the play is produced. In its own way Arthur Miller's *The Death of a Salesman* is fully as serious and as dignified for our world as *Hamlet* was for Elizabethan England, although it is a lesser play. Classical tragedy and romantic tragedy both emphasize the significance of a choice made by the PROTAGONIST but dictated by his "flaw," his hamartia; yet to insist that *tragedy* be confined to this particular view of man and life is to limit it in indefensible ways. Clearly *tragedy* defies specific definition, each age producing works that speak in the conventions and beliefs of that age the enduring sense that man seems to have of the tragic nature of his existence and of the grandeur of the human spirit in facing it.

In the Middle Ages the term *tragedy* did not refer to a drama but to any narrative which recounted how a person of high rank, through ill fortune or his own vice or error, fell from high estate to low. The *tragedies* recounted in Chaucer's "Monk's Tale," in Lydgate's *Fall of Princes*, and in the Renaissance collection, *The Mirror for Magistrates*, are of this sort. In the sixteenth century the influence of classical tragedy, particularly of Senecan tragedy, combined with notable elements of the medieval drama to produce English *tragedy*. In 1559 came the first translation of a Senecan tragedy, and in 1562 was acted Sackville and Norton's *Gorboduc*, "the first regular English *tragedy*." The genius for the stage which characterized the Elizabethan Age worked upon this form to produce the greatest flowering in the drama that England has known. Yet the *tragedy* which emerged was not the classical TRAGEDY of Aristotle's definition, despite the efforts of men like Ben Jonson to school it into being so, but plays of a heterogeneous character known as romantic tragedy—plays which tended to ignore the unities, which followed medieval tradition in mixing sadness and mirth, and which strove at any cost—including sub-plots and comic relief scenes—to satisfy the spectators with vigorous action and gripping spectacle. Shakespeare worked in the forms of the revenge tragedy, the domestic tragedy, and the chronicle play.

The seventeenth century saw the Elizabethan tragedy continued with a growing emphasis on violence and shock during its first half, to be replaced with the heroic drama, with its stylized conflict of love and honor, during its second half. The eighteenth century saw the development of a drama around middle-class figures, known as domestic tragedy, which was serious in intent but superficial in importance. With the emergence of Ibsen in the late nineteenth century came the concept of middle-class *tragedy* growing out of social problems and issues. In the twentieth century, middle-class and laboring-class characters are often portrayed in their circumstances as the victims of social, hereditary, and environmental forces. When, as often happens, they receive their fate with a self-pitying whimper, they can hardly be said to have tragic dimensions. But when, as also happens in much modern serious drama, they face their destiny, however evil and unmerited, with courage and dignity, they are probably as truly tragic, *mutatis mutandis*, as Oedipus was to Sophocles' Athenians or Hamlet was to Shakespeare's Englishmen.

INDEX